Anonymous

Fast Day Sermons

The Pulpit on the State of the Country

Anonymous

Fast Day Sermons
The Pulpit on the State of the Country

ISBN/EAN: 9783337099756

Printed in Europe, USA, Canada, Australia, Japan

Cover: Foto ©ninafisch / pixelio.de

More available books at **www.hansebooks.com**

FAST DAY SERMONS.

FAST DAY SERMONS:

OR

THE PULPIT

ON

THE STATE OF THE COUNTRY.

NEW YORK:

RUDD & CARLETON, 130 GRAND STREET.

M DCCC LXI.

CONTENTS.

PREFACE.

THE following Discourses are collected in a volume in the belief that they will have a historical interest. These are Revolutionary times. The country is profoundly agitated, not on a question of party, but of National existence. On the very brink of dissolution, we are led to pause and review the causes that have brought us to this. While the people attend eagerly to the appeals of their leaders, thoughtful men will listen silently for the calm voices of the Pulpit, from which they will expect a clearer statement of the principles which underlie all this popular turbulence.

The particular sermons here introduced, have been chosen not in the interest of any party, but as fairly representing the mind of the country, both North and South. In the very front of the book is placed the discourse of Dr. THORNWELL, the leading minister, if not the leading man, of South Carolina — one who is regarded by many as being, by his intellectual ascendency and influence, the natural successor of John C. Calhoun. His discourse contains the whole argument of Disunion. This abstract reasoning is carried out in the sermon which follows, by Dr. PALMER, of New Orleans, a native of South Carolina, and a former pupil of Dr. Thornwell. His appeal to the South to maintain its rights is most earnest and eloquent. In contrast with these fiery addresses, and to afford

the reader an interval of relief, we place next the milder counsels and gentler tones of Dr. DABNEY, of Virginia, who speaks
less as a Southern man than as a minister of the Prince of
Peace. Then follows a sharp rebuke of disunion from Dr.
ROBERT J. BRECKINRIDGE, of Kentucky.

Of the sermons of Northern preachers, the volume includes
those of directly opposite views. The learned Rabbi RA-
PHALL argues for the ancient Hebrew slavery, as ordained of
God, and thus as justifying the same institution in later
ages, and Rev. H. J. VAN DYKE assumes the same, while ex-
posing the character and influence of Abolitionism, a spirit
which he evidently thinks not from above, but from beneath.
To both of these Prof. TAYLER LEWIS replies, not as a vehe-
ment orator, but as a Christian scholar, in lucid style, and with
thoughts well set in logical array. Next, Dr. VINTON, the accomplished minister of Trinity, rebukes the spirit of Northern fanaticism, as an offset to which, Mr. BEECHER stoutly de-
fends the anti-slavery position of the North; and Dr. BEL-
LOWS argues that the present is a conflict between Civilization
and Barbarism. The collection closes with a middle-ground
sermon from Rev. Dr. ADAMS, of this city.

In reviewing these discourses, as they stand here side by
side, one cannot but see that the difference which now divides
the North and the South is not a mere misunderstanding; that
there is a real and profound difference of opinion. At the
same time, seeing how widely, and yet how honestly and sincerely, good men may differ, he will be apt to learn for himself
broader views and a kindlier charity.

NEW YORK, *Jan.* 1861.

OUR NATIONAL SINS

A SERMON PREACHED IN THE PRESBYTERIAN CHURCH, COLUMBIA, S. C.
ON THE DAY OF THE STATE FAST, NOV. 21, 1860.

BY REV. J. H. THORNWELL, D. D.

" And it came to pass, when King Hezekiah heard it, that he rent his clothes, and covered himself with sackcloth, and went into the house of the Lord."—*Isaiah* xxxvii : 1.

I have no design, in the selection of these words, to intimate that there is a parallel between Jerusalem and our own Commonwealth in relation to the Covenant of God. I am far from believing that we alone, of all the people of the earth, are possessed of the true religion, and far from encouraging the narrow and exclusive spirit which, with the ancient hypocrites denounced by the Prophet, can complacently exclaim, the temple of the Lord, the temple of the Lord, are we. Such arrogance and bigotry are utterly inconsistent with the penitential confessions which this day has been set apart to evoke. We are here, not like the Pharisee, to boast of our own righteousness, and to thank God that we are not like other men ; but we are here like the poor publican, to smite upon our breasts, and to say, God be merciful to us, sinners. My design, in the choice of these words, is to illustrate the spirit and temper with which a Christian people should deport themselves in

times of public calamity and distress. Jerusalem was
in great straits. The whole country had been ravaged
by a proud and insolent foe. The Sacred City remained as the last hold of the State, and a large army
lay encamped before its walls. Ruin seemed to be inevitable. *It was a day of trouble, and of rebuke, and
of blasphemy. The children had come to the birth, and
there was not strength to bring forth.* In the extremity
of the danger, the sovereign betakes himself to God.
Renouncing all human confidence, and all human allian-
ces, he rent his clothes, and covered himself with sackcloth, and went into the house of the Lord.

In applying the text to our own circumstances, widely
different in many respects from those of Jerusalem at the
time referred to, I am oppressed with a difficulty, which
you that are acquainted with my views of the nature and
functions of the Christian ministry can readily understand. During the twenty-five years in which I have fulfilled my course as a preacher — all of which have been
spent in my native State, and nearly all in this city — I
have never introduced secular politics into the instructions of the pulpit. It has been a point of conscience
with me to know no party in the State. Questions of
law and public administration I have left to the tribunals appointed to settle them, and have confined my ex-
hortations to those great matters that pertain immediately to the kingdom of God. I have left it to Cæsar
to take care of his own rights, and have insisted only
upon the supreme rights of the Almighty. The angry
disputes of the forum I have excluded from the house
of the Lord. And while all classes have been exhorted to the discharge of their common duties, as men, as

citizens, as members of the family — while the sanctions of religion have, without scruple, been applied to all the relations of life, whether public or private, civil or domestic — the grounds of dissension which divide the community into parties, and range its members under different banners, have not been permitted to intrude into the sanctuary. The business of a preacher, as such, is to expound the Word of God. He has no commission to go beyond the teaching of the Scriptures. He has no authority to expound to senators the Constitution of the State, nor to interpret for judges the law of the land. In the civil and political sphere, the dead must bury their dead. It is obvious, however, that religious sanctions cannot be applied to civil and political duties without taking for granted the relations out of which these duties spring. Religion cannot exact submission to the powers that be, without implying that these powers are known and confessed. It cannot enjoin obedience to Cæsar, without taking it for granted that the authority of Cæsar is acknowledged. When the Constitution of the State is fixed and settled, the general reference to it which religion implies, in the inculcation of civil and political duties, may be made without intruding into the functions of the magistrate, or taking sides with any particular party in the Commonwealth. The relations which condition duty are admitted, and the conscience instantly recognizes the grounds on which the minister of the Gospel exhorts to fidelity. The duties belong to the department of religion ; the relations out of which they spring belong to the department of political science ; and must be determined apart from the Word of God. The concrete cases, to which the law of God is to be applied, must always be given ; the law itself is all that the preacher can enforce as of Divine authority. As the law, without the facts, however, is a shadow without substance ; as the duty is unmeaning which is determined by no definite relations ; the preacher cannot inculcate civil obedience, or convict of national sin, without allusions, more or less precise, to the theory and structure of the government. He avoids presumption, by having it distinctly understood, that the theory which he assumes is not announced as the Word of God, but is to be proved, as any other facts of history and experience. He speaks here only in his own name, as a man, and promulges a matter of opinion, and not an article of faith. If the assumptions which he makes are true, the duties which he enjoins must be accepted as Divine commands. The speculative antecedents being admitted, the practical consequents cannot be avoided. There are cases in which the question relates to a change in the government, in which the question of duty is simply a question of revolution. In such cases the minister has no commission from God to recommend or resist a change, unless some moral principle is immediately involved. He can explain and enforce the spirit and temper in which revolution should be contemplated and carried forward or abandoned. He can expound the doctrine of the Scriptures in relation to the nature, the grounds, the extent and limitations of civil obedience ; but it is not for him, as a preacher, to say when evils are intolerable, nor to prescribe the mode and measure of redress. These points he must leave to the State itself. When a revolution has once been achieved, he can enforce the duties which spring from the new condition of affairs.

Thus much I have felt bound to say, as to my views of the duty of a minister in relation to matters of State. As a citizen, a man, a member of the Commonwealth, he has a right to form and express his opinions upon every subject, to whatever department it belongs, which affects the interests of his race. As a man, he is as free as any other man; but the citizen must not be confounded with the preacher, nor private opinions with the oracles of God. Entertaining these sentiments concerning the relations of the sacred office to political affairs, I am oppressed with the apprehension, that in attempting to fulfil the requisitions of the present occasion, I may transgress the limits of propriety, and merge the pulpit into the rostrum. I am anxious to avoid this error, and would, therefore, have it understood, in advance, that whatever theory may be assumed of the nature and structure of our Government, is assumed upon the common grounds of historical knowledge, and is assumed mainly as fixing the points from which I would survey the sins of the country. If true — and no man has a right to reject them, without being able to disprove them — my conclusions in reference to our national guilt are irrefragably established. If not true, we must either deny that we are sinners, or must seek some other relations in which to ground the consciousness of sin. If that consciousness should be thoroughly grounded, the services of this day will not be in vain. I can truly say that my great aim is not to expound our complex institutions, but to awaken the national conscience to a sense of its responsibility be-

fore God. It is not to enlighten your minds, but to
touch your hearts; not to plead the cause of States
rights or Federal authority, but to bring you as penitents before the Supreme Judge. This is no common
solemnity. The day has been set apart by the constituted authorities of this Commonwealth, by joint reso-
lution of both branches of the Legislature, and proclaimed by the Chief Magistrate of the State, as a day
of fasting, humiliation and prayer. South Carolina,
therefore, as an organized political community, pros-
trates herself this day before God. It is a time of
danger, of blasphemy and rebuke, and, imitating the
example of Hezekiah, she rends her clothes, covers herself with sackcloth, and comes into the House of the
Lord. The question is, how she should demean herself
under these solemn circumstances. Every minister,
this day, becomes her organ, and he should instruct the
people as to the attitude we should all assume in the
presence of Jehovah. It is a day of solemn worship,
in which the state appears as a penitent, and lays her
case before the Judge of all the earth.

The points to which I shall direct your attention,
are, first, the spirit in which we should approach God,
and second, the errand on which we should go.

I. As the individual, in coming to God, must believe
that He is, and that He is the rewarder of them that
diligently search Him, so the State must be impressed
with a profound sense of His all-pervading providence,
and of its responsibility to Him, as the moral Ruler of
the world. The powers that be are ordained of Him.
From Him the magistrate receives his commission, and
in His fear, he must use the sword as a terror to evil

doers and a praise to them that do well. Civil government is an institute of Heaven, founded in the character of man as social and moral, and is designed to realize the idea of justice. Take away the notion of mutual rights and the corresponding notions of duty and obligation, and a commonwealth is no more conceivable among men than among brutes. As the State is essentially moral in its idea, it connects itself directly with the government of God. It is, indeed, the organ through which that government is administered in its relations to the highest interests of earth. A State, therefore, which does not recognize its dependence upon God, or which fails to apprehend, in its functions and offices, a commission from heaven, is false to the law of its own being. The moral finds its source and centre only in God. There can be no rights without responsibility, and responsibility is incomplete until it terminates in a supreme will. The earthly sanctions of the State, its rewards and punishments, are insufficient either for the punishment of vice or the encouragement of virtue, unless they connect themselves with the higher sanctions which religion discloses. If the State had to deal only with natures confessedly mortal ; if its subjects were conscious of no other life than that which they bear from the cradle to the grave ; if their prospect terminated at death ; if they were only brutes of a more finished make, but equally destined to everlasting extinction, who does not see that the law would lose its terror, and obedience be stripped of its dignity. The moral nature of man is inseparably linked with immortality, and immortality as inseparably linked with religion. Among Pagan idolaters, the instinct of immortality, though not developed into a doctrine, nor realized as a fact in reflection, is yet the secret power which, in the spontaneous workings of the soul, gives efficacy to punishment, and energy to rewards. Man feels himself immortal, and this feeling, though operating blindly, colors his hopes and his fears. The State, therefore, which should undertake to accomplish the ends of its being, without taking into account the religious element in man, palsies its own arm. Subjects that have no religion are incapable of law. Rules of prudence they may institute ; measures of precaution they may adopt; a routine of coercion and constraint they may establish ; but laws they cannot have. They may be governed like a lunatic asylum ; but where there is no nature which responds to the sentiment of duty, there is no nature which confesses the majesty of law. Every State, therefore, must have a religion, or it must cease to be a government of men. Hence no Commonwealth has ever existed without religious sanctions. " Whether true or false, sublime or ridiculous," says the author of the Consulate and the Empire, " man must have a religion. Every where, in all ages, in all countries, in ancient as in modern times, in civilized as well as in barbarian nations, we find him a worshipper at some altar, be it venerable, degraded, or blood-stained."

It is not only necessary that the State should have a religion ; it is equally necessary, in order to an adequate fulfilment of its own idea, that it have the true religion. Truth is the only proper food of the soul, and though superstition and error may avail for a time as external restraints, they never generate an inward

principle of obedience. They serve as outward motives, but never become an inward life, and when the
falsehood comes to be detected, the mind is apt to
abandon itself to unrestrained licentiousness. The
reaction is violent in proportion to the intensity of the
previous delusion. The most formidable convulsions in
States are those which have been consequent upon the
detection of religious imposture. "When a religion,"
says McCosh, "waxes old in a country — when the circumstances which at first favored its formation or introduction have changed — when in an age of reason it is
tried and found unreasonable — when in an age of
learning it is discovered to be the product of the grossest ignorance — when in an age of levity it is felt to be
too stern — then the infidel spirit takes courage, and,
with a zeal in which there is a strange mixture of
scowling revenge and light-hearted wantonness, of deep-
set hatred and laughing levity, it proceeds to level all
existing temples and altars, and erects no others in
their room." The void which is created is soon filled
with wantonness and violence. The State cannot be
restored to order until it settles down upon some form
of religion again. As the subjects of a State must
have a religion in order to be truly obedient, and as it
is the true religion alone which converts obedience into
a living principle, it is obvious that a Commonwealth
can no more be organized, which shall recognize all
religions, than one which shall recognize none. The
sanctions of its laws must have a centre of unity some
where. To combine in the same government contra-
dictory systems of faith, is as hopelessly impossible as
to constitute into one State men of different races and

languages. The Christian, the Pagan, Mohammedan ;
Jews, Infidels and Turks, cannot coalesce as organic
elements in one body politic. The State must take its
religious type from the doctrines, the precepts, and the
institutions of one or the other of these parties.

When we insist upon the religious character of the
State, we are not to be understood as recommending or
favoring a Church Establishment. To have a religion is
one thing — to have a Church Establishment is another ; and perhaps the most effectual way of extinguishing the religious life of a State is to confine the expression of it to the forms and peculiarities of a single sect.

The Church and the State, as visible institutions, are
entirely distinct, and neither can usurp the province of
the other without injury to both. But religion, as a
life, as an inward principle, though specially developed
and fostered by the Church, extends its domain beyond
the sphere of technical worship, touches all the relations of man, and constitutes the inspiration of every
duty. The service of the Commonwealth becomes an
act of piety to God. The State realizes its religious
character through the religious character of its subjects ; and a State is and ought to be Christian, because
all its subjects are and ought to be determined by the
principles of the Gospel. As every legislator is bound
to be a Christian man, he has no right to vote for any
laws which are inconsistent with the teachings of the
Scriptures. He must carry his Christian conscience
into the halls of legislation.

In conformity with these principles, we recognize
Christianity to-day as the religion of our Commonwealth. Our standard of right is that eternal law

which God proclaimed from Sinai, and which Jesus
expounded on the Mount. We recognize our responsibility to Jesus Christ. He is head over all things to
the Church, and the nation that will not serve Him is
doomed to perish. Before men we are a free and sovereign State; before God we are dependent subjects;
and one of the most cheering omens of the times is the
heartiness with which this truth has been received. We
are a Christian people, and a Christian Commonwealth.
As on the one hand we are not Jews, Infidels or Turks,
so on the other, we are not Presbyterians, Baptists,
Episcopalians, or Methodists. Christianity, without
distinction of sects, is the fountain of our national life.
We accept the Bible as the great moral charter by
which our laws must be measured, and the Incarnate
Redeemer as the Judge to whom we are responsible.

In contending that Christianity is the organic life of
the State, we of course do not exclude from the privileges of citizens, nor from the protection of the laws,
those who do not acknowledge the authority of Jesus.
They do not cease to be men, because they are not
Christians, and Christian principle exacts that their
rights should be sacredly maintained by an institute
which is founded in the idea of justice. As, moreover,
the religion of the State realizes itself through the religious life of its subjects, it is not to be supported by
arbitrary tests or by civil pains and disabilities. Religion is essentially free and spontaneous. It cannot be
enacted as a law, nor enforced by authority. When the
State protects its outward institutions, such as the sanctity of the Sabbath, it enjoins nothing which does violence to any man's conscience. It is only giving vent

to the religious life of the people, without exacting from others what they feel it sinful to perform ; and so long as freedom of conscience and the protection of their rights are secured to men, they have no reason to complain that they are not permitted to unsettle the principles upon which all law and order ultimately rest. As long as they are not required to profess what they do not believe, nor to do what their consciences condemn ; as long as they are excluded from no privilege and deprived of no right, they cannot complain that the spirit and sanction of the laws are a standing protest against their want of sympathy with the prevailing type of national life. If Christianity be true, they ought certainly to be Christians. The claim of this religion, in contradistinction from every other, or from none at all, is founded only in its truth. If true, it must be authoritative, and the people who accept it as true would be traitors to their faith if they did not mould their institutions in conformity with its spirit. It is only as a sanction, and not as a law, that we plead for its influence ; and how a Christian people can have any other than Christian institutions, it surpasses our intelligence to compass. That the State should treat all religions with equal indifference, is to suppose that the subjects of the State can have a double life, flowing in parallel streams, which never approach nor touch — a life as citizens, and a life as men. It is to forget the essential unity of man, and the convergence of all the energies of his being to a religious centre. It is to forget that religion is the perfection of his nature, and that he realizes the idea of humanity in proportion as religion pervades his whole being. A godless State is, in fact, a contradistinction in terms; and if we must have some god, or cease to be citizens because we have ceased to be men, who will hesitate between the God of the Bible and the absurd devices of human superstition and depravity?

It is, then, before the Supreme Jehovah that we prostrate ourselves to-day. We come as a Commonwealth ordained by him. We come as His creatures and His subjects. The sword by which we have executed justice, we received from His hands. We believe that He is — that He is our God; that His favor is life, and His loving kindness better than life. We ascribe to His grace the institutions under which we have flourished. We trace to His hands the blessings which have distinguished our lot. Under Him the foundations of the State were laid, and to Him we owe whatsoever is valuable in our laws, healthful in our customs, or precious in our history. We come this day to acknowledge our dependence, swear our allegiance, and confess our responsibility. By Him we exist as a State, and to Him we must answer for the manner in which we have discharged our trust. *"God standeth in the congregation of the mighty. He judgeth among the gods.*

II. Having explained the spirit in which we should approach God, let me call your attention, in the next place, to the ERRAND which brings us before Him this day — fasting, humiliation, and prayer. These terms define the worship which we are expected to present. Fasting is the outward sign; penitence and prayer are the inward graces. In fasting, we relinquish for a season the bounties of Providence, in token of our conviction, that we have forfeited all claim to our daily bread. It is a symbolical confession that we deserve to be stripped of every gift, and left to perish in hunger, nakedness, and want. On occasions of solemn moment, and particularly when "manifestations of the Divine anger appear, as pestilence, war, and famine, the salutary custom of all ages has been for pastors to exhort the people to public fasting and extraordinary prayer." Through such a solemnity Nineveh was saved; and if we are equally penitent, who shall say that we may not also be delivered from the judgments which our sins have provoked? Fasting, apart from inward penitence, is an idle mockery. *Is it such a fast as I have chosen? a day for a man to afflict his soul? is it to bow down his head as a bulrush, and to spread sackcloth and ashes under him? wilt thou call this a fast and an acceptable day to the Lord? Is not this the fast that I have chosen? to loose the bands of wickedness, to undo the heavy burdens, and to let the oppressed go free, and that ye break every yoke? Is it not to deal thy bread to the hungry, and that thou bring the poor that are cast out to thy house? when thou seest the naked that thou cover him; and that thou hide not thyself from thine own flesh?* The great thing with us to-day is, to be impressed with a sense of our sins as a people; to confess them humbly before God; to deprecate His judgments, and to supplicate his favor. We are too apt to restrict the notion of sin in its proper sense to the sphere of the individual; to regard it as altogether private and personal, and not capable of being predicated of the mal-administration of the State. But if the State is a moral institute, responsible to God, and existing for moral and spiritual ends, it is certainly a subject capable of sin. It may endure, too, the penalty of sin, either in its organic capacity, by national judgments, by war, pestilence, weakness, and dissolution, or in its individual subjects, whose offences as citizens are as distinctly transgressions as any other forms of iniquity, and enter into the grounds of the Divine dispensations towards them. The State exists under a law which defines its duty. It is a means to an end, which limits its powers and determines its functions. It is the realization of an idea. Like an individual, it may sin by defect in coming short of its duty, and sin by positive contradiction to it. It may fail to comprehend its vocation; it may arrogate too much, or claim too little. It may be wanting in public spirit, or it may give public spirit a wrong direction. It may subordinate the spiritual to the material, and, in encouraging the increase of national wealth, neglect to foster national greatness. In aspiring to be rich and increased in goods, it may forget that the real glory of a nation is to be free, intelligent, and virtuous. The power which it has received as an instrument of good, it may pervert into an engine of tyranny. It may disregard the welfare and prosperity of its subjects, and degenerate into a tool for the selfish purposes of unscrupulous rulers. It may seek to aggrandize factions, instead of promoting the well-being of the people. The State, too, as a moral person, stands in relations to other States, in consequence of which it may be guilty of bad faith, of inordinate ambition, of covetousness, rapacity, and selfishness. The same vices which degrade the individual among his fellows, may degrade a commonwealth among surrounding nations. It may be mean, voracious, insolent, extortionary. It may cringe to the strong, and oppress the weak. It may take unworthy advantages of the necessities of its neighbors, or make unworthy concessions for temporary purposes. The same laws regulate, and the same crimes disfigure, the intercourse of States with one another, which obtain in the case of individuals. The political relations of the one are precisely analogous to the social relations of the other. The same standard of honor, of integrity and magnanimity which is incumbent upon their subjects, is equally binding upon the States themselves, and character ought to be as sacred among sovereign States as among private individuals.

The true light, therefore, in which national defects and transgressions should be contemplated, is formally that of sin against God. Their injustice to their people is treachery to Him, and their failure to comprehend or to seek to fulfil the end of their being, is contempt of the Divine authority. We take too low a view, when we regard their errors simply as impolitic; their real magnitude and enormity we can never apprehend until we see them in the light of sins.

It is to be feared that this notion of sin has not the hold which it should have of the public conscience. We are not accustomed to judge of the State by the same canons of responsibility which we apply to individuals. In some way or other, the notion of sovereignty, which only defines the relation of a State to earthly tribunals, affects our views of its relations to God; and, whilst we charge it with errors, with blunders, with unfaithfulness to its trust, and deplore the calamities which its misconduct brings upon its subjects as public evils, we lose sight of the still more solemn truth, that these aberrations are the actions of a moral agent, and must be answered for at the bar of God. The moral law is one, and the State is bound to do its duty, under the same sanctions which pertain to the individual. When the State fails, or transgresses, its offences are equally abominations in the sight of God. It is clearly idle to talk of national repentance, without the consciousness of national sin. This doctrine, therefore, I would impress upon you in every form of statement, that the misconduct of the State is rebellion against God, and that a nation which comes short of its destination, and is faithless to its trust, is stained with sin of the most malignant dye. God may endure it in patience for a season, but it is loathsome and abominable in His eyes, and the day of reckoning will at last come. Sin must either be pardoned or punished, confessed and forsaken, or it will work death. Sin has been the ruin of every Empire that ever flourished and fell. Assyria, Persia, Greece, and Rome, have paid the penalties to the Divine law. The only alternative with States, as with their subjects, is, repent or perish. The first duty, therefore, which, as a Christian people, we should endeavor to discharge this day, is to confess our national sins with humility and penitence. We should endeavor to feel their magnitude and enormity, not as injuries to man, but as offences against the majesty of God. Our language should be that of David : *Against Thee, Thee only, have we sinned, and done this evil in thy sight.*

Another errand which it behooves us equally to prosecute to-day is, to seek Divine guidance and Divine strength for the future. *It is not in man that walketh to direct his steps*, and States are no more competent than individuals to discharge their duties without the grace of God. Let us endeavor to cherish a sense of our dependence, and aspire to the distinction of that happy people whose God is the Lord. It is a great thing to contemplate our civil duties in the light of obedience to Him; and when they are undertaken in the spirit of worship, they are likely to be performed in the spirit of faithfulness. If we are truly penitent, and truly sensible of our dependence upon God; if it is the reigning desire of our hearts to know His will, and our fixed purpose, in reliance on His strength, to do it, He may give us an answer of peace, He may bring light out of darkness, and extract safety from danger.

Having indicated the spirit in which we should approach God, and pointed out the purposes for which we should go, it remains that we apply the truth to our present circumstances, by signalizing the sins which it behooves us to confess, and by designating the blessings which it behooves us to implore. The conscience is never touched by vague generalities; we must come to particulars; thus and thus hast thou done. The State appears as a penitent this day. She has, therefore, sins to confess. There is a burden upon her heart which must needs be relieved. What are these sins? What is this burden? The completeness of our answer to these questions will measure the extent and sincerity of our repentance.

To understand our sins we must look at ourselves in a double light: first, as a member of this Confederacy, as part and parcel of the people of these United States;

and, in the next place, as a particular Commonwealth, a
perfect State in ourselves. As long as we are members
of this Confederacy we cannot detach ourselves from a
personal interest in the sins and transgressions of the
whole people ; and, though there may be offences in which
we have had no actual participation, we are not at liberty
to indulge in a self-righteous temper, nor to employ the
language of recrimination and reproach. The spectacle of sin is always sad. The fall of none should be
contemplated with exultation or with triumph. We
should look upon the errors of our brethren with pity
and with sorrow, and, as Daniel confessed, in humility
and contrition, and with deep commiseration for their
misery, the sins of his people, so we should endeavor
this day to deplore the shortcomings of our common
country, as a matter of personal distress to ourselves.
When we come before God, we should endeavor to contemplate the moral aspects of the country in the light
of His awful holiness. And the more profoundly we
are impressed with the malignity of our national guilt,
the deeper should be our concern for the transgressors
themselves. Sinners cannot triumph over sinners. Those
whose only plea is mercy to themselves, ought not to be
unmerciful to others. Much more should we be filled
with sorrow when the sins we deplore are likely to
prove the ruin of a great nation. To behold a vast,
imperial republic, like ours, bequeathed to us by a noble
ancestry, consecrated by a noble history, the work of
illustrious statesmen and patriots, falling a prey to national degeneracy and corruption, is enough to make
angels weep, and should wring from our hearts tears of
bitterness and blood. The sin must be enormous where

the punishment is so fearful. In less than a century we have spoiled the legacy of our fathers. A Christian people, with Christian institutions, the envy and admiration of the world, have not lived to the age of pagan Greece. Surely, God has a controversy with us, and it becomes us to inquire, with all solemnity, into the cause of His fierce anger. The union, which our fathers designed to be perpetual, is on the verge of dissolution. A name once dear to our hearts, has become intolerable to entire States. Once admired, loved, almost adored, as the citadel and safeguard of freedom, it has become, in many minds, synonymous with oppression, with treachery, with falsehood, and with violence. The government to which we once invited the victims of tyranny from every part of the world, and under whose ample shield we gloried in promising them security and protection — that government has become hateful in the very regions in which it was once hailed with the greatest loyalty. Brother has risen up against brother, State against State; angry disputes and bitter criminations and recriminations abound, and the country stands upon the very brink of revolution. Surely, it is time to come to ourselves; to look our follies and our wickednesses in the face; time for every patriot to rend his garments, cover himself with sackcloth, and come into the house of the Lord. Let us deal faithfully this day: let us survey the sins of the land, not to accuse one another, but to humble ourselves under the mighty hand of God.

1. To appreciate the sins which attach to us in our unity as a confederated people, we must advert for a moment to the peculiar structure of our government.

When we came out of the Revolution, it is admitted on all hands that we were separate and independent States. Each was sovereign — that is, completely a nation in itself; but our fathers looked around them, and saw that the grounds of unity were as conspicuous as the elements of diversity. The people were of one blood, one language, one religion. They were, in short, one race. They surveyed the continent from north to south, from east to west, and its geography indicated that it ought to be the dwelling-place of a united population. While there were differences in soil, climate, and productions, that would naturally develop different types of industry, and give rise to different forms of interest, there were great connecting bonds in the mighty rivers which traversed the country, that as clearly signified that the diversity was not inconsistent with unity. The problem, accordingly, which the wisdom of our ancestors undertook to solve was, to harmonize this diversity with unity; to make the people, who were already many, at the same time, one. One nation, in the strict and proper sense, they could never become; that would be to absorb the diversity in unity. Many nations, in all the relations of sovereign States, they could not be; that would be to abolish the unity altogether. The problem was solved by a happy application of the federal principle. The diversity existed already in the many States which had just achieved their independence. These many States, in the exercise of their sovereignty, formed an alliance, which cemented them together in one body politic. This alliance was, in its principle, a treaty, and in its result, a government. In its principle it was a treaty, because it was a compact among sovereigns. In its result it was a government, because it created organs of political power which, under certain conditions, acted immediately upon the people of all the States, without the formal ratification of their own Legislatures, and in all foreign relations stood as the representative of their common sovereignty. It is obvious that the ultimate ground of the authority of federal legislation is the consent of the confederating States. The laws of Congress bind me, only because South Carolina has consented that I should be bound. The rights of Congress are only the concessions of the sovereign States. This will appear from a moment's reflection. It is obvious that the States might have required that no measures of the Federal Government should be of force within their own borders, without the formal sanction of their own Legislatures. In that case, there could have been no dispute as to the ultimate ground of obedience. The difficulties of such an arrangement are too obvious to be enumerated, but how were these difficulties to be avoided? By surrendering the principle on which the authority of Congress depended, or by changing the mode of its application? To have surrendered the principle would have been to abjure their own sovereignty. There was evidently, then, only a change in the mode of its application. That change consisted in defining the conditions under which consent might be presumed beforehand. The Constitution of the United States, in its grants of power to Congress, is only a device by which a general description is given, in advance, of the kind of legislation that each State will allow to be obligatory on its own people. The provisions of the Constitution are really anticipations of the concurrence of the States. They are formal declarations to the Federal Legislature, that within such and such limits, you have our consent to bind our people. In this way our fathers organized a government that united us for all common purposes, and left us in our original diversity to prosecute our separate and local interests. Congress is, therefore, only the creature of the States, and acts only through them. It is their consent, their treaty, which gives to its enactments the validity of law. As the Federal Legislature was clearly designed to realize the unity of the people, its powers are restricted, from the very necessities of the case, to those points in which all the States have a common interest. The creature of a treaty, in which the contracting parties were all equal, it is manifestly the servant, and not the master, of the States. It is an agent, and not a principal.

If this view of the subject be correct, the Federal government is preëminently a government, whose very existence depends upon a scrupulous adherence to good faith. It requires the sternest integrity to work it. Its very life-blood is honor. Now, there are two respects in which it may fatally err. In the first place Congress may transcend its powers, and thus be guilty of a breach of trust, and of disloyalty to its own masters. It may presume upon the consent of the States, where no consent has been given. It may forget that it is a servant, and aspire to be lord. It may forget that it is an agent, and arrogate to itself the rights and authority of the principal. When it surveys the extent of its jurisdiction, the amount of its patronage, and the weight of its influence abroad, it may become dazzled with the contemplation of its own greatness, and attribute to itself the light that is reflected upon it. Its one people it may construe into one nation, and, unmindful of its origin, treat the sovereignties which created it as dependent provinces. Treating upon a footing of equality with foreign powers, it may insensibly ascribe to itself the authority of Kings and Emperors. All this is conceivable ; to some extent it is inevitable, unless the most scrupulous integrity should reign in the Federal Councils. But to sin in any of these respects is fraud, and fraud connected with treason. In the next place, the States may break faith with one another. They may refuse to fulfil their engagements. They may pervert the Federal authorities to the accomplishment of selfish and sectional ends. They may undertake to make their common agent the minister of partial advantages, or they may use lawful powers for unlawful purposes. Here, too, in the relation of the States to each other, is wide scope for fraud.

In one, or in both these directions, we may look for instances of national transgression ; and on this day, we should solemnly review the history of the Republic, for the purpose of bringing our consciences before the tribunal of God. Perfidy, under all circumstances, is an aggravated sin ; but when it brings in its train the destruction of institutions which have been the hope and admiration of the world ; when it subverts the foundations of a great empire, scattering the seeds of dissension, bitterness and strife ; when it arms house against house, and State against State, and converts a happy union into a scene of implacable and deadly feuds, language is hardly competent to describe the enormity of the guilt. The fraud which makes our government a failure, must darken the prospects of liberty throughout the world. No policy can be devised which shall perpetuate freedom among a people that are dead to honor and integrity. Liberty and virtue are twin sisters, and the best fabric in the world, however ingeniously framed, and curiously balanced, can be no security against the corroding influences of bad faith. Perfidy is always weakness; and a government whose basis is the faith of treaties, must inevitably perish before it. The combination of the federal principle with the sovereignty of States, is the only principle which can maintain free institutions upon a broad scale. This combination can secure freedom to a continent; it might even govern the world. The day of small States is passed, and as the federal principle is the only one which can guarantee freedom to extensive territories, the federal principle must constitute the hope of the human race. It was the glory of this country to have first applied it to the formation of an effective government, and, had we been faithful to our trust, a destiny was before us which it has never been the lot of any people to inherit. It was ours to redeem this continent, to spread freedom, civilization and religion through the whole length of the land. Geographically placed between Europe and Asia, we were, in some sense, the representatives of the human race. The fortunes of the world were in our hand. We were a city set upon a hill, whose light was intended to shine upon every people and upon every land. To forego this destiny, to forfeit this inheritance, and that through bad faith, is an enormity of treason equalled only by the treachery of a Judas, who betrayed his master with a kiss. Favored as we have been, we can expect to perish by no common death. The judgment lingers not, and the damnation slumbers not, of the reprobates and traitors, who, for the wages of unrighteousness, have sapped the pillars and undermined the foundations of the stateliest temple of liberty the world ever beheld. Rebellion against God, and treason to man, are combined in the perfidy. The innocent may be spared, as Lot was delivered from the destruction of Sodom ; but the guilty must perish with an aggravated doom. The first instances of transgression may seem slight and insignificant, but when they strike at the principle of good faith, like a puncture of the heart, they strike at the root of our national life. The Union was conceived in plighted faith, and can only be maintained by a complete redemption of the pledge. The moment faith is broken, the Union is dissolved. Entertaining these views of the radical relations of good faith to the success and stability of our government, I would impress upon the country the flagrant iniquity of dealing loosely with its covenants. It is here that our dangers are concentrated, and here we should look for the sins that have provoked the judgments of God. Here is the secret of our bitter strifes, our furious contention, our deadly animosities ; and, should this Government be destined to fall, the epitaph which may be written on its tomb, is a memorial of broken faith.

The foregoing remarks are general, and designed to bring no railing accusation against any section of the country, but to excite every part of it to a faithful review of its dealings under the Constitution. There is one subject, however in relation to which the non-slaveholding States have not only broken faith, but have justified their course upon the plea of conscience. We allude to the subject of slavery. They have been reluctant to open the Territories to the introduction of slaves, and have refused to restore fugitives to their masters, and have vindicated themselves from blame by appealing to a higher law than the compacts of men. The doctrine of a higher law, properly interpreted and applied, we are far from repudiating. God is greater than man, and no human covenants can set aside or annul the supreme obligations of His will. But, in the present case, the plea is improperly applied. If it is wrong to countenance slavery by restoring fugitives to their masters, or by permitting it to enter into the Territories, then the true method is to abrogate the contract which requires both. We repent of sin by forsaking it, and the only way to undo a wicked bargain is to cancel it. If the non-slaveholding States cannot in conscience redeem their faith, they are bound in honor to take back their pledges, to withdraw from the Union, and to release their confederates from all the conditions of the contract. No other course can they pursue without sin. To swear to observe the Constitution, when the Constitution binds them to do what they believe to be wicked, is an oath which, whether broken or kept, cannot be taken without dishonor. To keep it, is to violate the conscience in the unlawful article. To break it, is to be guilty of perjury. The only escape from this dilemma is, not to take it at all.

But, in truth, even upon the supposition that slavery is immoral, there is nothing wrong in the oath to observe the Constitution. The responsibility of slavery is not upon the non-slaveholding States. It is not created by their laws, but by the laws of the slaveholding States; and all they do in the case of the fugitive from his master, is to remand him to the jurisdiction of the laws from which he has escaped. They have nothing to do with the justice or injustice of the laws themselves. They are simply required to say that the accident of being on their soil shall not dissolve the relation between a subject and its government. The treaty existing among the States, in reference to this point, is precisely analogous to a treaty among foreign nations, requiring the surrender of criminals that have fled from justice. The country surrendering passes no judgment upon the merits of the case. It leaves the whole of the responsibility to the laws of the country claiming jurisdiction. All that it does is not to interpose and arrest the operation of those laws. Surely, there is nothing unrighteous in this; nothing unrighteous in refusing to screen a man from the authority of the code under which Providence has cast his lot. There is no obligation to do it without a treaty; but there is nothing inherently unlawful in making such a treaty, and in strictly adhering to it when made. The plea of conscience proceeds from a palpable misapprehension of the nature of the case.

The plea is still more flagrantly inadequate when applied to the exclusion of slavery from the Territories. All the States have confessedly an equal right of property in them. They are a joint possession. The citizens of any State may go there and take up their abode, and, without express contract to the contrary among the proprietors, they are at liberty to observe the customs of their own States. It is as if the land were distributed, and each State had a part. In that case, each State would evidently put its part under the jurisdiction of its own laws. The joint possession, to the extent of the partnership, places the Territory in the same relation to the laws of all the States. One has no more right to introduce its peculiarities than another, and without positive contract the peculiarities of none can be excluded. The case is as if a Christian and a Pagan people should acquire a common territory. Would it be competent for the Christian people, in the absence of a positive stipulation, to say to their Pagan neighbors, You shall not bring your idols into this land? You may come yourselves, but you come only on condition that you renounce your worship? If there is any wrong, it is in making the treaty at first; but if Christians and Pagans can enter into treaties at all, there is no crime in observing them. If they can lawfully acquire joint possession of a soil, the Pagan has as much right to introduce his idols as the Christian his purer worship. In respect to the question of slavery, if there is wrong any where, it is in the union of slaveholding and non-slaveholding States in one confederacy; but, being confederate, there can be no just scruple as to the fulfillment of their contracts. It is a mistake to suppose that the North sanctions slavery by doing justice to the South. It leaves the whole responsibility of the institution where God has placed it, among the people of the South themselves. We do not ask the North to introduce it upon their own soil; we do not ask them to approve it; we do not ask them to speak a single

word in its defence : we only ask them to execute in
good faith the contract which has been solemnly ratified
betwixt us.   We ask them not to interfere with the
jurisdiction of our own laws over our own subjects, nor
with the free use of our own property upon our own
soil.   This is the head and front of our pretensions, and
when these reasonable demands are met by the plea of
conscience and the authority of a higher law, they must
pardon our dullness, if we cannot understand that delicate sensibility to honor which makes no scruple of an
oath that it does not mean to observe, and holds to the
profit, without fulfilling the conditions, of the contract.
When they ask to be released from their engagements,
and, in token of their sincerity, are willing to release
us from ours ; when they are willing to abandon the
Union rather than ensnare their consciences ; when
they abhor the wages, as sincerely as the deeds, of unrighteousness — then, and not till then, they may expect
their plea to be admitted.

2. In the next place, we shall find ample ground of
humiliation, if we consider the manner in which the organs of Government have been perverted from their
real design, and changed in their essential character.
All our institutions are representative.   We legislate
by parliaments, we judge by courts, and we execute by
officers appointed for the purpose.   The people in their
collective capacity do nothing but choose their representatives.   They enact no laws ; they conduct no
trials ; they execute no sentences.   Now, what is the
genius and spirit of a representative assembly ?   Is
it to give expression to the popular will ?   Is it to
find out and do what the people, if assembled in

mass, would do? Is it simply a contrivance to avoid the inconveniences of large convocations, and bound to seek the same results which these convocations would be likely to effect? This doctrine I utterly and absolutely deny. Representatives are appointed, not to ascertain what the will of the people actually is, but what it ought to be. The people are not permitted to legislate *en masse*, because their passions and caprices are likely to prove stronger than reason and truth. Representation is a check upon themselves. Every State is bound to realize the idea of justice. This requires calm deliberation and sober thought. To provide for this deliberation, to protect themselves from their own prejudices and passions, and to cause the voice of reason to be heard, they retire from the scene, aad leave the inquiry and decision of their duty to chosen men, in whose wisdom they have confidence. This is the true theory of parliamentary government. Courts are appointed to interpret the law, and officers to execute the decrees of the courts, in order that justice and not passion may rule in every trial. The supremacy of reason and justice is the supremacy of law and order. Contemplated in this light, parliamentary government is the most perfect under heaven. It avoids equally the extremes of the despotism of a single will, which is sure to terminate in tyranny, and of the still more hateful despotism of mobs, which is sure to terminate in anarchy. It gives rise to a free commonwealth. It aims at the true and right, and truth and rectitude are the safeguards of freedom. Such is the genius of our own institutions. But how has the gold become dim, and the fine gold changed! Has the Congress of these United States fulfilled its high idea? Called together to deliberate, to discuss, to inquire after truth ; bound to listen to no voice but the voice of wisdom and justice — has it always presented the spectacle of gravity, decorum, and candor, which we expect to behold in the Senate of a free people? What shall we say, when gold has usurped the authority of truth, when votes have been bought and sold, and the interests of a faction allowed to outweigh the rights and interests of a whole people? What shall we say, when blows have taken the place of argument, and our halls of legislation have been converted into an arena for the combats of fierce gladiators? What shall we say, when, instead of the language of calm deliberation, the representatives of the people have vied with each other in vituperation and abuse, and, when they have exhausted the dialect of Billingsgate, have rushed upon each other with the ferocity of tigers, or with the fury of the bulls of Bashan? The offence is rank, and smells to heaven. Such an awful prostitution of high functions cannot take place with impunity. The hall which should have inscribed upon its portals *the scene of wisdom and of high debate*, cannot become a den of robbers, or a rendezvous for bullies and hectors, without provoking the just judgments of God. It is a lamentation, and shall be for a lamentation, that the Federal Legislature, which ought to have been a model of refined, impartial and courteous debate — a model to which we could always point with an honest pride, has made itself a scandal to a civilized people. The day of reckoning was obliged to come. The country is brought to the brink of dissolution.

The corruption is of the same kind when the tribunals of the law are set aside, and mobs usurp the jurisdiction of the courts. There may be occasions when the established order is unable to check a threatening evil. In such cases, the necessities of self-defence may justify society in falling back upon its primordial rights. But these occasions are rare. But when society assumes, without necessity, the functions of judges and magistrates, it is guilty of an abuse which, if not arrested, must end in anarchy. *There* only is security where the law is supreme; and the worst of all social evils is where the populace is stronger than the law — where the sentence of courts is annulled by the phrenzy of mobs, and the officers of justice are insulted and restrained in the execution of their functions.

In these respects, all of which resolve themselves into the abuse of the representative principle, we have national sins to confess. We have poisoned the springs of our government. We have given to faction what is due to truth. We have dethroned reason and justice, and made our legislation a miserable scramble for the interests of sections and parties. We have deified the people, making their will, as will, and not as reasonable and right, the supreme law; and they, in turn, have deified themselves, by assuming all the attributes of government, and exercising unlimited dominion. They have become at once legislators, judges, juries, and executioners. The last form of evil has been only occasional, but unless checked and repressed, it may strengthen and expand. In proportion as it increases, reverence for law and for the forms of law loses its power. The tendency to sink our institutions into a pure democracy has been steadily growing. We are rapidly losing even the notion of a representative, by merging it into that of a deputy; and it is but the natural product of this error, that Congress should be the battle-ground of conflicting wills, and that its sole inquiry should become : what says the voice of the majority? *Vox populi, vox Dei.*

I have said, I think, enough to show that in our federal relations, we have reason to be humbled in the presence of God. Our Government is a noble one. Human wisdom could not have devised a better. With all our unfaithfulness it has made us great and prosperous. It has won for us the homage and respect of the world; and had we been faithful to its principles, the blessings it has already conferred upon us would be but the beginning of its triumphs. Could we continue a united people, united in heart as well as in form; could the government be administered according to the real genius of our federal and representative institutions, imagination can hardly conceive the scene of prosperity, influence and glory which would dawn upon our children a hundred years hence. When we contemplate that we might become, and then look at the prospect which is now before us, we have reason to put our hands on our mouths, and our mouths in the dust, and to exclaim : *God be merciful to us sinners !* Let us weep for the country. Let us confess our own sins and the sins of the people. God may hear the cry of the penitent, and say to them, as He said to Moses, when he deplored the sins of his people, *I will make of thee a great nation.*

3. There are other forms of sin which, though not

national in the sense that they pertain to the administration of the government, are national in the sense
that they are widely diffused among the people: they
enter into the grounds of the Divine controversy with
us; and, if not repented of and forsaken, must end in
national calamities. Conspicuous among these is the sin
of profaneness. The name of God is constantly on our
lips, and if the frequency with which it is used were any
sign of religion, ours might pass for the most devout
people under heaven. We introduce it into every subject, and upon all occasions. A sentence is never complete without it. If we are earnest, it enlivens our discourse; if we are angry, it affords a vent to our passions;
if we are merry, it quickens our enjoyments, and if we
are sad, it relieves our misery. Like those particles in
the Greek tongue, which to the philologist give a delicate turn to the meaning, but which to the common
reader might be removed without being missed, the name
of God is indispensable in the vulgar dialect of the
people, but it takes a practised ear to detect the shade
which it gives to the sentence. Many persons would
be dumb if they were not allowed to be profane. The
only words which, as nimble servitors, are ready to obey
their bidding, are the names of God and the awful
terms in which He announces the final doom of the
guilty. These are their vocabulary. Judging from the
discourse which he is likely to hear in the streets, a
stranger might infer that the name was all that we had
left of God; that we were a nation of atheists, who had
at last discovered that He was only a word, and,
determined to make reprisals for the terrors with which
superstition had clothed Him, we were degrading even

the name by the lowest associations. That a puny
mortal should thus trifle with the majesty of God, and
make a jest of the Divine judgments, is a spectacle
which may well astonish the angels, and ought to confound ourselves. Devils hate, but they dare not make
light of God. It is only here upon earth, where the
patience of God is as infinite as His being, that the
name which fills heaven with reverence and hell with
terror is an idle word. Profaneness naturally leads to
licentiousness, by dissolving the sentiment of reverence.

Closely connected with levity in the use of the Divine
name, is the profaneness which treats with contempt the
positive institution of the Sabbath. Here the government is implicated in the sin. It encourages the dese-
cration of the Lord's Day by the companies which
carry its mails. The Sabbath, as an external institute,
is absolutely essential to the maintenance and propaga-
tion of Christianity in the world, and until the Christian religion is disproved, and the supremacy of Christ
set aside, no government on earth can annul it with
impunity.

It is also characteristic of our people that they are
self sufficient and vainglorious, to a degree that makes
them ridiculous. They love to boast, and they love to
sacrifice to their own drag and to burn incense to their
own net. They feel themselves competent for every
enterprise. They can scale heaven, weigh the earth,
and measure the sea. Their own arms and their own
right hand will get them the victory in every under-
taking. Even the style of their conversation is grandi-
loquent. The hyperbole is their favorite figure, and the
superlative their favorite degree of comparison. To

hear their self-laudations, you would never dream that they acknowledged a Providence, or depended on any superior power. All this is the grossest atheism. The consequence of this self-sufficiency is a want of reverence for any thing. We honor neither God nor the king. We revile our rulers, and speak evil of dignities, with as little compunction as we profane the ordinances of religion. Nothing is great but ourselves. It is enough to indicate these types of sin, without dwelling upon them. The important thing is to feel that they are sins. They are so common that they cease to impress us, and in some of their aspects they are so grotesque, they provoke a smile more readily than a tear.

4. Having adverted to the sins which belong to us as members of the Confederacy, let us now turn to those which belong to us as a particular Commonwealth. I shall restrict myself to our dealings with the institution which has produced the present convulsions of the country, and brought us to the verge of ruin. That the relation betwixt the slave and his master is not inconsistent with the word of God, we have long since settled. Our consciences are not troubled, and have no reason to be troubled, on this score. We do not hold our slaves in bondage from remorseless considerations of interest. If I know the character of our people, I think I can safely say, that if they were persuaded of the essential immorality of slavery, they would not be backward in adopting measures for the ultimate abatement of the evil. We cherish the institution not from avarice, but from principle. We look upon it as an element of strength, and not of weakness, and confidently antici-

pate the time when the nations that now revile us would gladly change places with us. In its last analysis, slavery is nothing but an organization of labor, and an organization by virtue of which labor and capital are made to coincide. Under this scheme, labor can never be without employment, and the wealth of the country is pledged to feed and clothe it. Where labor is free, and the laborer not a part of the capital of the country, there are two causes constantly at work, which, in the excessive contrasts they produce, must end in agrarian revolutions and intolerable distress. The first is the tendency of capital to accumulate. Where it does not include the laborer as a part, it will employ only that labor which will yield the largest returns. It looks to itself, and not to the interest of the laborer. The other is the tendency of population to outstrip the demands for employment. The multiplication of laborers not only reduces wages to the lowest point, but leaves multitudes wholly unemployed. While the capitalist is accumulating his hoards, rolling in affluence and splendor, thousands that would work if they had the opportunity are doomed to perish of hunger. The most astonishing contrasts of poverty and riches are constantly increasing. Society is divided between princes and beggars. If labor is left free, how is this condition of things to be obviated? The government must either make provision to support people in idleness, or it must arrest the law of population and keep them from being born, or it must organize labor. Human beings cannot be expected to starve. There is a point at which they will rise in desperation against a social order which dooms them to nakedness and famine, whilst

their lordly neighbor is clothed in purple and fine linen,
and faring sumptuously every day. They will scorn
the logic which makes it their duty to perish in the
midst of plenty. Bread they must have, and bread
they will have, though all the distinctions of property
have to be abolished to provide it. The government,
therefore, must support them, or an agrarian revolution
is inevitable. But shall it support them in idleness?
Will the poor, who have to work for their living, consent to see others as stout and able as themselves clothed and fed like the lilies of the field, while they toil
not, neither do they spin? Will not this be to give a
premium to idleness? The government, then, must find
them employment; but how shall this be done? On
what principle shall labor be organized so as to make it
certain that the laborer shall never be without employment, and employment adequate for his support? The
only way in which it can be done, as a permanent arrangement, is by converting the laborer into capital;
that is, by giving the employer a right of property in
the labor employed; in other words, by slavery. The
master must always find work for his slave, as well as
food and raiment. The capital of the country, under
this system, must always feed and clothe the country.
There can be no pauperism, and no temptations to agra-
rianism. That non-slaveholding States will eventually
have to organize labor, and to introduce something so
like slavery that it will be impossible to discriminate
between them, or to suffer from the most violent and
disastrous insurrections against the system which creates and perpetuates their misery, seems to be as certain as the tendencies in the laws of capital and popu-

lation to produce the extremes of poverty and wealth.
We do not envy them their social condition. With
sanctimonious complacency they may affect to despise
us, and to shun our society as they would shun the in-
fection of a plague. They may say to us, *Stand by —
we are holier than thou;* but the day of reckoning
must come. As long as the demand for labor transcends the supply, all is well: capital and labor are
mutual friends, and the country grows in wealth with
mushroom rapidity. But when it is no longer capital
asking for labor, but labor asking for capital ; when it
is no longer work seeking men, but men seeking work
— then the tables are turned, and unemployed labor
and selfish capital stand face to face in deadly hostility.
We desire to see no such state of things among ourselves, and we accept as a good and merciful constitution the organization of labor which Providence has
given us in slavery. Like every human arrangement, it
is liable to abuse ; but in its idea, and in its ultimate
influence upon the social system, it is wise and beneficent. We see in it a security for the rights of property and a safeguard against pauperism and idleness,
which our traducers may yet live to wish had been en-
grafted upon their own institutions. The idle declama-
tion about degrading men to the condition of chattels,
and treating them as cows, oxen, or swine; the idea
that they are regarded as tools and instruments, and
not as beings possessed of immortal souls, betray a
gross ignorance of the real nature of the relation. Slavery gives one man the right of property in the labor
of another. The property of man in man is only the
property of man in human toil. The laborer becomes

capital, not because he is a thing, but because he is the exponent of a presumed amount of labor. This is the radical notion of the system, and all legislation upon it should be regulated by this fundamental idea.

The question now arises, Have we, as a people and a State, discharged our duty to our slaves? Is there not reason to apprehend that in some cases we have given occasion to the calumnies of our adversaries, by putting the defence of slavery upon grounds which make the slave a different kind of being from his master? Depend upon it, it is no light matter to deny the common brotherhood of humanity. The consequences are much graver than flippant speculators about the diversity of races are aware of. If the African is not of the same blood with ourselves, he has no lot nor part in the Gospel. The redemption of Jesus Christ extends only to those who are partakers of the same flesh and blood with Himself. The ground of his right to redeem is the participation, not of a like, but of a common nature. Had the humanity of Jesus been miraculously created apart from connection with the human race, though it might in all respects have been precisely similar to ours, He could not, according to the Scriptures, have been our Redeemer. He must be able to call us brethren before He can impart to us His saving grace. No Christian man, therefore, can give any countenance to speculations which trace the negro to any other parent but Adam. If he is not descended from Adam, he has not the same flesh and blood with Jesus, and is therefore excluded from the possibility of salvation. Those who defend slavery upon the plea

3

that the African is not of the same stock with ourselves, are aiming a fatal blow at the institution, by bringing it into conflict with the dearest doctrines of the gospel. To arm the religious sentiment against it, is to destroy it. When the question at stake is, whether a large portion of mankind can be saved, we want something more than deductions from doubtful phenomena. Nothing but the Word of God can justify us in shutting the gates of mercy upon any portion of the race. The science, falsely so called, which proffers its aid upon such conditions, is such a friend to slavery as Joab to Amasa, who met him with the friendly greeting, *Art thou in health, my brother?* and stabbed him under the fifth rib. I am happy to say that such speculations have not sprung from slavery. They were not invented to justify it. They are the offspring of infidelity, a part of the process by which science has been endeavoring to convict Christianity of falsehood; and it is as idle to charge the responsibility of the doctrine about the diversity of species upon slaveholders, as to load them with the guilt of questioning the geological accuracy of Moses. Both are assaults of infidel science upon the records of our faith, and both have found their warmest advocates among the opponents of slavery. Our offence has been, that in some instances we have accepted and converted into a plea, the conclusions of this vain deceit. Let us see to it that we give our revilers no handle against us; above all, that we make not God our enemy. Let us not repudiate our kindred with the poor brethren whom He has scattered among us, and entrusted to our guardianship and care. Let us receive them as bone of our bone, and flesh of our flesh. Let us recognize them as having the same Father, the same Redeemer, and the same everlasting destiny.

Let us inquire, in the next place, whether we have rendered unto our servants that which is just and equal. Is our legislation in all respects in harmony with the idea of slavery? Are our laws such that we can heartily approve them in the presence of God? Have we sufficiently protected the person of the slave? Are our provisions adequate for giving him a fair and impartial trial when prosecuted for offences? Do we guard as we should his family relations? And, above all, have we furnished him with proper means of religious instruction? These and such questions we should endeavor to answer with the utmost solemnity and truth. We have come before the Lord as penitents. The people whom we hold in bondage are the occasion of all our troubles. We have been provoked by bitter and furious assailants to deal harshly with them, and it becomes us this day to review our history, and the history of our legislation, in the light of God's truth, and to abandon, with ingenuous sincerity, whatever our consciences can not sanction. Let not the taunts of our revilers shake us from our propriety. Let it be our first care to commend ourselves to God, and, if He be for us, what does it signify who is against us? Our slaves are a solemn trust, and while we have a right to use and direct their labor, we are bound to feed, clothe and protect them, to give them the comforts of this life, and to introduce them to the hopes of a blessed immortality. They are moral beings, and it will be found that in the culture of their moral nature we reap

the largest reward from their service. The relation itself is moral, and in the tender affections and endear-
ing sympathies it evokes, it gives scope for the exercise
of the most attractive graces of human character.
Strange as it may sound to those who are not familiar
with the system, slavery is a school of virtue, and no
class of men have furnished sublimer instances of heroic devotion than slaves in their loyalty and love to their
masters. We have seen them rejoice at the cradle of
the infant, and weep at the bier of the dead; and there
are few amongst us, perhaps, who have not drawn their
nourishment from their generous breasts. Where the
relations are so kindly, there is every motive of fidelity
on our part. Let us apply with unflinching candor the
golden rule of our Saviour. Have we rendered to our
slaves what, if we were in their circumstances, we
should think it right and just in them to render to us.
We are not bound to render unto them what they may in
fact desire. Such a rule would transmute morality into
arbitrary caprice. But we are bound to render unto
them what they have a right to desire: that is, we are
bound to render unto them that which is just and equal.
The Saviour requires us to exchange places, in order
that we may appreciate what is just and equal, free
from the benumbing influences which are likely to pervert the judgment when there is no personal interest in
the decision. I need not say that it is our duty as a
Commonwealth to develop all the capabilities of good
which the relation of slavery contains. They have
never yet been fully unfolded. We have had to attend
so much to the outer defences, that we have not been in
a condition to give full play to the energies of the in-

ward life. This is the problem to which Christian statesmen should hereafter direct their efforts.

II. This day is a day of *prayer*, as well as of humiliation and confession. There are blessings which in our present circumstances we urgently need, and we should make them the burden of importunate supplications. The first is the grace of magnanimity, that our moderation may be known unto all men. By moderation, I do not mean tameness and servility of spirit; and by magnanimity I do not mean what Aristotle seems to understand by it — a consciousness of worth which feels itself entitled to great rewards. The true notion of it is, a just sense of what is due to the dignity of the State, and an humble reliance upon God to make it equal to every occasion. The mind that feels the responsibility of its spiritual endowments, and aims at the perfection of its nature in the consummation of an end which satisfies the fulness of its being, while it arrogates nothing of merit to itself, but ascribes all its capacities to the unmerited bounties of God; the mind that is conscious of what is due to mind, and intent upon fulfilling its own idea — is truly great; and the more thoroughly it is penetrated with this consciousness, the more deeply it is humbled under the conviction of its manifold shortcomings, and the more earnest in its cries for grace to enable it to win the prize. To know our true place in the universe, to feel that we are possessed of noble powers, and that we are bound to pursue an end that is worthy of them, is not pride, but sobriety of judgment. Pride emerges when we attribute to ourselves the excellence of our gifts; when we cherish a spirit of independence and self-sufficiency, and rob God of the glory which is due to His bounty. Humility is not a confession that mind is intrinsically little: it is only the conviction of its absolute dependence upon God, and of its relative nothingness when compared with Him. A Commonwealth is magnanimous when it comprehends the vocation of a State, when it rises to the dignity of its high functions, and seeks to cherish a spirit in harmony with the great moral purposes it was ordained to execute. A magnanimous State can not be the victim of petty passions. It is superior to rashness, to revenge, to irritation, and caprice. It has an ideal which it aims to exemplify ; cultivates a mind upon a level with its calling, and, turning neither to the right nor to the left, presses with undeviating step to the goal before it. It is calm, collected, self-possessed, resolved. It dares do all that may become a State. It will attempt nothing more ; it will be content with nothing less. That we, as a Commonwealth, in the trying circumstances in which we are placed, may be able to exhibit this spectacle of magnanimity to the world ; that we may command its admiration by the dignity and self-respect of our bearing, even though we should not secure its assent to the wisdom of our policy ; that we may make all men see and feel that we are actuated by principle, and not by passion, should be a subject of our fervent supplications this day. Wisdom and courage are the inspiration of God.

In the next place, we should look to Him to raise up for us, as guides and leaders in the present emergency, men of counsel and understanding. Statesmen in the State, as Apostles in the Church, are special ministers of God. They arise at His bidding, and execute His behests. Moses and Joshua, Solon and Lycurgus, the Prince of Orange and Washington, were anointed and commissioned of Heaven for the work they so happily performed. To construct a Government of any kind, is a work of no ordinary magnitude ; but the Government of a free people, with its complicated checks and balances, it is given only to the loftiest minds to be able to conceive, much less to create. If ever there was a time, since the adoption of the Federal Constitution, when the whole country needed the counsel and guidance of patriotic statesmen, it is now, when, under the lead of demagogues, factions and politicians, we have corrupted every principle of our polity, and brought the Government to the brink of dissolution. No human arm is equal to the crisis. No human eye can penetrate the future. Our only help is in God ; from Him alone cometh our salvation. The highest proof of patriotism in the present conjuncture, is in penitence and humility to seek His favor, and if it is his purpose to redeem and save us, in answer to our prayers, He will cause the men to stand forth, and the people to honor and accept them whom He has commissioned to conduct us through the wilderness. In the meantime, let us scrupulously resist every influence that is unfriendly to the influence of His Spirit. Let us mortify every thought, and subdue every passion, upon which we cannot sincerely invoke His blessing. If we are to lay the foundations of a new empire, or to readjust the proportions of the old, the only pledge of permanent success is the Divine favor. Happy is that people, and that people alone, whose God is the Lord.

Finally, let us pray that our courage may be equal to

every emergency. Even though our cause be just, and
our course approved of Heaven, our path to victory
may be through a baptism of blood. Liberty has its
martyrs and confessors, as well as religion. The oak is
rooted amid wintry storms. Great truths come to us
at great cost, and the most impressive teachers of mankind are those who have sealed their lessons with their
blood. Our State may suffer; she may suffer grievous-
ly; she may suffer long: Be it so: we shall love her
the more tenderly and the more intensely, the more bitterly she suffers. It does not follow, even if she should
be destined to fall, that her course was wrong, or her
sufferings in vain. Thermopylæ was lost, but the moral
power of Thermopylæ will continue as long as valor
and freedom have a friend; and reverence for law is
one of the noblest sentiments of the human soul. Let
it be our great concern to know God's will. Let *right*
and *duty* be our watchword; liberty, regulated by law,
our goal; and, leaning upon the arm of everlasting
strength, we shall achieve a name, whether we succeed
or fall, that posterity will not willingly let die.

SLAVERY A DIVINE TRUST.

DUTY OF THE SOUTH TO PRESERVE AND PERPETUATE IT

A SERMON PREACHED IN THE FIRST PRESBYTERIAN CHURCH OF
NEW ORLEANS, LA., NOV. 29, 1860

BY REV. B. M. PALMER, D. D.

———

Shall the throne of iniquity have fellowship with thee, which frameth
mischief by a law? — *Psalm* xciv, 20.

All the men of thy confederacy have brought thee even to the border;
the men that were at peace with thee have deceived thee, and prevailed
against thee; they that ate thy bread have laid a wound under thee;
there is none understanding in him. — *Obadiah* v.

THE voice of the Chief Magistrate has summoned us
to-day to the house of prayer. This call, in its annual
repetition, may be, too often, only a solemn state-form ;
nevertheless, it covers a mighty and a double truth.

It recognizes the existence of a personal God, whose
will shapes the destiny of nations, and that sentiment
of religion in man which points to Him as the needle to
the pole. Even with those who grope in the twiligh
natural religion, natural conscience gives a voice t
the dispensations of Providence. If in autumn " extensive harvests hang their heavy head," the joyous reaper,
" crowned with the sickle and the wheaten sheaf," lifts
his heart to the " Father of lights, from whom cometh
down every good and perfect gift." Or, if pestilence

and famine waste the earth, even pagan altars smoke
with bleeding victims, and costly hecatombs appease the
divine anger which flames out in such dire misfortunes.
It is the instinct of man's religious nature, which, among
Christians and heathen alike, seeks after God — the
natural homage which reason, blinded as it may be,
pays to a universal and ruling Providence.   All classes
bow beneath its spell, especially in seasons of gloom,
when a nation bends beneath the weight of a general
calamity, and a common sorrow falls upon every heart.
The hesitating skeptic forgets to weigh his scruples, as
the dark shadow passes over him and fills his soul with
awe.   The dainty philosopher, coolly discoursing of the
forces of nature and her uniform laws, abandons for a
time his atheistical speculations, abashed by the proofs
of a supreme and personal will.

Thus the devout followers of Jesus Christ, and those
who do not rise above the level of mere theism, are
drawn into momentary fellowship; as, under the pressure of these inextinguishable convictions, they pay a
public and united homage to the God of nature and
grace.

In obedience to this great law of religious feeling, not
less than in obedience to the civil ruler who represents
this Commonwealth in its unity, we are now assembled.
Hitherto, on similar occasions, our language has been
the language of gratitude and song. "The voice of
rejoicing and salvation was in the tabernacles of the
righteous."   Together we praised the Lord "that our
garners were full, affording all manner of store ; that
our sheep brought forth thousands and tens of thousands in our streets ; that our oxen were strong to labor,

and there was no breaking in nor going out, and no
complaining was in our streets." As we together surveyed the blessings of Providence, the joyful chorus
swelled from millions of people, " Peace be within thy
walls, and prosperity within thy palaces." But, to-day,
burdened hearts all over this land are brought to the
sanctuary of God. We " see the tents of Cushan in
affliction, and the curtains of the land of Midian do
tremble." We have fallen upon times when there are
" signs in the sun, and in the moon, and in the stars;
upon the earth distress of nations, with perplexity; the
sea and the waves roaring; men's hearts failing them
for fear, and for looking after those things which are
coming" in the near, yet gloomy, future. Since the
words of this proclamation were penned by which we
are convened, that which all men dreaded, but against
which all men hoped, has been realized; and in the triumph of a sectional majority, we are compelled to read
the probable doom of our once happy and united confederacy. It is not to be concealed, that we are in the
most fearful and perilous crisis which has occurred in
our history as a nation. The cords which, during four-
fifths of a century, have bound together this growing
Republic, are now strained to their utmost tension —
they just need the touch of fire to part asunder forever.
Like a ship laboring in the storm, and suddenly grounded upon some treacherous shoal, every timber of this
vast confederacy strains and groans under the pressure.
Sectional divisions, the jealousy of rival interests, the
lust of political power, a bastard ambition, which looks
to personal aggrandizement rather than to the public
weal, a reckless radicalism, which seeks for the subver-

sion of all that is ancient and stable, and a furious
fanaticism, which drives on its ill-considered conclusions
with utter disregard of the evil it engenders — all these
combine to create a portentous crisis, the like of which
we have never known before, and which puts to a cru-
cifying test the virtue, the patriotism, and the piety of
the country.

You, my hearers, who have waited upon my public
ministry, and have known me in the intimacies of pastoral intercourse, will do me the justice to testify that I
have never intermeddled with political questions. Interested as I might be in the progress of events, I have
never obtruded, either publicly or privately, my opinions upon any of you ; nor can a single man arise and
say that, by word or sign, have I ever sought to warp
his sentiments or control his judgment upon any political subject whatsoever. The party questions which have
hitherto divided the political world, have seemed to me
to involve no issue sufficiently momentous to warrant my
turning aside, even for a moment, from my chosen calling. In this day of intelligence, I have felt there were
thousands around me more competent to instruct in
statesmanship ; and thus, from considerations of modes
ty, no less than prudence, I have preferred to move
among you as a preacher of righteousness belonging to
a kingdom not of this world.

During the heated canvass which has just been
brought to so disastrous a close, the seal of a rigid and
religious silence has not been broken. I deplored the
divisions amongst us, as being, to a large extent, imper-
tinent in the solemn crisis which was too evidently impending. Most clearly did it appear to me that but

one issue before us ; an issue soon to be presented in a
form which would compel the attention. That crisis
might make it imperative upon me, as a Christian and
a divine, to speak in language admitting no misconstruc-
tion. Until then, aside from the din and strife of parties, I could only mature, with solitary and prayerful
thought, the destined utterance. That hour has come.
At a juncture so solemn as the present, with the destiny
of a great people waiting upon the decision of an hour,
it is not lawful to be still. Whoever may have influence to shape public opinion, at such a time must lend
it, or prove faithless to a trust as solemn as any to be
accounted for at the bar of God.

Is it immodest in me to assume that I may represent
a class whose opinions in such a controversy are of cardinal importance — the class which seeks to ascertain
its duty in the light simply of conscience and religion,
and which turns to the moralist and the Christian for
support and guidance? The question, too, which now
places us upon the brink of revolution, was, in its origin, a question of morals and religion. It was debated
in ecclesiastical councils before it entered legislative
halls. It has riven asunder the two largest religious
communions in the land ; and the right determination
of this primary question will go far toward fixing the
attitude we must assume in the coming struggle. I sincerely pray God that I may be forgiven if I have mis-
apprehended the duty incumbent upon me to-day ; for I
have ascended this pulpit under the agitation of feeling
natural to one who is about to deviate from the settled
policy of his public life. It is my purpose — not as
your organ, compromiting you, whose opinions are for

the most part unknown to me, but on my sole responsibility — to speak upon the one question of the day; and to state the duty which, as I believe, patriotism and religion alike requires of us all. I shall aim to speak with a moderation of tone and feeling almost judicial, well befitting the sanctities of the place and the solemnities of the judgment-day.

In determining our duty in this emergency, it is necessary that we should first ascertain the nature of the trust providentially committed to us. A nation often has a character as well-defined and intense as that of the individual. This depends, of course, upon a variety of causes, operating through a long period of time. It is due largely to the original traits which distinguish the stock from which it springs, and to the providential training which has formed its education. But however derived, this individuality of character alone makes any people truly historic, competent to work out its specific mission, and to become a factor in the world's progress. The particular trust assigned to such a people becomes the pledge of Divine protection, and their fidelity to it determines the fate by which it is finally overtaken. What that trust is must be ascertained from the necessities of their position, the institutions which are the outgrowth of their principles, and the conflicts through which they preserve their identity and independence. If, then, the South is such a people, what, at this juncture, is their providential trust? I answer, that it is *to conserve and to perpetuate the institution of slavery as now existing.* It is not necessary here to inquire whether this is precisely the best relation in which the hewer of wood and drawer of water can stand to his employer; although this proposition may perhaps be successfully sustained by those who choose to defend it. Still less are we required, dogmatically, to affirm that it will subsist through all time. Baffled as our wisdom may now be, in finding a solution of this intricate social problem, it would, nevertheless, be the height of arrogance to pronounce what changes may or may not occur in the distant future. In the grand march of events, Providence may work out a solution undiscoverable by us. What modifications of soil and climate may hereafter be produced, what consequent changes in the products on which we depend, what political revolutions may occur among the races which are now enacting the great drama of history ; — all such inquiries are totally irrelevant, because no prophetic vision can pierce the darkness of that future. If this question should ever arise, the generation to whom it is remitted will doubtless have the wisdom to meet it, and Providence will furnish the lights in which it is to be resolved. All that we claim for them and for ourselves is liberty to work out this problem, guided by nature and God, without obtrusive interference from abroad. These great questions of providence and history must have free scope for their solution ; and the race whose fortunes are distinctly implicated in the same is alone authorized, as it is alone competent, to determine them. It is just this impertinence of human legislation, setting bounds to what God only can regulate, that the South is called this day to resent and resist. The country is convulsed simply because " the throne of iniquity frameth mischief by a law." Without, therefore, determining the question of duty for future generations, I simply say, that for us, as now situated, the duty is plain of conserving and transmitting the system of slavery, with the freest scope for its natural development and extension. Let us, my brethren, look our duty in the face. With this institution assigned to our keeping, what reply shall we make to those who say that its days are numbered? My own conviction is, that we should at once lift ourselves, intelligently, to the highest moral ground, and proclaim to all the world that we hold this trust from God, and in its occupancy we are prepared to stand or fall as God may appoint. If the critical moment has arrived at which the great issue is joined, let us say that, in the sight of all perils, we will stand by our trust: and God be with the right!

The argument which enforces the solemnity of this providential trust is simple and condensed. It is bound upon us, then, by the *principle of self-preservation*, that " first law" which is continually asserting its supremacy over others. Need I pause to show how this system of servitude underlies and supports our material interests? That our wealth consists in our lands, and in the serfs who till them? That from the nature of our products they can only be cultivated by labor which must be controlled in order to be certain? That any other than a tropical race must faint and wither beneath a tropical sun? Need I pause to show how this system is interwoven with our entire social fabric? That these slaves form parts of our households, even as our children; and that, too, through a relationship recognized and sanctioned in the scriptures of God even as the other? Must I pause to show how it has fashioned our modes of life, and determined all our habits of thought

and feeling, and moulded the very type of our civilization? How, then, can the hand of violence be laid upon it without involving our existence? The so-called
free States of this country are working out the social
problem under conditions peculiar to themselves. These
conditions are sufficiently hard, and their success is too
uncertain, to excite in us the least jealousy of their lot.
With a teeming population, which the soil cannot support — with their wealth depending upon arts, created
by artificial wants — with an eternal friction between
the grades of their society — with their labor and their
capital grinding against each other like the upper and
nether millstones — with labor cheapened and displaced
by new mechanical inventions, bursting more asunder
the bonds of brotherhood; amid these intricate perils
we have ever given them our sympathy and our prayers,
and have never sought to weaken the foundations of
their social order. God grant them complete success
in the solution of all their perplexities! We, too, have
our responsibilities and our trials; but they are all
bound up in this one institution, which has been the object of such unrighteous assault through five and twenty years. If we are true to ourselves, we shall, at this
critical juncture, stand by it, and work out our destiny.

This duty is bound upon us again *as the constituted
guardians of the slaves themselves.* Our lot is not
more implicated in theirs, than is their lot in ours; in
our mutual relations we survive or perish together.
The worst foes of the black race are those who have intermeddled on their behalf. We know better than
others that every attribute of their character fits them
for dependence and servitude. By nature, the most

affectionate and loyal of all races beneath the sun, they are also the most helpless; and no calamity can befall them greater than the loss of that protection they enjoy under this patriarchal system. Indeed, the experiment has been grandly tried of precipitating them upon freedom, which they know not how to enjoy; and the dismal results are before us, in statistics that astonish the world. With the fairest portions of the earth in their possession, and with the advantage of a long discipline as cultivators of the soil, their constitutional indolence has converted the most beautiful islands of the sea into a howling waste. It is not too much to say, that if the South should, at this moment, surrender every slave, the wisdom of the entire world, united in solemn council, could not solve the question of their disposal. Their transportation to Africa, even if it were feasible, would be but the most refined cruelty; they must perish with starvation before they could have time to relapse into their primitive barbarism. Their residence here, in the presence of the vigorous Saxon race, would be but the signal for their rapid extermination before they had time to waste away through listlessness, filth and vice. Freedom would be their doom; and equally from both they call upon us, their providential guardians, to be protected. I know this argument will be scoffed abroad as the hypocritical cover thrown over our own cupidity and selfishness; but every Southern master knows its truth and feels its power. My servant, whether born in my house or bought with my money, stands to me in the relation of a child. Though providentially owing me service, which, providentially, I am bound to exact, he is, nevertheless, my brother and my friend; and I am to him a guardian and a father. He leans upon me for protection, for counsel, and for blessing; and so long as the relation continues, no power, but the power of almighty God, shall come between him and me. Were there no argument but this, it binds upon us the providential duty of preserving the relation that we may save him from a doom worse than death.

It is a duty which we owe, further, *to the civilized world.* It is a remarkable fact, that during these thirty years of unceasing warfare against slavery, and while a lying spirit has inflamed the world against us, that world has grown more and more dependent upon it for sustenance and wealth. Every tyro knows that all branches of industry fall back upon the soil. We must come, every one of us, to the bosom of this great mother for nourishment. In the happy partnership which has grown up in providence between the tribes of this confederacy, our industry has been concentrated upon agriculture. To the North we have cheerfully resigned all the profits arising from manufacture and commerce. Those profits they have, for the most part, fairly earned, and we have never begrudged them. We have sent them our sugar, and bought it back when refined; we have sent them our cotton, and bought it back when spun into thread or woven into cloth. Almost every article we use, from the shoe-latchet to the most elaborate and costly article of luxury, they have made and we have bought; and both sections have thriven by the partnership, as no people ever thrived before since the first shining of the sun. So literally true are the words of the text, addressed by Obadiah to Edom, "All the

men of our confederacy, the men that were at peace
with us, have eaten our bread at the very time they
have deceived and laid a wound under us." Even beyond this — the enriching commerce which has built the
splendid cities and marble palaces of England as well
as of America, has been largely established upon the
products of our soil; and the blooms upon Southern
fields, gathered by black hands, have fed the spindles
and looms of Manchester and Birmingham not less than
of Lawrence and Lowell. Strike now a blow at this
system of labor, and the world itself totters at the
stroke. Shall we permit that blow to fall? Do we not
owe it to civilized man to stand in the breach and stay
the uplifted arm? If the blind Samson lays hold of
the pillars which support the arch of the world's industry, how many more will be buried beneath its ruins
than the lords of the Philistines? "Who knoweth
whether we are not come to the kingdom for such a
time as this?"

Last of all, in this great struggle, *we defend the cause
of God and religion.* The Abolition spirit is undeni-
ably atheistic. The demon which erected its throne
upon the guillotine in the days of Robespierre and
Marat, which abolished the Sabbath, and worshipped
reason in the person of a harlot, yet survives to work
other horrors, of which those of the French revolution
are but the type. Among a people so generally religious as the American, a disguise must be worn; but it
is the same old threadbare disguise of the advocacy of
human rights. From a thousand Jacobin clubs here, as
in France, the decree has gone forth which strikes at
God by striking at all subordination and law. Availing

itself of the morbid and misdirected sympathies of men,
it has entrapped weak consciences in the meshes of its
treachery ; and now, at last, has seated its high-priest
upon the throne, clad in the black garments of discord
and schism, so symbolic of its ends. Under this spe-
cious cry of reform, it demands that every evil shall be
corrected, or society become a wreck — the sun must be
stricken from the heavens, if a spot is found on his disk.
The Most High, knowing his own power, which is
infinite, and his own wisdom, which is unfathomable,
can afford to be patient. But these self-constituted
reformers must quicken the activity of Jehovah, or compel his abdication. In their furious haste, they trample
upon obligations sacred as any which can bind the conscience. It is time to reproduce the obsolete idea that
Providence must govern man, and not that man should
control Providence. In the imperfect state of human
society, it pleases God to allow evils which check others
that are greater. As in the physical world, objects are
moved forward, not by a single force, but by the composition of forces ; so in his moral administration, there
are checks and balances whose intimate relations are
comprehended only by himself. But what reck they of
this — these fierce zealots who undertake to drive the
chariot of the sun ? working out the single and false
idea which rides them like a nightmare, they dash
athwart the spheres, utterly disregarding the delicate
mechanism of Providence ; which moves on wheels
within wheels, with pivots, and balances, and springs,
which the great designer alone can control. This spirit
of atheism, which knows no God who tolerates evil, no
Bible which sanctions law, and no conscience that can

be bound by oaths and covenants, has selected us for its victims, and slavery for its issue. Its banner-cry rings out already upon the air — "Liberty, equality, fraternity," which, simply interpreted, mean bondage, confiscation and massacre. With its tricolor waving in the breeze, it waits to inaugurate its reign of terror. To the South the highest position is assigned, of defending, before all nations, the cause of all religion and of all truth. In this trust, we are resisting the power which wars against constitutions, and laws and compacts, against Sabbaths and sanctuaries, against the family, the State and the church ; which blasphemously invades the prerogatives of God, and rebukes the Most High for the errors of his administration, which, if it cannot snatch the reins of empire from his grasp, will lay the universe in ruins at his feet. Is it possible that we shall decline the onset ?

This argument, then, which sweeps over the entire circle of our relations, touches the four cardinal points of duty *to ourselves, to our slaves, to the world, and to almighty God.* It establishes the nature and solemnity of our present trust to *preserve and transmit our existing system of domestic servitude, with the right, unchanged by man, to go and root itself wherever Providence and nature may carry it.* This trust we will discharge in the face of the worst possible peril. Though war be the aggregation of all evils, yet, should the madness of the hour appeal to the arbitration of the sword, we will not shrink even from the baptism of fire. If modern crusaders stand in serried ranks upon some plain of Esdraelon, there shall we be in defence of our trust. Not till the last man has fallen behind the last rampart, shall it drop from our hands; and then only in surrender to the God who gave it.

Against this institution a system of aggression has been pursued through the last thirty years. Initiated by a few fanatics, who were at first despised, it has gathered strength from opposition until it has assumed its present gigantic proportions. No man has thoughtfully watched the progress of this controversy without being convinced that the crisis must at length come. Some few, perhaps, have hoped against hope, that the gathering imposthume might be dispersed, and the poison be eliminated from the body politic by healthful remedies. But the delusion has scarcely been cherished by those who have studied the history of fanaticism, in its path of blood and fire through the ages of the past. The moment must arrive when the conflict must be joined, and victory decide for one or the other. As it has been a war of legislative tactics, and not of physical force, both parties have been maneuvering for a position; and the embarrassment has been, while dodging amidst constitutional forms, to make an issue that should be clear, simple and tangible. Such an issue is at length presented in the result of the recent Presidential election. Be it observed, too, that it is an issue made by the North, not by the South; upon whom, therefore, must rest the entire guilt of the present disturbance. With a choice between three national candidates, who have more or less divided the vote of the South, the North, with unexampled unanimity, have cast their ballot for a candidate who is sectional, who represents a party that is sectional, and the ground of that sectionalism, prejudiced against the established and constitutional rights and immunities and institutions of the South. What does this declare — what can it declare — but that from henceforth this is to be a government of section over section ; a government using constitutional forms only to embarrass and divide the section ruled, and as fortresses through whose embrasures the cannon of legislation is to be employed in demolishing the guaranteed institutions of the South ? What issue is more direct, concrete, intelligible than this ? I thank God that, since the conflict must be joined, the responsibility of this issue rests not with us, who have ever acted upon the defensive ; and that it is so disembarrassed and simple that the feeblest mind can understand it.

The question with the South to-day is not what issue shall *she* make, but how shall she meet that which is prepared for her ? Is it possible that we can hesitate longer than a moment ? In our natural recoil from the perils of revolution, and with our clinging fondness for the memories of the past, we may perhaps look around for something to soften the asperity of this issue, for some ground on which we may defer the day of evil, for some hope that the gathering clouds may not burst in fury upon the land.

It is alleged, for example, that the President elect has been chosen by a fair majority, under prescribed forms. But need I say, to those who have read history, that no despotism is more absolute than that of an unprincipled democracy, and no tyranny more galling than than that exercised through constitutional formulas ? But the plea is idle, when the very question we debate is the perpetuation of that constitution now converted into

an engine of oppression, and the continuance of that
union which is henceforth to be our condition of vassalage. I say it with solemnity and pain, this union of
our forefathers is already gone. It existed but in mutual confidence, the bonds of which were ruptured in
the late election. Though its form should be preserved,
it is, in fact, destroyed. We may possibly entertain
the project of reconstructing it ; but it will be another
union, resting upon other than past guarantees. " In
that we say a new covenant, we have made the first old,
and that which decayeth and waxeth old is ready to
vanish away " — " as a vesture it is folded up." For
myself, I say, that under the rule which threatens us, I
throw off the yoke of this union as readily as did our
ancestors the yoke of King George III., and for causes
immeasurably stronger than those pleaded in their celebrated declaration.

It is softly whispered, too, that the successful com-
petitor for the throne protests and avers his purpose to
administer the government in a conservative and national spirit. Allowing him all credit for personal integrity in these protestations, he is, in this matter,
nearly as impotent for good as he is competent for evil.
He is nothing more than a figure upon the political
chess-board — whether pawn, or knight, or king, will
hereafter appear — but still a silent figure upon the
checkered squares, moved by the hands of an unseen
player. That player is the party to which he owes his
elevation ; a party that has signalized its history by the
most unblushing perjuries. What faith can be placed
in the protestations of men who openly avow that their
consciences are too sublimated to be restrained by the

4

obligation of covenants or by the sanctity of oaths?
No: we have seen the trail of the serpent five and
twenty years in our Eden; twined now in the branches
of the forbidden tree, we feel the pangs of death already begun, as its hot breath is upon our cheek, hissing
out the original falsehood, "Ye shall not surely die."

Another suggests, that even yet the electors, alarmed
by these demonstrations of the South, may not cast the
black ball which dooms their country to the execution-
er. It is a forlorn hope. Whether we should counsel
such breach of faith in them, or take refuge in their
treachery — whether such a result would give a President chosen by the people according to the Constitution
— are points I will not discuss. But that it would
prove a cure for any of our ills, who can believe? It
is certain that it would, with some show of justice, exasperate a party sufficiently ferocious — that it would
doom us to four years of increasing strife and bitterness — and that the crisis must come at last, under
issues posssibly not half so clear as the present. Let
us not desire to shift the day of trial by miserable sub-
terfuges of this sort. The issue is upon us; let us meet
it like men, and end this strife forever.

But some quietist whispers, yet further, this majority
is accidental, and has been swelled by accessions of men
simply opposed to the existing administration; the party is utterly heterogeneous, and must be shivered into
fragments by its own success. I confess, frankly, this
suggestion has staggered me more than any other, and
I sought to take refuge therein. Why should we not
wait and see the effect of success itself upon a party
whose elements might devour each other in the very

distribution of the spoil ? Two considerations have dissipated the fallacy before me. The first is, that, however mixed the party, Abolitionism is clearly its informing and actuating soul ; and fanaticism is a blood-hound that never bolts its track when it has once lapped blood. The elevation of their candidate is far from being the consummation of their aims ; it is only the beginning of that consummation ; and, if all history be not a lie, there will be cohesion enough till the end of the beginning is reached, and the dreadful banquet of slaughter and ruin shall glut the appetite. The second consideration is a principle which I cannot blink. It is nowhere denied that the first article in the creed of the new dominant party is the restriction of slavery within its present limits. It is distinctly avowed by their organs, and in the name of their elected chieftain, as will appear from the following extract from an arti-cle written to pacify the South, and to reassure its fears : —

"There can be no doubt whatever in the mind of any man, that Mr. Lincoln regards slavery as a moral, social and political evil, and that it should be dealt with as such by the Federal Government, in every in-stance where it is called upon to deal with it at all. On this point there is no room for question — and there need be no misgivings as to his official action. The whole influence of the Executive Department of the Government, while in his hands, will be thrown against the extension of slavery into the new territories of the Union, and the reopening of the African slave trade. On these points he will make no compromise, nor yield one hair's breadth to coercion from any quarter or in any shape. He does not accede to the alleged decision of the Supreme Court, that the Constitution places slaves upon the footing of other property, and protects them as such wherever its jurisdiction extends ; nor will he be, in the least degree, governed or controlled by it in his executive action. He will do all in his power, personally and officially, by the di-rect exercise of the powers of his office, and the indirect influence in separable from it, to arrest the tendency to make slavery national and perpetual, and to place it in precisely the same position which it held in the early days of the Republic, and in the view of the founders of the Government."

Now, what enigmas may be couched in this last sentence, the sphinx which uttered them can perhaps resolve ; but the sentence in which they occur is as big as the belly of the Trojan horse which laid the city of Priam in ruins.

These utterances we have heard so long, that they fall stale upon the ear; but never before have they had such significance.   Hitherto they have come from Jacobin conventicles and pulpits, from the rostrum, from the hustings, and from the halls of our national Congress ; but always as the utterances of irresponsible men, or associations of men.   But now the voice comes from the throne ; already, before clad with the sanctities of office, ere the anointing oil is poured upon the monarch's head, the decree has gone forth that the institution of Southern slavery shall be constrained within assigned limits.   Though nature and Providence should send forth its branches like the banyan-tree, to take root in congenial soil, here is a power superior to both, that says it shall wither and die within its own charmed circle.

What say you to this, to whom this great providential trust of conserving slavery is assigned ? " Shall the throne of iniquity have fellowship with thee which frameth mischief by a law ? "   It is this that makes the crisis.   Whether we will or not, this is the historic moment when the fate of this institution hangs suspended in the balance.   Decide either way, it is the moment of

our destiny — the only thing affected by the decision is
the complexion of that destiny. If the South bows before this throne, she accepts the decree of restriction
and ultimate extinction, which is made the condition of
her homage.

As it appears to me, the course to be pursued in this
emergency is that which has already been inaugurated.
Let the people in all the Southern States, in solemn
counsel assembled, reclaim the powers they have dele-
gated. Let those conventions be composed of men
whose fidelity has been approved — men who bring the
wisdom, experience and firmness of age to support and
announce principles which have long been matured.
Let these conventions decide firmly and solemnly what
they will do with this great trust committed to their
hands. Let them pledge each other, in sacred covenant, to uphold and perpetuate what they cannot resign
without dishonor and palpable ruin. Let them, further,
take all the necessary steps looking to separate and independent existence, and initiate measures for framing
a new and homogeneous confederacy. Thus, prepared
for every contingency, let the crisis come. Paradoxi-
cal as it may seem, if there be any way to save, or
rather to reconstruct, the Union of our forefathers, it is
this.

Perhaps, at the last moment, the conservative portions of the North may awake to see the abyss into
which they are about to plunge. Perchance they may
arise and crush out forever the Abolition hydra, and
cast it into a grave from which there shall never be a
resurrection.

Thus, with restored confidence, we may be rejoined a

united and happy people.   But, before God, I believe
that nothing will effect this but the line of policy which
the South has been compelled in self-preservation to
adopt.   I confess frankly I am not sanguine that such
an auspicious result will be reached.   Partly, because I
do not see how new guarantees are to be grafted upon
the constitution, nor how, if grafted, they can be more
binding than those which have already been trampled
under foot; but, chiefly, because I do not see how such
guarantees can be elicited from the people at the North.
It cannot be disguised that, almost to a man, they are
antislavery where they are not Abolition.   A whole
generation has been educated to look upon the system
with abhorrence as a national blot.   They hope, and
look, and pray for its extinction within a reasonable
time, and cannot be satisfied unless things are seen
drawing to that conclusion.   We, on the contrary, as
its constituted guardian, can demand nothing less than
that it should be left open to expansion, subject to no
limitations save those imposed by God and nature.   I
fear the antagonism is too great, and the conscience of ,
both parties too deeply implicated to allow such a composition of the strife.   Nevertheless, since it is within
the range of possibility in the providence of God, I
would not shut out the alternative.

Should it fail, what remains but that we say to each
other, calmly and kindly, what Abraham said to Lot:
" Let there be no strife, I pray thee, between me and
thee, and between my herdmen and thy herdmen, for
we be brethren.   Is not the whole land before thee?
Separate thyself I pray thee, from me — if thou wilt
take the left hand, then I will go to the right, or if thou

depart to the right hand, then I will go to the left." Thus, if we cannot save the Union, we may save the inestimable blessings it enshrines ; if we cannot preserve the vase, we will preserve the precious liquor it contains.

In all this, I speak for the North no less than for the South ; for on our united and determined resistance at this moment depends the salvation of the whole country — in saving ourselves we shall save the North from the ruin she is madly drawing down upon her own head.

The position of the South is at this moment sublime. If she has grace given her to know her hour, she will save herself, the country, and the world. It will involve, indeed, temporary prostration and distress ; the dikes of Holland must be cut to save her from the troops of Philip. But I warn my countrymen, the historic moment once passed, never returns. If she will arise in her majesty, and speak now as with the voice of one man, she will roll back for all time the curse that is upon her. If she succumbs now, she transmits that curse as an heir-loom to posterity.

We may, for a generation, enjoy comparative ease, gather up our feet in our beds, and die in peace ; but our children will go forth beggared from the homes of their fathers. Fishermen will cast their nets where your proud commercial navy now rides at anchor, and dry them upon the shore now covered with your bales of merchandise. Sapped, circumvented, undermined, the institutions of your soil will be overthrown ; and within five and twenty years, the history of St. Domingo will be the record of Louisiana. If dead men's bones can tremble, ours will move under the muttered curses of sons and daughters, denouncing the blindness and love of ease which hath left them an inheritance of woe.

I have done my duty under as deep a sense of responsibility to God and man as I have ever felt. Under a full conviction that the salvation of the whole country is depending upon the action of the South, I am impelled to deepen the sentiment of resistance in the Southern mind, and to strengthen the current now flowing toward a union of the South in defence of her chartered rights. It is a duty which I shall not be recalled to repeat, for such awful junctures do not occur twice in a century.

Bright and happy days are yet before us; and before another political earthquake shall shake the continent, I hope to be " where the wicked cease from troubling and where the weary are at rest."

It only remains to say that, whatever be the fortunes of the South, I accept them for my own. Born upon her soil, of a father thus born before me — from an ancestry that occupied it while yet it was a part of England's possessions — she is, in every sense, my mother. I shall die upon her bosom; she shall know no peril but it is my peril — no conflict but it is my conflict — and no abyss of ruin into which I shall not share her fall. May the Lord God cover her head in this her day of battle!

THE CHRISTIAN'S BEST MOTIVE FOR PATRIOTISM.

A SERMON PREACHED IN THE COLLEGE CHURCH, HAMPDEN SIDNEY, VA., ON A GENERAL FAST DAY, NOVEMBER 1, 1860.

BY ROBERT L. DABNEY, D. D.

" Because of the house of the Lord our God, I will seek thy good."— *Psalms* cxxii : 9.

The true Christian feels the claims of patriotism as sensibly as any other man, though he holds them subject to the limitations of justice and charity to others. Thus, King David resolves that he will seek the peace of Jerusalem, the capital city of the Hebrew Commonwealth ; not only as a patriotic king, but from an additional religious motive. So the Christian has a motive for patriotism far stronger and holier than those of all other men. Additional to theirs, he has this reason to pray for the peace of Jerusalem ; for his brethren and companions' sakes, and because of the house of the Lord his God which is in it. The kingdom of Jesus Christ — that blessed kingdom whose sceptre is peace, righteousness, meekness and truth ; in whose prosperity the hopes of a suffering race are all involved, which alone can arrest the flood of sins and woes which now sweeps generation after generation into ruin — is committed by its Divine Head to human hands, and is partially dependent on the course of human events. This spiritual commonwealth among us, as is proper, has no legal ties to the secular, and no other relations than those of mutual good will and courtesy. But still, inasmuch as Christ is pleased to leave to second causes their natural influence over his Church, it is largely dependent on our secular governments. Now there are few things which can affect the interests of Zion so disastrously as political convulsions and war. Let the Christian weigh their influences.

First : We are taught, even by experience of customary party excitements, that a season of political agitation is most unfavorable to spiritual prosperity. Few experienced pastors expect revivals during excited presidential canvasses. The mind is absorbed by agitating secular topics, angry and unchristian emotions are provoked, and the tender dew of heavenly-mindedness is speedily evaporated by the hot and dusty turmoil of the popular meeting and the hustings. Few men who traffic habitually in such scenes exhibit much grace. We suspect that the Christian, returning from a day of such excitement, is little inclined to the place of secret prayer. But how much must all these evil influences be exasperated when the subjects of political strife assume a violent and convulsive aspect ? When every mind is filled by eager, secular concerns — when angry passions rage in every heart, dividing brother against brother in Zion — when unscrupulous haste precipitates multitudes into words and acts of injustice and wrong, agitating and defiling their own consciences, and provoking the hot tumults of resentment on either side — what room is there for the quiet and sacred voice of the Holy Spirit ? It has been remarked by wise historians, that a time of political convulsions is a time of giant growth for all forms of vice. And just to that degree it is a time of barrenness for the Christian graces. ˑ

But when political strife proceeds to actual war, then indeed do "the ways of Zion mourn." War is the grand and favorite device of him who was a liar and murderer from the beginning, to obstruct all spiritual good, and to barbarize mankind. To all the above agitations, distractions and evil passions, raised now to actual phrenzy, must be added the interruptions of Sabbath rest and of public worship, while the sacred hours are profaned with the tumult of preparations, marchings, or actual combats. Domestic life, that most fruitful source of all wholesome restraints, is broken up by danger, fear, waste of property and separations. The youth hurry from that peaceful domain of humanizing and pious influences into the rude noise and gross corruptions of camps, whence they return, if they return at all, depraved by military license, unused to peaceful industry, and hardened to all evil, to poison society at home. Colleges and schools are scattered, the voice of science is silenced, the hopes of peaceful industry are violently destroyed, till recklessness and resentment turn the very husbandman into a bandit. And, above all, Death holds his cruel carnival, and not only by the sword, but yet more by destitution, by vice, by pestilence, hurries his myriads unprepared, from scenes of guilty woe on earth, into everlasting despair below. Need we wonder that the Heavenly Dove should spread its gentle wings, and fly far from such abhorrent scenes?

But civil feud has ever been known as the most bitter of all. " A brother offended is harder to be won than

a strong city: and their contentions are like the bars
of a castle." The very tenderness of brothers' love
makes them more tender to the injury. The strength
of the mutual obligations, which should have bound
them to kindness, enhances the hot indignation at mutual outrage. When the twin lands which now lie so
intimately side by side, parted by a line so long, so
faint, so invisible, that it does not separate, begin to
strike each other, the very nearness and intimacy make
each more naked to the other's blows. How dire, then,
would be the conflagration of battle which would rage
along this narrow line across the whole breadth of a
continent? How deadly the struggle, when the republican hardihood and chivalry, the young, giant strength,
and teeming wealth, which begin to make the mightiest
despots respectful, are turned against each other. Some
seem to delight in placing the relative prowess of the
North and South in odious comparison. Should we
not, my brethren, rather weep tears of blood at the
wretched and wicked thought, that the common prowess with which the North and South have so often side
by side carried dismay and rout into the ranks of common enemies — that terrible prowess which, in North
and South alike, withstood the force of the British Lion
while we were yet in the gristle of our youth, and
which ever since has overthrown and broken every enemy, with the lion's force and the eagle's swiftness combined — should hereafter be expended in fratricidal
blows? And, then, this vast frontier must be forted
and guarded. This hostile neighborhood, so dangerous
because so intimate, must be watched on either hand by
armies; and these armies become, as among the unhap-

py and suspicious nations of Europe, as much the machines of internal oppression as of outward defence. Our future growth of men and wealth would be swallowed up by the devouring maw of strife. These teeming fields, whose increase fills the granaries of the famishing nations, and makes their owners' bosoms to overflow with wealth, must go to feed the barren waste of warlike preparation and labor. The source of half the missionary activities which now gladden the waste places of the earth would be dried up. Farewell to the benign career of imperial *Peace*, by which we had hoped the Empire Republic would teach the angry nations nobler triumphs than those of war. A long farewell to that dream we had indulged — dream not unworthy surely to have been inspired by the *Prince of Peace* — that here a nation was to grow up on this soil, which God had kept till "the fullness of time was come," wrapped in the mysteries of pathless seas, and untainted by the steps of civilized despots, or organized crime ; a nation composed of the strong, the free, the bold, the oppressed of every people, and, like the Corinthian brass, more precious than any that composed it ; which should come, by the righteous arts of peace, to a greatness such as at last to shame and frighten war away from the family of kingdoms ; which should work out the great experiment of equal laws and a free conscience, for the first time, for the imitation of the world ; and from whose bosom a free Church, unstained by the guilt of persecution, and unburdened by the leaden protection of the State, should send forth her light and salvation to the ends of the earth to bring the millenial morning. This cunning machine of law, which now

regulates our rights, would be wrecked amidst the
storms of revolution. The stern exigencies of danger,
would compel both the rivals, perhaps, to substitute the
strong, but harsh will of the soldier, for the mild protection of constitutions. And the oppressors of soul
and body, from every stronghold of absolutism throughout the earth, would utter their jubilant and scornful
triumph: "Lo! the vain experiment of man's self-
government has drowned itself in its own blood and
ruin!" The movement of the world's redemption
might be put back for ages, and the enthroning of the
Prince of Peace over his promised dominion, so long
ravaged by sin and woe, would be postponed, while
eternal death preyed upon yet more of the teeming generations.

Now, in view of this tremendous picture of possible
crime and misery, would to God that I could reach
the ear of every professed servant of Jesus Christ in
the whole land! I would cry to them: Christians of
America — Brothers — Shall all this be? Shall this
Church of thirty thousand evangelical ministers, and
four millions of Christian adults — this Church, so
boastful of its influence and power; so respected and rev-
erenced by nearly all; so crowned with the honors of
literature, of station, of secular office, of riches; this
Church, which moulds the thought of three-fourths of
our educated men through her schools, and of all, by her
pulpit and her press, this Church; which glories in having just received a fresh baptism of the Spirit of Heaven
in a national revival — permit the tremendous picture
to become reality? Nay, shall they aid in precipitating the dreaded consummation, by traitorously in-

flaming the animosities which they should have allayed,
and thus leave the work of their Master to do the
Devil's ? Then, how burning the sarcasm, which this
result will contain upon your Christianity in the eyes of
posterity ! Why, they will say, was there not enough
of the majesty of moral weight in these four millions of
Christians, to say to the angry waves, " Peace : be
still ? " Why did not these four millions rise, with a
LOVE so Christ-like, so beautiful, so strong, that strife
should be paralyzed by it into reverential admiration ?
Why did they not speak for their country, and for the
House of the Lord their God which was in it, with a wisdom before whose firm moderation, righteousness, and
clear light, passion and folly should scatter like the mist ?
Were not all these strong enough to throw the arms of
their loving mediation around their fellow citizens, and
keep down the weapons that sought each other's hearts ;
or rather to receive them into their own bosoms than
permit our mother-country to be slain ? Did this
mighty Church stand idly by, and see phrensy immolate
so many of the dearest hopes of man, and of the rights
of the Redeemer, on her hellish altar ? And this Church
knew too, that the fiend had borrowed the torch of discord from the altar of Christianity, and that therefore
Christians were bound, by a peculiar tie, to arrest her
insane hand, before the precious sacrifice was wrapped
in flames. Then, shame on the boasted Christianity of
America, and of the nineteenth century ! With all its
parade of evangelism, power, and light, wherein has it
been less impotent and spurious than the effete religion
of declining Rome, which betrayed Christendom into
the dark ages ; or than the baptized superstitions which,

in those ages, sanctioned the Crusades and the Inquisition? In the sight of Heaven's righteous Judge, I believe that if the Christianity of America now betrays the interest of man and God to the criminal hands which threaten them, its guilt will be second only to that of the apostate Church which betrayed the Saviour of the world; and its judgment will be rendered in calamities second only to those which avenged the Divine blood invoked by Jerusalem on herself and her children.

How, then, shall Christians seek the good of their country, for the Church's sake? This raises the more practical question of present duty, and introduces the more practical part of my discourse.

And first — Christians should everywhere begin to pray for their country. "Because of the house of the Lord our God, let us seek its good." The guilty Churches of all our land should humble themselves before a holy God, for their Christian backslidings, and our national sins. "Blow the trumpet in Zion, sanctify a fast, call a solemn assembly: Gather the people, sanctify the congregation, assemble the elders, gather the children, and those that suck the breasts; let the bridegroom go forth of his chamber, and the bride out of her closet. Let the priests, the ministers of the LORD, weep between the porch and the altar; and let them say, Spare thy people, O LORD, and give not thy heritage to reproach."

And along with this should go humble confessions of our sins, individual and social. And here, let me distinctly warn you, that I am not about to point your attention to sins of fellow-citizens of another quarter of

the Confederacy, from whose faults some may suppose
the present fear arises. Whether they have committed
faults, or how great, it is not my present concern to
say. Our business is to-day with our own sins. It
will do our hearts no good to confess to God the sins
of our fellow-men : He already knows them, and esti-
mates them more fairly than perhaps our prejudice will
permit us to do. It is for our own sins alone that we
are responsible to God. It is our own sins alone that
we have the means of reforming, by the help of His
grace. Let each man then consider, and forsake his
personal transgressions ; for as your persons help to
swell the aggregate of this great people, so your individual sins have gone to form that black cloud of guilt,
which threatens to hide from us the favorable light of
our Heavenly Father's face. But let us remember, and
confess also, our social sins ; that general worldliness,
which hath set up the high-places of its covetous idola-
tries all over the good land God hath given us ; that
selfish profusion and luxury, which have squandered on
the pride of life so much of the goods of our stewardship ; that Heaven-daring profanity and blasphemy by
reason of which the land mourneth. And let me not
forget faithfully to protest, on such a day as this, against
that peculiar sin of the Southern country, the passion
for bloody retaliation of personal wrong, which has been
so often professed and indulged among us, unwhipped
of justice. You have allowed too often the man of
violence, the duellist, professing his pretended " code
of honor " — most hateful and deceitful pretence of that
Father of Lies, who was a murderer from the beginning
— to stalk through the land with wrongs upon his angry

tongue, and blood upon his hand, while his crime was winked at by justice, and almost applauded by a corrupt public opinion. " So ye have polluted the land wherein ye are ; for blood, it defileth the land, and the land cannot be cleansed of the blood that is shed therein, but by the blood of him that shed it." Let us remember also, that our innocence or rightfulness in the particular point of present differences and anticipated collisions, gives no assurance that God may not chastise us for our sins by those very events. Often has His manifold, wise and righteous providence permitted an unjust aggressor to make himself the instrument, wherewith to lash His sinning people, even when he afterwards punished the invader himself.

Second : We would say, with all the earnestness and emphasis which the most solemn feeling can inspire, let each individual Christian in our land, whether he sits in our halls of legislature, or rules as a magistrate, or guides public opinion through the press, or merely fills the station of the private citizen, consider his own personal concern in this matter. We would affectionately individualize each man, and say to him, my brother, " Thou art the man. Consider what would God have *you* to do ? " Every Christian man, whether law-maker or law-executor or voter, should carry his Christian conscience, enlightened by God's word, into his political duty, in another manner than we have been accustomed to do. We must ask less, what party caucuses and leaders dictate, and more, what duty dictates. For the day is at hand, when we shall be brought to an awful judgment for the thoughtless manner in which we exercise our civic function. My brethren, the Christians of

this land are able to control the selection of reckless
and wicked men for places of trust, if they please, and
will do their duty. Here are four millions of men and
women, chiefly adults, among a people of twenty-six
millions of men, women, children and slaves — four millions who profess to be supremely ruled by principles
of righteousness, peace and love, and to be united to
each other in the brotherhood of a heavenly birth. If
even the voters among these would go together to the
polls, to uphold the cause of peace, they would turn the
scale of every election. Where is the community in all
our land, where the male citizens who are professors of
Christianity would not give the victory to that party to
which they gave their united support? But alas! how
often have we gone on Monday to the hustings, after
having appeared on Sabbath as the servants of the
Prince of Peace, and brethren of all his servants, and
in our political heats speedily forgotten that we were
Christians? Let each Christian citizen have his independent political predilections, and support them with
decision, if you please. Let them, if need be, render
that enlightened and moderate allegiance to the party
of their choice, which is supposed to be essential in free
governments. But when their party demands of them
that they shall sustain men of corrupt private morals or
reckless passions, because of their supposed party orthodoxy, let all Christians say: " Nay, verily, we would
fain yield all reasonable party fidelity; but we are also
partisans in the commonwealth of King Jesus, and our
allegiance to Him transcends all others. Unless you
will present us a man who to party orthodoxy unites
private virtues, we cannot sustain him." Then would

their reasonable demand be potential in every party,
and the abuse would be crushed. And this stand, if
taken by Christian citizens, we affirm, would infringe
no personal or associated rights. For, is there any
party who would admit that it had not a single member
respectable, virtuous and sober enough to deserve the
suffrages of Christian men? If there is, surely it is
time it should slink away from the arena of political
competition, and hide itself in oblivion! Here, then, is
a prominent duty, if we would save our country, that we
shall carry our citizenship in the kingdom of Heaven
everywhere, and make it dominate over every public act.
We must obey the law of God rather than the unrighteous behests of party, to " choose out of all the
people *able men, such as fear God, men of truth, hating
covetousness, and place such over them to be rulers,*"
or God will assuredly avenge himself for our violated
allegiance to him. The Christians of this country must
sternly claim that wicked or reckless men shall no longer hold the helm of State ; that political orthodoxy
shall no longer atone for that worst offence against citizenship, a wicked life. And along with rulers, I would
include the directors of the public press, as being of the
general class of " leaders of the people." Even while
you boast of the potency of this engine of the nineteenth
century, you have allowed it to fall in many cases into
most incompetent and dangerous hands. See who have
held this responsible lever in our land in these latter
days! Some are honorable and patriotic ; but more are
unreliable ; some mere half-educated youths, without
any stake of family, estate, or reputation in the commu-

nity; some fiery denouncers, some touching the springs
of public affairs with a drunken hand, and many the
open advocates and practitioners of the duellist's murderous code — these men you have permitted and even
upheld and salaried, in your easy thoughtlessness, to
misrepresent, misdirect and inflame the public sentiment
of the nation!

There are many reasons which demand of every
God-fearing citizen that he shall sustain, directly or
indirectly, none but honest and prudent men in places
of influence. When you elevate a bad man, you give
to him a hundred-fold more power of example to corrupt your sons, and your neighbors' sons, by his evil
acts. Those acts are a hundred-fold more conspicuous
and more weighty to attract notice and imitation, than
if you had left him in his deserved obscurity. When
you delegate your money, influence, or civic power, to
a bad man, you make his wicked official acts and influence your own; he is your chosen agent, and acts for
you, and be assured a jealous God will not forget to
visit the people for the guilt thus contracted.

But especially should you remember, at such a period
as this, the boundless mischief wrought by the habit of
reckless vituperation, and the political violence, in
which bad and foolish or inexperienced men indulge, to
further political ends. It is this which chiefly has created our present unhappy dangers, by misrepresenting
each section to the other. You have heard descriptions
of the *reign of terror* in the first French Revolution,
and perhaps as you saw the frightful and murderous
violence of political factions there displayed, you have

exclaimed : " Were these men or devils ? " They were
men, my brethren; " men of like passions with us."
Read the narrative of the philosophic *Thiers*, and you
will learn the source of these rivers of blood.   Unscrupulous leaders of parties and presses, in order to
carry their favorite projects and overpower political rivals, resorted to the *trick* of imputing odious and malignant motives to all adversaries ; democrats denouncing Girondists and royalists as traitorous plotters of
foreign invasion, and national sack ; royalists denouncing democrats as agrarians and robbers, till by dint of
bandying the outrageous charges backwards and forwards, all minds were gradually embittered and prepared to believe the worst.   Hence the bloody political
proscriptions ; hence the frightful butcheries of the
Septembriseurs; because misguided men were taught to
believe that no less trenchant remedy would anticipate
the treason designed against the country.

Now I say to you in all faithfulness, that the reckless
and incapable men whom you have weakly trusted with
power or influence, have already led us far on towards
similar calamities.   They have bandied violent words,
those cheap weapons of petulant feebleness ; they have
justified agression ; they have misrepresented our tem-
pers and principles — answered, alas, by equal misrep-
resentations and violence in other quarters — until
multitudes of honest men, who sincerely suppose themselves as patriotic as you think yourselves, are really
persuaded that in resisting your claims, they are but
rearing a necessary bulwark against lawless and arrogant agressions.   Four years ago, an instance of unjust

and wicked insolence was avenged, on the floor of the Senate of the United States, by an act of violence most unrighteous and ill-judged. And now, not so much that rash and sinful act of retaliation, but the insane, wicked, and insulting justification of it generally made by Southern secular prints, directed by reckless boys, or professed duellists, a justification abhorred and condemned by almost all decent men in our section, is this day carrying myriads of votes, (of men who, if not thus outraged, might have remained calm and just towards us,) for the cause whose triumph you deprecate. Thus the miserable game goes on ; until at last, blood breaks out, and the exhausted combatants are taught in the end, by mutually inflicted miseries, to pause and consider, that they are contending mainly for a misunderstanding of each other.

Now I well know, my brethren and fellow-citizens, that if I should speak to you in private, you would all concur in my honest reprobation of this folly and injustice : I know that I have but expressed the common sentiments of all good men among us. Yet, in your dislike to be troubled, in your easy good nature, you let things take their course, under the wretched mismanagement of the hands into which they have fallen ; you even permit your money and your influence to go indirectly, in support of these agents of mischief and misrule, who thus misrepresent your characters, and aims, and rights. If the public interests cannot arouse you from this good natured sin, let me see if I cannot touch you more nearly. Whereunto can all this mutual violence grow ? Do not the increasing anger and preju-

dice, which seems so fast ripening on both sides for a
fatal collision, tell you too plainly? And when these
rash representatives of yours in our halls of legislation
and our newspapers, shall have sown the wind, who
will reap the whirlwind? When they have scattered
the dragon's teeth, who must meet that horrent crop
which they will produce? Not they alone; but you,
your sons, your friends and their sons. So that these
misleaders of the people, while you so weakly connive
at their indiscretions, may be indirectly preparing the
weapon which is to pierce the bosom of your fair-haired
boy; and summoning the birds of prey, which are to
pick out those eyes whose joy is now the light of your
happy homes, as he lies stark on some lost battle-field.
For God's sake, then — for your own sakes, for your
children's sake, arise — declare that from this day, no
money, no vote, no influence of yours, shall go to the
maintenance of any other counsels than those of moderation, righteousness, and manly forbearance.

Last: Every Christian must study the things which
make for peace. All must resolve that they will demand of others nothing more than their necessary
rights, and that, in the tone of moderation and forbearance. Yea, that they will generously forego all except
what duty forbids them to forego, rather than have
strife with brethren. We must all be magnanimous
enough to forbear the language of threatening and reproach, (language which evinces no courage,) to acknowledge the excesses of ourselves and our friends,
and to make reparation for it, whether such reparation
be offered on the other side or not. Instead of complain-

ing in vindictive and bitter spirit of the extravagances of misguided men on the opposite side, each man should enquire whether there are not sinful extravagances on his own side; and when it is necessary to remonstrate, do it in the tone of wounded love, rather than of insane threatening. In one word; let each one resolve to grant all that is right, and ask nothing else; "and lo, there will be a great calm."

[The reader of this sermon will notice that its date, before the late Presidential election, accounts in part for its topics and also for its omissions. He is also requested to bear in mind that the professed attitude of the people to whom it was preached,—that of penitents before the Most High, rendered aliusions to their own sins alone appropriate at that time ; and hence the sermon contains no implication that they are the only, or the chief offenders, in those particulars.—R. L. D.]

THE UNION TO BE PRESERVED.

A DISCOURSE DELIVERED AT LEXINGTON, KY., ON THE DAY OF THE NATIONAL FAST, JAN. 4, 1861.

BY ROBERT J. BRECKINRIDGE, D. D.

It is in circumstances, my friends, of terrible solemnity, that this great nation presents herself in an attitude of humiliation before the Lord God of Hosts; in circumstances of great solemnity, that she stands before the bar of all surrounding nations, under that universal public opinion which gives fame or stamps with infamy, and hardly less solemn than both is her attitude at the bar of distant ages, and especially our own posterity, that awful tribunal whose decrees can be reversed only by the decree of God.

It is the first of these three aspects, either passing by in silence or touching very slightly the other two, that I am to consider before you now. And what I shall chiefly attempt to show is, that our duties can never be made subordinate to our passions without involving us in ruin; and that our rights can never be set above our interests without destroying both.

In taking this direction, let us bear in mind that the proclamation of the Chief Magistrate of the Republic which calls us to this service, asserts, in the first place, that ruin is impending over our national institutions; and asserts, in the second place, that so far as appears

to him, no human resources remain that are adequate to
save them; and, in the third place, that the whole nation, according to his judgment, ought to prostrate itself before God and cry to Him for deliverance. Upon
this I have to say, in the great name of God, and by
the authority of Jesus Christ the Saviour of the world,
these two things: 1. That national judgments never
come except by reason of national sins; nor are they
ever turned aside except upon condition of repentance
for the sins which produced them; and, 2. That repentance for sin, as it is the absolute and universal, so
it is the infallible condition of divine pardon and acceptance, not only in the case of individuals, but more
obviously still and more immediately in the case of nations, since nations, as such, have no existence in a future life. Wherefore, if we are in the way of fearful
evils we are also in the way of clear duty, and therein
we may hope for assured deliverance in the degree, 1.
That every one will go before another in earnest en-
deavors to rectify in himself all that is abominable to
God; and, 2. That every one will evince towards others the forbearance which he desires that God should
extend to him. Wherefore, also we may boldly say
that the remedy from God to us need not be expected
to manifest itself by means of political parties, or by
means of combinations of political leaders, or by means
of new political compacts, or by means of additional
legal enactments, or by means of more explicit constitutional provisions; but that it must come from God to
us and be made manifest through a profound movement
in the source of all power in free governments, namely: 1. In the hearts of individual men turning from

L. of C

their sins, their follies and their madness; and, 2. In the uprising of an irresistible impulse thus created, which over the length and breadth of the land shall array itself in the power of God against every endeavor to bring upon us the evils which we are imploring God to avert.

The first and greatest of these evils that we beseech God to avert, and that we should strive with all our might to prevent, is the annihilation of the nation itself, by tearing it into fragments. Men may talk of rights perpetually and outrageously violated; they may talk of injuries that are obliged to be redressed; they may talk of guarantees without which they can submit to no further peace; and there is doubtless much that has force and much more that is captivating to ardent minds in such expositions of our sad condition; for what problem half so terrible was ever agitated upon which it was not easy to advance much on every side of it? I will not consume the short time allowed to me in examining such views. What I assert in answer to them all, is that we have overwhelming duties and incalculable interests which dictate a special line of conduct, the chief aim of which should be the preservation of the American Union, and therein of the American nation.

To be more explicit, it seems to me that there are inestimable blessings connected with the preservation of our National Union, and that there are intolerable evils involved in its destruction. For the blessings — there is the blessing of peace amongst ourselves; there is the blessing of freedom to ourselves and to our posterity; .there is the blessing of internal prosperity secured by that peace and freedom, never before excelled if attained by any people ; there is the blessing of our national independence, secured by our invincible strength against all the powers of the earth combined ; there is the blessing of our glorious example to all nations and to all ages ; there is the blessing of irresistible power to do good to all peoples, and to prevent evil over the face of the whole earth ; there is the blessing of an unfettered Gospel, and an open Bible, and a divine Saviour, more and more manifested in our whole national life as that life deepens and spreads, subduing and possessing the widest and the noblest inheritance ever given to any people, and overflowing and fructifying all peoples besides. It is the problem sought to be solved from the beginning of time, and, to say the least, the highest approximation made to its solution, namely, the complete possession of freedom united with irresistible national force, and all directed to the glory of God and the good of man. And this is that glorious estate now declared to be in fearful peril, and which we are called upon to beseech God to preserve unto us.

On the other hand, the evils of rending this nation : Which of the blessings that I have enumerated — and I have enumerated only those which appeared to me to be the most obvious — which of these is there, peace, freedom, prosperity, independence, the glory of our example, the power to do good and to prevent evil, the opportunity to give permanent efficiency all over this continent, and in a certain degree all over this earth to the Gospel of God ; which of these blessings is there that may not be utterly lost to vast portions of the nation ; which of them may not be jeoparded over this whole continent; which of them is there that may not depart forevermore from us and our posterity, in the attempt to destroy our oneness as a people, and in the results of that unparalleled self-destruction? Besides all this, how obvious and how terrible are the evils over and above, which the very attempt begets, and which our after progress must necessarily make permanent if that attempt succeeds. 1. We have already incurred the perils of universal bankruptcy before the first act is achieved by one of the least important of the thirty-three States. 2. We have already seen constitutional government, both in its essence and in its form, trampled under foot by the convention of that State; and all the powers of sovereignty itself, both ordinary and extraordinary, assumed by it in such a manner that life, liberty and property have no more security in South Carolina than anywhere under heaven where absolute despotism or absolute anarchy prevails, except in the personal characters of the gentlemen who hold the power. 3. We have already seen that small community preparing to treat with foreign nations, and, if need be, introduce foreign armies into this country, headlong in the career in which she disdains all counsel, scorns all consultation and all entreaty, and treats all ties, all recollections, all existing engagements and obligations as if her ordinance of secession had not only denationalized that community, but had extinguished all its past existence. 4. We see the glorious flag of this Union torn down and a colonial flag floating in its place; yea, we see that community thrown into paroxysms of rage, and the cabinet at Washington thrown into confusion because in the harbor of Charleston our national flag, instead of being still further dishonored, yet floats over a single tower! What, then, did they expect who sent to the harbor of Charleston, to occupy the national fortresses there, the son of a companion of Washington, a hero whose veins are full of revolutionary blood and whose body is covered with honorable scars, won in the service of his country? Why did they send that Kentucky hero there if they did not intend the place they put into his hands to be kept to the last extremity? But I need not enlarge upon this terrible aspect of what is coming to us all if the Union is destroyed. These are but the beginnings of sorrows. The men and parties who initiate the reign of lawless passion, rarely escape destruction amid the storms they create, but are unable to control. Law comes from the depth of eternity, and in its sublime sway is the nexus of the universe. Institutions *grow;* they are not *made.* Desolated empires are never restored; all history furnishes no such example. If we desire to perish, all we have to do is to leap into this vortex of disunion. If we have any just conception of the solemnity of this day, let us beseech God that our country shall not be torn to pieces; and under the power of these solemnities let us quit ourselves like men, in order to avert that most horrible of all national calamities.

Let us consider, in the next place, those rights, as they are called, by means of which, and in their extreme exercise, all the calamities that threaten us are to be brought upon us at any moment; nay, are to be so brought upon us, that our destruction shall be perfectly regular, perfectly legal, perfectly constitutional. In which case a system like ours, a system the most enduring of all others, whether we consider the history of the past, or the laws which enter into its composition; a system the hardest of all others to be deranged, and the easiest of all to be readjusted when deranged; such a system is alleged to have a secret in it, designed expressly to kill it, at the option of the smallest fragment of it. I allude to the claim of the right of nullification, and the claim of the right of secession, as being Constitutional rights; and I desire to explain myself briefly in regard to them.

According to my apprehension, there is a thorough and fundamental difference between the two. The power of nullification, supposing it to exist, would be an extreme right within the Union, and is necessarily temporary in its effects, and promptly tends to the termination of the difficulty upon which it arises. And this settlement may occur by the action of our complex system of government in various ways. It may be in the way of some compromise of existing difficulties; or in the way of repeal, by one party or the other; or the modification of the obnoxious laws; or in the way of some judicial decision settling the difficulty or — which is the true remedy — instead of nullification, by an appeal to the people at the polls, who are the source of all power in free governments, and by obedience to their decision when rendered by voting instead of by fighting, or, at the worst, by an appeal to arms; but even in that case the result necessarily secures the continuance of the preëxisting system of government on the restoration of peace, let that peace be by victory on which side you please. The doctrine of nullification stands related to the doctrine of State Rights, precisely

as the doctrine of consolidation stands related to the
old Federal doctrine of a strong Central Government.
In both cases the theory of a great party has been
pushed to a logical absurdity, which subverted our political system. That the will of the greater part should
prevail, and that the smaller parts should have the
power of appeal to this will, at the polls, and in judgment upon every principle of civil and political liberty
— was the ultimate form in which this great doctrine
entered into the political creed of that old Republican
party which came into power with Mr. Jefferson in
1801, and was expounded as they held it in those famous resolutions of Kentucky and Virginia in the latter
part of the last century. Its connection with the whole
theory of every mixed political system is not only absolute but is vital. More especially is it so with our
complex system. It has been carried — as it stands
connected with the constitutional, and much more with
the reserved rights of the States, to an extreme on that
side — opposite to the extreme of consolidation. But
even in its extremest form, it bears no proportion in
mischief to the doctrine of secession. Considered in its
true and original form, I judge it to be indispensable to
the preservation of our political system; and that the
opposite mode of interpreting our political duties, and
rights, and remedies, terminates in subjugating the
States to the General Government, and in subjugating
both the General Government and the exposition of
every political principle to the Supreme Court of the
United States. The former system is natural and permanent, the latter is absurd, and invites rebellion.
This great phenomenon has occurred in this country,

that, by reason of the extraordinary ability of some of the advocates of the system which passed away in 1801, it has assumed a new form and a new life in general opinion, and seconded by the peculiar constitution of the Supreme Court of the United States, the old Republican or Democratic notions upon this great subject, though constantly triumphant in the country, have been constantly allowed in the interpretations of that Court. I judge that the doctrine of secession is an extreme reaction against this Federal interpretation of the relations of the States to each other and to the nation. For when you arrive at an interpretation which is final, and hateful to immense parties and interests; and there is no remedy but arms, secession, or absolute submission; the expression of the popular will against the interpretation you have made, brings society to a condition, that in an excitable race and amongst a free people, can hardly be expected to be safe or easy to be managed. You have, therefore, this perilous and extraordinary claim of the right of secession under this extreme reaction, differing absolutely from the idea of the old State Rights party, and differing absolutely even from nullification itself.

Secession is a proceeding which begins by tearing to pieces the whole fabric of Government, both social and political. It begins by rendering all redress of all possible evils utterly impossible under the system that exists, for its very object is to destroy that existence. It begins by provoking war, and rendering its occurrence apparently inevitable and its termination well nigh impossible. Its very design is not to reform the administration of existing laws, not to obtain their repeal or modification ; but to annihilate the institutions of the country, and to make many nations out of one. If it is the Constitutional right of any State to do this, then we have no national Government and never had any. Then, also, it is perfectly idle to speak of new Constitutions, since the new Constitutions can have no more force than the Constitution already despised and disobeyed. Then, also, the possibility is ended — ended in the very theory of the case, and illustrated in the utter failure of its practice — of uniting Republican freedom with national strength in any country or under any form of government. But according to my belief, and according to the universal belief of the American people but a little while ago, no such right, legal or Constitutional, as that of secession, does or can exist under any form of government, and least of all under such institutions as ours.

And, first of all, no State in this Union ever had any sovereignty at all, independent of, and except as they were, *United* States. When they speak of recovering their sovereignty — when they speak of returning to their condition as sovereigns in which they were before they were members of the Confederacy called at first the United Colonies and then the United States ; they speak of a thing that has no existence — they speak of a thing that is historically without foundation. They were not States ; they were colonies of the British, the Spanish, the French, the Dutch Governments ; they were colonies granted by Royal charter to particular individuals or particular companies. Pennsylvania was the estate, the property of William Penn ; Georgia, the larger part, perhaps the whole of it, of Gen. Oglethorpe. They were settled under charters to individuals and to companies — settled as colonies of foreign kings and States by their subjects; as such they revolted; as such, before their revolt, they united in a Continental Government more or less complete. As such United Colonies, they pronounced that famous Declaration of Independence which, after a heroic struggle of seven years, still as United Colonies, they made good.

The great Washington, who led that great war, was the Commander-in-Chief for and in behalf of these United Colonies. As such they were born States. The treaty of peace, that made them independent States, was concluded with them all together as the United States. What sovereignty did Kentucky ever have except the sovereignty that she has as a State of these United States, born at the same moment a State of the American Union and a separate sovereign State? We were a district of Virginia. We became a State, and we became one of the United States at the same moment, for the same purpose, and for good and all. What I mean by this is to point out the fact that the complex system of government which we have in this country, did always, does now, and in the nature of the case, must contemplate these States as united into a common Government, and that common Government as really a part of our political system, as the particular institutions of the separate sovereignties are a part of our political system. And while, as you will observe, I have attempted, while repudiating the doctrine of nullification, to vindicate that doctrine of State rights, which, as I firmly believe, is an integral and indispensable part of our political system; yet on the other

hand, that the doctrine that we are a nation, and that
we have a national government, is, and always was,
just as truly a part of our system as the other. And
our political system always stood as much upon the basis that we are a nation, as it stood upon the basis that
that nation is composed of sovereign States. They
were born into both relations; so born that each State
is equally and forever, by force of its very existence
and the manner thereof, both a part of this American
nation and also a sovereign State of itself. The people, therefore, can no more legally throw off their national alleigance than they can legally throw off their
State allegiance. Nor can any State any more legally
absolve the allegiance of its people to the nation, than
the nation can legally absolve the allegiance due by the
people to the State they live in. Either attempt, considered in any legal, in any constitutional, in any historical light, is pure madness.

Now the pretext of founding the right of secession
upon the right to change or abolish the government,
which is constitutionally secured to the people of the
nation and the States, seems to me — and I say it with
all the respect due to others — to be both immoral and
absurd. Absurd, since they who claim to exercise it
are, according to the very statement of the case, but an
insignificant minority of those in whom the real right
resides. It is a right vested by God, and recognized
by our Constitutions as residing in the greater part of
those who are citizens under the Constitution which
they change or abolish. But what in the name of God,
and all the possible and all the imaginable arrogance of
South Carolina, could lead her to believe that she is the

major part of all the people that profess allegiance to the Constitution of the United States? And it is immoral, because it is trifling with the sacred rights of others, with the most solemn obligations on our own part, and the most vital interests of all concerned. And it is both immoral and absurd in one, because as a political pretext, its use in this manner invalidates and renders perilous and odious, the grandest contribution of modern times to the science of government, and therein to the peace of society, the security of liberty and the progress of civilization; namely, the giving constitutional validity to this natural right of man to change or to abolish the government under which they live, by voting, when the major part see fit to do so. It is trifling with this great natural right, legalized in all our American Constitutions, fatally caricaturing and recklessly converting it into the most terrible engine of organized legal destruction. More than that; it is impossible, in the very nature of the case and in the very nature of government, that any such legal power or any such constitutional right could exist; because its existence presupposes law to have changed its nature and to have become a mere device; and presupposes government to have changed its nature, and ceasing to be a permanent ordinance of God, to become a temporary instrument of evil in the hands of factions as they successively arise. Above all places under heaven, no such right of destruction can exist under our American Constitutions, since it is they that have devised this very remedy of voting instead of fighting; they that have made this natural right a Constitutional right; they that have done it for the preservation and not for the ruin of society. And it has preserved it for more than seventy years the noblest form of human society, in constant security; and it could, if justly exercised, preserve it forever.

But let us go a little deeper still. It cannot be denied that the right of self-preservation, both in men and States, is a supreme right. In private persons, it is a right regulated by law in all communities that have laws. Amongst nations, there is no common supreme authority, and it must be regulated in their intercourse with each other, by the discretion of each; and arms are the final appeal. In our system of government, there is ample provision made. In all disputes between any State and foreign nation, the General Government will protect and redress the State.

In disputes between two States, the Supreme Court is the Constitutional arbiter. It is only in disputes that may arise between the General Government and a particular State, that any serious difference of opinion as to the remedy, has manifested itself in this country; and on that subject it is the less necessary that I add anything to what has been said when speaking of nullification, as the grounds of our existing difficulties are not between the disaffected States and the General Government chiefly if at all; but they are difficulties, rather founded on opposite states of public opinion touching the institution of negro slavery, in the Northern and in the Southern States. It may confidently be asserted that if the power of nullification, or the power of secession, or both of them, were perfectly constitutional rights, neither of them should be, under any circumstances, wantonly exercised. Nor should either of them, most especially the

right of secession, ever be exercised except under extreme necessity.   But if these powers, or either of
them, is a mere usurpation founded upon no right whatever, then no State may resort to rebellion or revolution, without, in the first place, such a just and necessary cause as may not be otherwise maintained; or, in
the second place, without such a prospect of success as
justifies the evil of rebellion or revolution; or else such
intolerable evils as justify the most desperate attempts.
Now it is my profound conviction that nothing has occurred, that nothing exists, which justifies that revolution which has occurred in South Carolina, and which
seems to be impending in other Southern States.   Beyond all doubt, nothing has occurred of this description,
connected with any other interest or topic, except that
of negro slavery; and connected with that, my deep
assurance is, that the just and necessary cause of the
slave States, may be otherwise maintained than by secession, revolution or rebellion; nay, that it may be
incomparably better maintained otherwise; nay, that it
cannot be maintained in that way at all, and that the
attempt to do so will be fatal as regards the avowed
object, and pregnant with incalculable evils besides.

In such discussions as these, the nature of the institution of slavery is perfectly immaterial.   So long as
the union of the States survives, the constitutional guar-
anty and the Federal power, which have proved adequate for more than seventy years, are that much added
to whatever other force States or sections may possess
to protect their rights.   Nor is there, in the nature of
the case, any reason why States with slaves, and States
without slaves should not abide together in peace, as

portions of the same great nation, as they have done from the beginning. The unhallowed passions of men, the fanaticism of the times, the mutual injuries and insults which portions of the people have inflicted on each other, the cruel use which political parties have made of unnatural and transient popular excitements, and, I must add, the unjust, offensive and unconstitutional enactments by various State Legislatures at the North; the repeal of the Missouri Compromise by Congress; the attempt of the Supreme Court to settle political principles, deemed to be of vast importance by all parties, in the Dred Scott case, which principles were not in the case at all; the subsequent conduct of the Federal Government, and of the people in Kansas; the total overthrow of the Whig and American parties, the division and defeat of the Democratic party, and the triumph of the Republican party; the ordinance of secession of South Carolina; the agitation pervading the whole nation, especially the greater part of the Southern States; and to crown all and if possible, to make all desperate, the amazing conduct of the President of the United States amidst these great disorders. This is the sad outline of this slavery agitation, the posture of which for a moment is thus exhibited, no one knowing how soon new and fatal steps may hurry us still farther. What I assert in the face of so much that is painful and full of peril, and what I confidently rely will be the verdict of posterity, is that all this, terrible as it is, affords no justification for the secession of any single State of the Union — none for the disruption of the American Union. They who make the attempt will find in it no remedy for the evils from which they flee. They who goad others to this fatal step, will find that they have themselves erred exceedingly. They who have had the lead in both acts of madness, have no hope for good from coming ages, half so great as that they may be utterly forgotten. Posterity will receive with scorn every plea that can be made for thirty millions of free people, professing to be Christian, in extenuation of the unparalleled folly of their self-destruction, by reason that they could not deal successfully with three or four millions of African slaves, scattered amongst them. Oh ! everlasting infamy, that the children of Washington did not know how to be free. Oh ! degradation still deeper, that the children of God did not know how to be just and to forbear with one another.

It is said, however, it is now too late. The evil is already done. South Carolina has already gone ; Florida, it is most likely went yesterday, or will go to-day, even while we are pleading with one another, and with God, to put a better mind in her. Soon, it may be possible within the present month, all the cotton States will go. We, it is added, by reason of being a slave State, must also go. Our destiny, they say, our interest, our duty, our all, is bound up with theirs, and we must go together. If this be your mind, distinctly made up, then the whole services of this day are a national mockery of God ; a national attempt to make our passionate impulses assume the dignity of divine suggestions, and thus seduce the Ruler of the universe into complicity with our sins and follies, through which all our miseries are inflicted upon us. Let it be admitted that a certain number of States, and that considerable, will attempt to form a Southern Confederacy, or to form as

many new sovereignties as there are seceding States.
Let it be assumed that either of those results is achieved, and that either by way of peace or war. Let all be
admitted. What then ? Thirteen States by their del-
egates formed the present Constitution more than seventy years ago. By the terms of the Constitution itself,
it was to be enforced when any nine of those thirteen
States adopted it, whether by convention of their people or otherwise, is immaterial to the present matter.
Thirteen States made the Constitution by their dele-
gates ; a clause is inserted in it that it shall go into effect when any nine of the thirteen States adopt it, let
any four refuse as they might. If they had refused
what would have happened, would have been, that these
four States, born States, and born United States, by the
Declaration of Independence, by the war of the revolution, by the peace with Great Britain, and by the articles of confederation, would by a common agreement
among the whole thirteen have refused to go further, or
to make any stronger national government, while the
other nine would have gone further, and made that a
stronger national government. But such was the desire
of all parties that there should be no separation of the
States at all, that the whole thirteen unanimously
adopted the new Constitution, putting a clause into it
that it should not go into effect unless a majority so
great as nine to four would sign it. I say if a minority
of States had not adopted the new Constitution, it
would have occurred that they would have passed, by
common consent, into a new condition, and, for the first
time, have become separate sovereign States. As you
well know, none of them refused permanently. What

I make this statement for, is to show that, taking that principle as just and permanent, as clearly laid down in the Constitution, it requires at least eleven States of the existing thirty-three States, to destroy, or affect in the slightest degree, the question as to whether or not the remaining States are the United States of America under the same Constitution. Twenty-two States, according to that principle, left after the eleven had seceded, would be as really the United States of America under that Federal Constitution, as they were before, according to the fundamental principle involved in the original mode of giving validity to the Constitution. Kentucky would still be as really one of these United States of America as she was at first, when, as a district of Virginia, which was one of the nine adopting States, she became, as such district, a part thereof; and, by consequence, a secession of less than eleven States, can, in no event, and upon no hypothesis, even so much as embarrass Kentucky in determining for herself what her duty, her safety and her honor require her to do.

This fact is so perfectly obvious that, I presume, if the New England States, instead of the cotton States, were to revolt and establish a separate confederacy, there is not a man in the State of Kentucky who would be led thereby to suppose that our relations with the Union and the Constitution were in the slightest degree affected; or that they were on that account under the slightest obligation to revolt also. It may sound harsh, but I am very much inclined to think that there are many thousands of men in Kentucky, who might be apt to suppose that the secession of the New England States would be a capital reason why nobody else should secede. It is the principle, however, which I am attempting to explain.

The answer to this view, I am aware is, that we are a slave State, and that our relations are, therefore, necessarily different with respect to other slave States, as compared with the free States, or with the nation at large. The reply to which is various: First. The institution of slavery as it exists in this country presents a threefold and very distinct aspect. First, the aspect of it in those States whose great staples are rice, sugar and cotton commonly, and well enough expressed by calling them the cotton States. Then the aspect of it presented by those States in portions of which those fabrics are raised, and in other portions of which they are not, which we may well enough call the mixed portion of the slave States. And then its aspect in those Slave States which are not producers of those great staples, in the midst of which, and out of which these great commotions come. What I assert is, that the relation of slavery to the community, and the relation of the community by reason of slavery to the General Government and the world, is widely different in all three of these classes of States. The relation of slavery to the community, to the government and to our future, in Kentucky, in Virginia, in Maryland, in Delaware, is widely different from the relation of slavery in all these respects, in Louisiana, in South Carolina, and in all the other cotton States. In the meantime, also, the relation is different from both of those, wherein it exists in what I have called the mixed States; in Arkansas, part of which is a farming country, and a part of which thoroughly planting; in Tennessee, part cotton, and the

eastern part a mountainous and farming country; in
Texas and North Carolina where similar facts exist,
and, perhaps, in some other States. What I desire is
that you get the idea I have of the matter; that while
it is true all the slave States have certain ties and sympathies between them which are real, and ought not to
be broken, yet, on the other hand, it is extremely easy
to carry this idea to a fatal and a false extent, and to
ruin ourselves forever under the illusion begotten thereby. In Kentucky the institution of slavery exists about
in the proportion of one slave to four white people, and
the gap between the two races is widening at every census. In South Carolina there are about five slaves to
three white persons, and the increment is on the slave
side. In the cotton States I know of no way in which
the institution of slavery can be dealt with at all, except by keeping the relation as it stands, as an integral
portion of the body politic, unmanageable except in the
present relation of the negro to the white man; and in
this posture it is the duty of the nation to protect and
defend the cotton States. In regard to Kentucky, the
institution of slavery is in such a position that the people of Kentucky can do with it whatever they may see
fit, both now and at any future period, without being
obliged, by reason of it, to resort to any desperate ex-
pedient, in any direction.

The state of things I have sketched, necessarily produces a general resemblance indeed, because slavery is
general; but, at the same time, innumerable diversities,
responsive to the very condition of slavery, of its products, and of its relative influence in the body politic
in the different slave States. And you never commit-

ted a greater folly than you will commit, if, disregarding these things, you allow this single consideration — that you are a slave State — to swallow up every other consideration, and control your whole action in this great crisis. We in Kentucky are tolerant of opinion. Inform yourselves of what is passing of an opposite character throughout South Carolina, and reflect on the change that must pass on you, before you would be prepared to tear down the most venerable institutions, to insult the proudest emblems of your country's glory, and to treat constitutions and laws as if they were playthings for children ; before you are prepared to descend from your present noble posture, and surrender yourself to the guidance and dictation of such counsels and such statesmen as rule this disunion movement. Nothing seems to me more obvious, and nothing is more important to be pressed upon your attention at this moment, than that the non-cotton States stand in a position radically different, in all respects, from the position in which the cotton States stand, both with regard to the institution of slavery, and with regard to the balance of the nation. The result is that all these States, the cotton States, and the mixed States, and the non-cotton slave States, and the free States, may enjoy peace, and may enjoy prosperity under a common government, and in a common Union, as they have done from the beginning ; where the rights of all and the interests of all may be respected and protected, and yet where the interests of every portion must be regulated by some general consideration of the interests which are common to everybody. On the other hand, in a confederacy where cotton is the great idea and end, it

is utterly impossible for the mixed, much more for the
non-cotton States to protect adequately any of their
rights, except the right of slavery, to carry out any of
their purposes except purposes connected with slavery,
to inaugurate any system of policy, or even to be free,
otherwise than as they servilely follow the lead, and
bow to the rule of the cotton States. The very instant
you enter a confederacy in which all is regulated and
created by the supreme interest of cotton, everything
precious and distinctive of you is jeoparded. Do you
want the slave trade re-opened ? Do you want free
trade and direct taxation ? Do you want some millions
more of African cannibals thrown amongst you, broadcast throughout the whole slave States ? Do you want
to begin a war which shall end when you have taken
possession of the whole Southern part of this continent,
down to the Isthmus of Darien ?

If your design is to accept the principles, purposes
and policy which are openly avowed in the interest of
secession, and which you see exhibited on a small scale,
but in their essence, in South Carolina — if that is your
notion of regulated freedom and the perfect security of
life and property ; if that is your understanding of
high national prosperity, where the great idea is more
negroes, more cotton, direct taxes, free imports from
all nations, and the conquest of all outlying land that
will bring cotton ; then, undoubtedly, Kentucky is no
longer what she has been, and her new career, beginning with secession, leads her far away from her strength
and her renown.

The second suggestion I have to make to you is, that
if the slave line is made the line of division, all the

slave States seceding from the Union, and all the free States standing united by the Union; what I assert in that case is, that the possibility of the perpetuity of negro slavery in any border State, terminates at once. In our affected zeal for slavery, we will have taken the most effectual means of extinguishing it; and that in the most disastrous of all possible ways. On the contrary, if this Union is to be saved, it is by the cordial sympathy of the border States on the one side and on the other side of the slave line that it must be saved. We have nothing to hope for from the extreme States on either side — nothing from the passionate violence of the extreme South — nothing from the turbulent fanaticism of the extreme North. It is along that slave line and in the spirit of mutual confidence, and the sense of common interest of the people on the North and on the South of that line that the nation must seek the instruments of its safety. It is Ohio, Indiana, Illinois, Pennsylvania, New Jersey, on the one side; and Maryland, Delaware, Virginia, Kentucky, Missouri — God send that I might add, with confidence, Tennessee and North Carolina, on the other side: these are the States that are competent to save this Union. Nothing, therefore, can be more suicidal than for the border slave States to adopt any line of conduct which can justly deprive them of the sympathy and confidence of the border free States — now largely possessed by them. And nothing is more certain than that a patriotic devotion to the Union, and a willingness to do all that honorable men should do, or moderate men ask in order to preserve it, is as strongly prevalent at this moment amongst the people of the border free States as

among those of the border slave States.   The great
central States I have enumerated, must necessarily control the fate both of the nation and of the continent,
whenever they act in concert ;   and the fate, both of
the nation and of the continent, is utterly inscrutable
after the division of them on the slave line — except
that we know when Sampson is shorn of his strength,
the enemies of Israel and of God will make the land
desolate.   Fronting on the Atlantic Ocean through
many degrees of latitude, running back across the continent so as to include an area larger than all western
Europe, and finer than any of equal extent upon the
globe, embracing a population inferior to none on earth,
and sufficiently numerous at present to constitute a great
nation, it is this immense power, free, to a great extent, from the opposite and intractable fanaticisms of
the extreme States on both sides of it, that is charged
with the preservation of our national institutions, and
with them our national power and glory.   These are
two aspects of the case thus put — in either of which
secession by peaceful means is impossible: first, if these
great central States fail to apprehend this part of the
great mission committed to them ;   secondly, if the cotton States, following the example of South Carolina —
or the Northern States adhering to extreme purposes in
the opposite direction — by either means render all
peaceful adjustment impossible.

But even in that case, the mission of these great
States is not ended.   If under the curse of God and
the madness of the extreme Northern and Southern
States, the preservation of the Union should be impossible, then it belongs to this immense central power to

reconstruct the nation upon the slave line as its central idea, and thus perpetuate our institutions, our principles and our hopes, with an unchanged nationality. For even they who act in the mere interests of slavery, ought to see, that after the secession of the cotton States, the border slave States are obliged, even for the sake of slavery, to be destroyed, or to adhere to the Union as long as any Union exists; and that if the Union were utterly destroyed, its reconstruction upon the slave line is the solitary condition on which slavery can exist in security anywhere, or can exist at all in any border State.

I have considered three possible solutions of the existing state of things. The preservation of the Union as it is; the probable secession of the cotton slave States, and the effect thereof upon the Union, and upon the course Kentucky ought to take; the total destruction of the Union, and its reconstruction upon the slave line. I have considered the whole matter, from the point of view understood to be taken by the President of the United States, namely: that he judges there is no power in the General Government to prevent, by force, its own dissolution by means of the secession of the States; and I have done this, because however ruinous or absurd any one may suppose the views of the President to be, it is nevertheless under their sway that the first acts of our impending revolutions are progressing. Under the same helpless aspect of the General Government, there remain two more possible solutions of the posture and duty of Kentucky, and other States similarly situated. The first of these is, that in the progress of events, it may well become the border slave

States to unite themselves into a separate confederacy; the second is, that it may well become Kentucky, under various contingencies, to assume a separate sovereign position, and act by herself. Having clearly stated my own conclusions, I will only say that the first of these two results is not one to be sought as desirable itself, but only as an alternative to be preferred to more dangerous arrangements. For my unalterable conviction is, that the slave line is the only permanent and secure basis of a confederacy for the slave States, and especially for the border slave States; and that the Union of free and slave States, in the same confederacy, is the indispensable condition of the peaceful and secure existence of slavery. As to the possible isolation of Kentucky, this also, it seems to me, is not a result to be sought. If it should occur as the alternative to evils still greater, Kentucky ought to embrace it with calmness and dignity, and awaiting the progress of events, show by her wisdom, her courage, her moderation, her invincible rectitude, both to this age and to all that are to come, how fully she understood, in the midst of a gainsaying and backsliding generation, that no people ever performed anything glorious who did not trust in God, who did not love their country, and who were not faithful to their oaths.

It seems to me, therefore, that the immediate duty of Kentucky may clearly be stated in very few words:

1. To stand by the Constitution and the Union of the country to the last extremity. 2. To prevent, as for the moment the impending and immediate danger, all attempts to reduce her, all attempts to terrify her into the taking of any step, inconsistent with her own Con-

stitution and laws; any step disregardful of the Constitution and laws of the United States; any step which can possibly compromise her position or draw her on otherwise than by her own free choice, deliberately expressed at the polls, according to her existing laws and Constitution, whereby she will choose her own destiny. 3. To settle on her heart that the rending of this Union on the slave line is, for her, whatever it may be for others, the most fatal issue that the times can have, and the doing this in such a way as to subject her to the dominion of the cotton States for all time to come, is the very worst form of that fatal issue.

After all, my friends — after all, we have the great promise of God that all things shall work together for good to them that love him. I do not know but that it may be the mind of God, and his divine purpose, to break this Union up, and to make of it other nations, that shall at last be more powerful than it, unitedly, would have been. I do not know, I do not pretend to say, how the Lord will use the passions of men to glorify his name. He restrains the remainder of wrath and will cause the wrath of man to praise Him. We have His divine assurance that all nations that have gone before us, and all that will follow us, and we ourselves, by our rise, by our progress, and, alas! by our decay and ruin, are but instruments of His infinite purpose, and means in His adorable providence, whereby the everlasting reign of Messiah, the Christ of God, is to be made absolute and universal.

Great, then, is our consolation, as we tremble for our country, to be confident in our Lord! Great is our comfort as we bewail the miseries which have befallen our glorious inheritance, to know that the Lord God Omnipotent reigneth! Infinitely precious is the assurance, amidst the trials now impending, and the woes which threaten us, that the heroic self devotion with which our personal duty is discharged, is one part of our fitness to become partakers of the inheritance of the saints in light!

THE CHARACTER AND INFLUENCE OF ABOLITIONISM.

A SERMON PREACHED IN THE FIRST PRESBYTERIAN CHURCH, BROOKLYN, DECEMBER 9, 1860.

BY REV. HENRY J. VAN DYKE.

---

1. Let as many servants as are under the yoke count their own masters worthy of all honor, that the name of God and his doctrine be not blasphemed.

2. And they that have believing masters, let them not despise them, because they are brethren ; but rather do them service, because they are faithful and beloved, partakers of the benefit. These things teach and exhort.

3. If any man teach otherwise, and consent not to wholesome words, even the words of our Lord Jesus Christ, and to the doctrine which is according to godliness ;

4. He is proud, knowing nothing, but doting about questions and strifes of words, whereof cometh envy, strife, railings, evil surmisings,

5. Perverse disputings of men of corrupt minds, and destitute of the truth, supposing that gain is godliness : from such withdraw thyself.— 1 *Timothy* vi : 1–5.

I propose to discuss the character and influence of abolitionism. With this view, I have selected a text from the Bible, and purpose to adhere to the letter and spirit of its teaching. We acknowledge, in this place, but one standard of morals — but one authoritative and infallible rule of faith and practice ; for we are Christians here ; not blind devotees, to bow down to the dictation of any man or church ; not heathen phi-

losophers, to grope our way by the feeble glimmerings
of the light of nature ; not modern infidels, to appeal
from the written law of God to the corrupt and fickle
tribunal of reason and humanity ; but Christians, on
whose banner is inscribed this sublime challenge : —
" To the law and to the testimony ; if they speak not
according to this word, it is because there is no light in
them."

Let me direct your special attention to the language
of our text.   There is no dispute among commentators,
there is no room for dispute, as to the meaning of the
expression, " servants under the yoke."   Even Mr.
Barnes, who is himself a distinguished Abolitionist, and
has done more, perhaps, than any other man in this
country to propagate Abolition doctrines, admits, that
" the addition of the phrase ' under the yoke,' shows
undoubtedly that it (*i. e.*, the original word, *doulos*) is
to be understood here of slavery."*   Let me quote an-

* Mr. Barnes adopts a most extraordinary method to avoid the force
of the precept which commands slaves who have believing masters to "*do
them service, because they are faithful and beloved, partakers of the
benefit.*"   He says : " The passage before us only proves that Paul considered that a man who was a slaveholder *might* be converted and be
spoken of as a believer or a Christian.   Many have been converted in
similar circumstances, as many have been in the practice of *all other
kinds of iniquity.*   What was their duty *after* their conversion, was another question ; and what was the duty of their servants or slaves was
another question still."

Again he says : " The passage does not teach that a man *can* be a
Christian, and *continue* to hold others in bondage.   It does not teach
that he ought to be considered as maintaining a good standing in the
church if he *continues* to be a slaveholder.   The fact that a man might
be converted who was a slaveholder, no more proves that it would be
right and desirable that he should *continue* that relation, than the fact

other testimony on this point from an eminent Scotch divine. I mean Dr. McKnight, whose Exposition of

that Saul of Tarsus became a Christian when engaged in persecution proves that it would have been right for him to continue in that business, or that the conversion of the Ephesians, who used ' curious arts,' proved that it would have been proper for them to continue in that employment. Men who are doing wrong, are converted in order to turn them *from* that course of life, not to justify them *in* it." Now, in view of these extracts, I have three remarks to make. (1.) They illustrate the power of fanaticism to embitter the heart. Mr. Barnes well knew when he wrote these passages, that multitudes of the noblest and holiest men of this land have been, and are, slaveholders — that many of the founders of our government, with Washington at their head, were slaveholders — that there are now in our Southern States thousands of Christian masters who give every Scriptural evidence of piety ; and yet in a way that is all the more severe, because of its quiet and seemingly gentle manner, he teaches that slaveholding is a crime on a par with the imposture of the Ephesian sorcerers, with the slaughter of Saul the persecutor, a crime so obvious and enormous, that a convert from heathenism, without any inspired instruction upon the subject, at once, and instinctively, abandoned it. (2.) These extracts illustrate most pitiably how fanaticism warps the human intellect. The inspired Apostle commands *that slaves who have believing masters* (not masters *who might become* believers, as Mr. Barnes, with an amazing ingenuity, intimates, but *believing masters* — masters who *had been* converted) *should do them service.* And why? BECAUSE they are " faithful and beloved, partakers of the benefit." Because these masters had been converted, were beloved of God, were faithful in the discharge of their social duties, were partakers of the benefits of Divine grace — THEREFORE, their slaves were to be the more obedient and respectful in their deportment. Now does not any one see that such a precept *contemplates the continuance* of the relation between the Christian master and his slaves? Would Paul so stultify himself as to give commandments for the regulation of that relation, based upon the fact of the master's conversion, if he had expected and known this fact would instantly dissolve the relation itself? When he says, " Children, obey your parents in the Lord," does he not imply that the parental relation is to be continued? And so when, in the very same passage (Ephesians vi. 1—5), he says, " Servants (*douloi*, slaves), be obedient to them that are your masters according to the

the Epistles is a standard work in Great Britain and in this country, and whose associations must exempt him from all suspicion of pro-slavery prejudices. He introduces his exposition of this chapter with the following explanation : — " Because the law of Moses (Exodus xxi. 2) allowed no Israelite to be made a slave for life without his own consent, the Judaizing teachers, to allure slaves to their party, taught that under the gospel, likewise, involuntary slavery is unlawful. This doctrine the Apostle condemned here, as in his other epistles, (1 Cor. vii. 20 ; Col. iii. 22 ; Eph. vi. 5,) by enjoining Christian slaves to honor and obey their mas-

---

flesh," does he not intimate, in the strongest form, that he expects *that* relation to continue?

(3.) These passages cast an imputation upon the integrity and candor of the great Apostle. I do not say Mr. Barnes *meant* such an imputation; I speak of the effect of such interpretations upon those who imbibe their spirit. Mr. B puts slaveholding on a level with " all other kinds of iniquity," and indicates his estimate of its guilt by choosing persecution and sorcery to illustrate it. Very well, then; if this be true. Paul might treat " all other kinds of iniquity " in the same way. To be consistent, he should have said : " Sorcerers, use your curious arts and practice your impostures in a Christian way. Persecutors, when you hale men and women, and breathe out threatenings and slaughter against the Church, see to it that you strangle and beat and kill the saints in the most gentle and tender manner. Adulterers, give to your paramours that which is just. Adulteresses, be obedient and submissive to those whom you serve. Men who go down from Jerusalem to Jericho, do not despise the thieves among whom you fall, for they ' are faithful and beloved, partakers of the benefit.' " Who does not see the gross impiety of attributing such teaching to the great Apostle ? But upon whom is this impiety chargeable ? Let the text of this discourse answer the question. Let those who teach that Paul held back the truth in regard to an enormous crime, answer to their own conscience, and to the distracted country which they have embroiled in fraternal strife, by their unscriptural dogmas.

ters, whether they were believers or unbelievers, and by
assuring Timothy that if any person taught otherwise,
he opposed the wholesome precepts of Jesus Christ, and
the doctrine of the gospel, which in all points is conformable to godliness or sound morality, and was puffed
up with pride, without possessing any true knowledge
either of the Jewish or Christian revelation." Our
learned Scotch friend then goes on to expound the passage in the following paraphrase, which we commend to
the prayerful attention of all whom it may concern : —

"Let whatever Christian slaves are under the yoke of unbelievers pay their own masters all respect and obedience, that
the character of God whom we worship may not be calumniat-
ed, and the doctrine of the gospel may not be evil spoken of,
as tending to destroy the political rights of mankind. And
those Christian slaves who have believing masters, let them not
despise them, fancying that they are their equals because they
are their brethren in Christ; for, though all Christians are
equal as to religious privileges, slaves are inferior to their masters in station. Wherefore, let them serve their masters more
diligently, because they who enjoy the benefit of their service
are believers and beloved of God. These things teach, and
exhort the brethren to practise them. If any one teach differ-
ently, by affirming that, under the gospel, slaves are not bound
to serve their masters, but ought to be made free, and does not
consent to the wholesome commandments which are our Lord
Jesus Christ's, and to the doctrine of the gospel, which in all
points is conformable to true morality, he is puffed up with
pride, and knoweth nothing either of the Jewish or the Christian revelations, though he pretends to have great knowledge of
both ; but is distempered in his mind about idle questions and
debates of words, which afford no foundation for such a doctrine, but are the source of envy, contention, evil-speaking, un-

just suspicion that the truth is not sincerely maintained, keen disputings carried on contrary to conscience, by men wholly corrupted in their minds and destitute of the true doctrine of the gospel, who reckon whatever produces most money is the best religion. From all such impious teachers withdraw thyself, and do not dispute with them."

It would be easy for me to confirm the testimony of Dr. McKnight, by extracts from commentators of every name and nation. Suffer me to select a few as representatives of various religious denominations.

Dr. ADAM CLARK, who is the standard of biblical criticism among our Methodist brethren, and perhaps the most learned man that large and zealous denomination has ever produced, gives us the following clear exposition : —

" The word *douloi* (servants) here means *slaves* converted to the Christian faith ; and the *zugon* or yoke is *the state of sla-very*, and by *despotai*, masters, we are to understand the heathen masters of those christianized slaves. Even these, in such circumstances, and under such domination, are commanded to treat their masters with all honor and respect, that the name of God by which they were called, and the doctrine of God, Christianity, which they had professed, might not be blasphemed — might not be evilly spoken of in consequence of their improper conduct. Civil rights are never abolished by any communications from God's Spirit. The civil state in which a man was before his conversion, is not altered by that conversion ; nor does the grace of God absolve him from any claims which either the State or his neighbor may have on him. All these outward things continue unaltered. *And they that have believing masters let them not despise them*, supposing themselves to be their equals because they are their brethren in Christ : and grounding their opinion on this, that *in him there is neither male or female, bond nor free :* for, although all are equal as to their spiritual privileges and state, yet there still continues in the order of God's providence a great disparity in their station ; the master must ever be, in this sense, superior to the servant. *But rather do them service* — obey them the more cheerfully, because they are *faithful* and *beloved* — *faithful* to God's grace, *beloved* by Him and His true followers. *Partakers of the benefit.* This is generally understood as referring to the master's participation in the services of his slaves; or it may apply to the servants who are partakers of many benefits from their Christian masters. Others think that *benefit* here refers to the grace of the gospel, the common salvation of believing masters and slaves."

Dr. DODDRIDGE, a great light among the English Congregationalists, whose practical works are in almost every Christian family, and whose precious hymns are sung wherever the name of Christ is known, gives us the following paraphrase :

"Let, therefore, as many servants as are under *the yoke of bondage,* account their own masters worthy of all that civil honor and respect which suits the station in which they respectively are : not taking occasion from their own religious knowledge and privilege to despise and rebel against them ; that the name and doctrine of God which they profess may not be blasphemed by their insolence and pride. And as for those servants who are so happy as to have believing masters, let them not presume on that account to despise them because they are brethren, and with respect to sacred privileges equal in Christ their common Lord ; but let them rather serve them with so much the greater care and tenderness, because they are faithful and beloved, and partakers with them of the great and glorious benefit which the gospel brings to all its professors of whatever rank or station in life."

I will add one more testimony from OLSHAUSEN, (as continued by WIESINGER,) a work which stands deservedly high among the most evangelical productions of modern Germany.

" *Vs.* 1. 'As many under the yoke as are slaves,'—thus De Wette rightly renders the words, taking *douloi* as the predicate : for the distinction cannot be intended to be drawn between such slaves as are under the yoke and such as are not. A slave is *as such* under the yoke : the expression therefore does not imply harsh treatment ; nor can it in itself mark the distinction between such slaves as serve heathen and such as serve Christian masters. The expression is rather used by the apostle in opposition to the *false ideas that were held on the subject of emancipation.* Whosoever is under the yoke is to conduct himself according to this his position. They are to count their masters worthy of all honor, that the name of God and the doctrine be not blasphemed. One can easily conceive what danger there was lest the Christian slave should inwardly exalt himself above his heathen master, and look down upon him. To meet this danger, there is here required of him not merely outward subjection, but inward esteem.

" *Vs.* 2 treats of Christian slaves under Christian masters. Such slaves are not to see in the fact of their masters being their brethren in Christ, a reason for despising them, (for to place themselves on a level with those to whom they owe subjection is already to despise them ;) but they are rather to find in this circumstance a motive to serve the more, *i. e.*, to do all the more what their position as slaves lays upon them."

Dr. GILL, the well known Baptist Commentator, gives us substantially the same exposition.

The text, as thus expounded by the concurrent testimony of all the commentators, is a prophecy written for these days, and wonderfully applicable to our present circumstances. It gives us a lifelike picture of Aboli- tionism in its principles, its spirit, and its practice, and furnishes us plain instruction in regard to our duty in the premises. Before entering upon the discussion of the doctrine, let us define the terms employed. By Abolitionism, we mean the principles and measures of Abolitionists. And what is an Abolitionist? He is one who believes that slaveholding is sin, and ought therefore to be abolished. This is the fundamental, the characteristic, the essential principle of Abolitionism — that slaveholding is sin — that holding men in involun- tary servitude is an infringement upon the rights of man, a heinous crime in the sight of God. A man may believe, on political or commercial grounds, that slavery is an undesirable system, and that slave labor is not the most profitable; he may have various views as to the rights of slaveholders under the constitution of the country; he may think this or that law upon the statute books of the Southern States is wrong; but this does not constitute him an Abolitionist; to be entitled to this name, he must believe *that slaveholding is morally wrong*. The alleged sinfulness of slaveholding, as it is the characteristic doctrine, so it is the strength of Abo- litionism in all its ramified and various forms. It is by this doctrine that it lays hold upon the hearts and con- sciences of men, that it comes as a disturbing force into our ecclesiastical and civil institutions, and by exciting religious animosity, (which all history proves to be the strongest of human passions,) imparts a peculiar inten- sity to every contest into which it enters. And you will perceive it is just here that Abolitionism presents a

proper subject for discussion in the pulpit: for it is one
great purpose of the Bible, and therefore one great duty
of God's ministers in its exposition, to show what is sin
and what is not.

Those who hold the doctrine that slaveholding is sin,
and ought therefore to be abolished, differ very much in
the extent to which they reduce their theory to practice. In some this faith is almost without works. They
content themselves with only voting in such a way as in
their judgment will best promote the ultimate triumph
of their views. Others stand off at what they suppose
a safe distance, as Shimei did when he stood on an opposite hill to curse King David, and rebuke the sin, and
denounce Divine judgments upon the sinner. Others,
more practical, if not more prudent, go into the very
midst of the alleged wickedness, and teach "servants
under the yoke" that they ought not to count their
own masters worthy of all honor — that liberty is their
inalienable right — which they should maintain, if necessary, even by the shedding of blood. Now, it is not
for me to decide who, of all these, are the truest to
their own principles. It is not for me to decide
whether the man who preaches this doctrine in brave
words, amid applauding multitudes in the city of Brooklyn, or the one who, in the stillness of the night, and in
the face of the law's terrors, goes to practise the
preaching at Harper's Ferry, is the most consistent
Abolitionist, and the most heroic man. It is not for
me to decide which is the most important part of a tree;
and if the tree be poisonous, which is the most injurious,
the root, or the branches, or the fruit. But I am here
to-night, in God's name, and by His help, to show that

this tree of Abolitionism is evil, and only evil — root and branch, flower, and leaf, and fruit; that it springs from, and is nourished by, an utter rejection of the Scriptures; that it produces no real benefit to the enslaved, and is the fruitful source of division and strife, and infidelity, in both Church and State. I have four distinct propositions on the subject to maintain — four theses to nail up over this pulpit, and defend with the " word of God, which is the sword of the Spirit."

I. — Abolitionism has no foundation in the Scriptures.

II. — Its principles have been promulgated chiefly by misrepresentation and abuse.

III. — It leads in multitudes of cases, and by a logical process, to utter infidelity.

IV. — It is the chief cause of the strife that agitates, and the danger that threatens, our country.

I. — ABOLITIONISM HAS NO FOUNDATION IN SCRIPTURE.

Passing by the records of the patriarchal age, and waiving the question as to those servants in Abraham's family who, in the simple, but expressive language of Scripture, " were bought with his money," let us come at once to the tribunal of that law which God promulgated amid the solemnities of Sinai. What said the law and the testimony to that peculiar people over whom God ruled, and for whose institutions He has assumed the responsibility? The answer is in the twenty-fifth chapter of Leviticus, in these words : —

" And if thy brother that dwelleth by thee be waxen poor, and be sold unto thee, thou shalt not compel him to serve as a

bond-servant; but as a hired servant and a sojourner he shall
be with thee, and shall serve thee unto the year of jubilee, and
then shall he depart from thee, both he and his children with
him."

So far, you will observe, the law refers to the children of Israel, who by reason of poverty were reduced
to servitude. It was their right to be free at the year
of jubilee, unless they chose to remain in perpetual
bondage; for which case provision is made in other and
distinct enactments.* But not so with slaves of foreign
birth. There was no year of jubilee provided for
them. † For what says the law? Read the forty-
fourth to forty-sixth verses of the chapter.

"Both thy bondmen and thy bondmaids which thou shalt
have shall be of the heathen that are round about you. Of
them shall ye buy bondmen and bondmaids. Moreover, of the

---

* Exodus xxi. 5, 6: "And if the servant (i. e., the *Hebrew* servant,
as the context shows) shall plainly say, I love my master, my wife, and
my children; I will not go out free; then his master shall bring him
unto the judges; he shall also bring him to the door or unto the door-
post; and his master shall bore his ear through with an awl: AND HE
SHALL SERVE HIM FOREVER."

† The abolitionists have blown this jubilee trumpet with a zeal worthy
of a better cause. They have insisted that under the Levitical economy
slaves could only be held for *fifty years.* Now, inasmuch as the average
of human life is somewhere between thirty and forty years, some, at
least, of these slaves, according to the interpretation of the Abolitionists
themselves, must have ended their days in bondage. But the fact is, as
any one may see by a candid reading of the twenty-fifth chapter of Leviticus, the year of jubilee had no reference to bondmen of foreign
birth, but only to Hebrew landowners who were " waxen poor and fall-
en in decay." "They might purchase bondmen of the heathen nations
that were round about them, or of those strangers that sojourned among
them, and might claim a dominion over them, and entail them upon
their families, as an inheritance, *for the year of jubilee should give
them no discharge.*"— MATTHEW HENRY.

children of the strangers that do sojourn among you — of them
shall ye buy and of their families that are with you, which they
beget in your land; and they shall be your *possession*. And
ye shall take them as an inheritance for your children after you,
to *inherit them for a possession*; they shall be *your bondmen
forever.*"

There it is, plainly written in the Divine law. No
legislative enactment, no statute framed by legal skill,
was ever more explicit and incapable of perversion.
When the Abolitionist tells me that slaveholding is sin,
in the simplicity of my faith in the Holy Scriptures, I
point him to this sacred record, and tell him, in all candor, as my text does, that his teaching blasphemes the
name of God and His doctrine. When he begins to
dote about questions and strifes of words, appealing to
the Declaration of Independence, and asserting that the
idea of property in men is an enormity and a crime, I
still hold him to the record, saying, " Ye shall take
them as an inheritance for your children after you, to
inherit them for a possession." When he waxes warm,
as he always does if his opponent quote Scripture
(which is the great test to try the spirits whether they
be of God — the very spear of Ithuriel to reveal their
true character) — when he gets angry, and begins to
pour out his evil surmisings and abuse upon slaveholders, I obey the precept which says, " from such withdraw thyself," comforting myself with this thought:
that the wisdom of God is wiser than men, and the
kindness of God kinder than men. Philosophers may
reason, and reformers may rave till doomsday: they
never can convince me that God, in the Levitical law,
or in any other law, sanctioned sin; and as I know,

from the plain passage I have quoted, and many more like it, that He *did* sanction slaveholding among His ancient people, I know, also, by the logic of that faith which believes the Bible to be His word, that slaveholding is not sin.

Abolitionists are accustomed to answer this appeal to the Levitical law, by asserting that the Old Testament gives the same sanction to polygamy that it does to slaveholding; and I am sorry to observe that ministers of the gospel make this broad assertion in the pulpit, without condescending to give us the proof-texts. Suppose the Old Testament does sanction polygamy, what then? What is the purpose of the Abolitionist in making this assertion? Does he mean to cast contempt upon the Levitical law, by proving that it sanctions what all Christians under the gospel admit to be wrong? Or does he mean to maintain that both slaveholding and polygamy are relations on which the Divine sanction rests? If it can be proved that the law of God, as promulgated by Moses, *did* sanction polygamy, I am prepared at once to say that polygamy is in itself no sin; and if there has been no explicit repeal of that sanction, that it is still right to have a plurality of wives. I know of nothing as sin except that which transgresses God's law. But the fact is, this attempt to offset slaveholding with polygamy is mere assertion. We call for the proof. Point us in the divine law which came by Moses, a passage in reference to a plurality of wives, clear and explicit, like that we have quoted in reference to the purchase of bondmen from the heathen. It cannot be done. It is true some of the patriarchs had more wives than one; and this fact is recorded. And so David committed murder and adultery; and *that* fact is recorded. But did God sanction these sins for which the sweet singer poured out his broken heart in the fifty-first Psalm, as He did sanction slaveholding, by inserting in His law express directions as to how they were to be committed? There cannot be found anywhere in the Levitical law, either a permission that a man may have two wives, or any direction as to how he shall obtain them. The nearest approach to such a precept is found in Deut. xxi. 15, where it says, " if a man have two wives," he shall do thus and so with the children. If a man have two wives! Is that the same thing as to say a man *may* have two wives? When the law says, " *if* a man smite his servant till he die," is that the same thing as to sanction the beating of a slave to death?

The most that has ever been claimed for polygamy under the Levitical Law is a *bare toleration*. Michaelis, who is the great authority on that side of the question, says : " It does not appear that Moses permitted polygamy willingly, or as a matter of indifference, in either a moral or political view, but, as Christ expresses it, merely on account of the hardness of their hearts. In other words, he did not approve, but found it advisable to tolerate it as a point of civil expediency." — *Commentaries on the Laws of Moses*, vol. 2, p. 8.

Now, even if we admit that for expediency sake the inspired lawgiver tolerated polygamy, it must be evident to every candid reader, that slaveholding holds a very different position under the divine law. Slaveholding is there not merely by a silence which gives consent, but it is there as a matter of *express enact-*

ment. It was *anticipated* by the law. It is not true, as is so often asserted, that *Moses found slavery among the Israelites.* At the time when he came to set up their nationality under the most perfect theocracy the world ever saw, they had themselves been slaves for generations. When they went out of Egypt, they had no social or commercial ties to bind them to a relation which the cruelty of their heathen masters had so long used as an instrument of oppression. There was not one slave in all that mighty host who gathered around Mount Sinai, to receive the law by which their future institutions were to be moulded.

Regarding Moses (as Michaelis and other rationalistic commentators do) merely in the light of a human lawgiver, how easy it would have been for him, by the insertion of one positive prohibition into his code, or even by the preaching of one abolition sermon, to put the stigma of his disapprobation forever upon slaveholding! How easy for him to keep silence, as it is alleged he did, in reference to polygamy, and thus leave slaveholding on the footing of an *evil tolerated for expediency sake!* Or to speak more like a Christian minister, how easy it would have been for God, if he regards slaveholding as sinful, in those days when his chosen people trembled before Sinai, under the utterance of that law which was to shape their character and destiny as a nation, to write the doctrine of Abolitionism in His holy law, and grave it indelibly upon the inspired records of the world. The fact that he uttered no such doctrine, but, on the contrary, *instructed the chosen seed to purchase, and hold, and bequeath their bondmen to their posterity,* shuts every man up to the alternative, either to reject Abolitionism, or reject Moses as an inspired lawgiver.

It must be admitted that the Jewish Rabbis, who taught for commandments the doctrines of men, construed the law into a sanction of polygamy. But Christ, the true expounder, showed them how their traditions made void the'law. Read his declaration on this subject in Matt. xix. 3 — 9 ; Mark x. 11 ; Luke xvi. 18. He admits that Moses suffered a man to marry a second wife, provided he had previously divorced the first; but declares that even this permission was because of the hardness of their hearts ; and then referring them to the original and model marriage, by which twain were made one flesh, he promulgates that great divine law, which, however it is trampled on now by the legislatures of nominally Christian states, was strictly observed in the Apostolic Church, so that a Christian man as well as a Christian minister, was " the husband of one wife."

Admitting, for the sake of the argument, that the Levitical law gives no more sanction to slaveholding than it did to polygamy, we ask the advocates of Abolitionism if Christ ever rebuked the prevailing practice in regard to the one, as he did in reference to the other? Leaving Moses and the Prophets, let us turn now to Jesus and His Apostles.

There are men, even among professing Christians, and not a few ministers of the gospel, who answer the argument from the Old Testament Scriptures, by a simple denial of their authority. They do not tell us how God could ever or anywhere countenance that which is morally wrong, but they content themselves with saying that the Levitical law is no rule of action for us ; and

they appeal from its decisions to what they consider
the higher tribunal of the gospel.* Let us, therefore,
join issue with them before the bar of the New Testament Scriptures. Here there is no lack of witnesses in
the case. It is a historic truth, acknowledged on all
hands, that at the advent of Jesus Christ slavery existed
all over the civilized world, and was intimately interwoven with its social and civil institutions. In Judea,
in Asia Minor, in Greece, in all the countries where the
Saviour or his Apostles preached the gospel, slaveholding was just as common as it is to-day in South Carolina. It is not alleged by any one, or, at least, by any
one having any pretensions to scholarship or candor,
that the Roman laws regulating slavery were even as
mild as the very worst statutes which have been passed
upon the subject in modern times. It will not be denied
by any honest and well-informed man, that modern civilization and the restraining influences of the gospel,
have shed ameliorating influences upon the relation between master and slave, which were utterly unknown at
the advent of Christianity. And how did Jesus and
his Apostles treat this subject? Masters and slaves met
them at every step in their missionary work, and were
present in every audience to which they preached.
The Roman law, which gave the full power of life and

---

* Some years since Dr. Wayland publicly asserted that *the New Tes-*
tament is the only and sufficient rule of faith for Christians. The
editors of the New York *Observer* challenged this statement ; and, as I
have been informed, the late Dr. James Alexander offered to debate the
question in the columns of that journal. Dr. Wayland prudently declined the discussion, promising, however, that he would, at a conve-
nient season, explain and defend his views. The promised explanation
has not yet appeared.

death into the master's hand, was familiar to them ; and all the evils connected with the system surrounded them every day, as obviously as the light of heaven. And yet, it is a remarkable fact, which the Abolitionist does not, because he cannot deny, that the New Testament is utterly silent in regard to the alleged sinfulness of slaveholding. In all the instructions of the Saviour ; in all the reported sermons of the inspired Apostles ; in all the epistles they were moved by the Holy Spirit to write, for the instruction of coming generations — there is not one distinct and explicit denunciation of slaveholding, nor one precept requiring the master to emancipate his slaves. Every acknowledged sin is openly and repeatedly condemned, and in unmeasured terms. Drunkenness and adultery, theft and murder — all the moral wrongs which ever have been known to afflict society, are forbidden by name : and yet, according to the teaching of Abolitionism, this greatest of all sins — this sum of all villanies — is never spoken of except in respectful terms. How can this be accounted for ?

Let Dr. Wayland, whose work on moral science is taught in many of our schools, answer this question ; and let parents whose children are studying that book, diligently consider his answer. I quote from Wayland's Moral Science, page 213 : —

" The gospel was designed not for one race or for one time, but for all races and for all times. It looked not to the abolition of slavery for that age alone, but for its universal abolition. Hence the important object of its Author was to gain for it a lodgment in every part of the known world, so that, by its universal diffusion among all classes of society, it might, quietly and peacefully, modify and subdue the evil passions of men.

In this manner alone could its object — a universal moral revolution — have been accomplished.   For if it had forbidden the evil, instead of subverting the principle ; if it had proclaimed the unlawfulness of slavery, and taught slaves to resist the oppression of their masters, it would instantly have arrayed the two parties in deadly hostility throughout the civilized world ; its announcement would have been the signal of servile war, and the very name of the Christian religion would have been forgotten amidst the agitation of universal bloodshed. The fact, under these circumstances, that the gospel *does not forbid slavery*, affords no reason to suppose that it does not mean to prohibit it."

We pause not now to comment upon the admitted fact *that the gospel does not forbid slavery*, and that Jesus Christ and his Apostles pursued a course entirely different from that adopted by the Abolitionists, including the learned author himself ; nor to inquire whether the teaching of Abolitionism is not as likely to produce strife and bloodshed in these days as in the first ages of the Church.   What we now call attention to, and protest against, is the imputation here cast upon Christ and His Apostles.   Do you believe the Saviour sought to insinuate His religion into the earth by concealing its real design, and preserving a profound silence in regard to one of the very worst sins it came to destroy ?   Do you believe that when he healed the centurion's servant, (whom every honest commentator admits to have been a slave,*) and pronounced that precious eulogy upon the

---

* We know the centurion's servant was a *slave*, not only from the position and nationality of the master, but from the very name given in the original to the servant.   "*Doulos*" is derived from the verb *deo*, to *bind*, and always signifies a *bondman*.

Dr. Robinson, whose Lexicon is the great standard upon such ques-

master, " I have not seen so great faith in Israel " —
do you believe that Jesus suffered that man to live on in
sin because he deprecated the consequences of preaching Abolitionism ? When Paul stood upon Mars' Hill,
surrounded by ten thousand times as many slaveholders
as there were idols in the city, do you believe he kept
back any part of the requirements of the gospel because he was afraid of a tumult among the people ? We
ask these Abolition philosophers whether, as a matter
of fact, idolatry, and the vices connected with it, were
not even more intimately interwoven with the social and
civil life of the Roman empire than slavery was ? Did
the Apostles abstain from preaching against idolatry ?
Nay, who does not know that by denouncing this sin
they brought down upon themselves the whole power of
the Roman empire ? Nero covered the Christian martyrs with pitch, and lighted up the city with their burning bodies, just because they would not withhold or
compromise the truth in regard to the worship of idols.
In the light of that fierce persecution, it is a profane
trifling for Dr. Wayland, or any other man, to tell us
that Jesus or Paul held back their honest opinions of
slavery in order to avoid " a servile war, in which the
very name of the Christian religion would have been
forgotten." The name of the Christian religion is not
so easily forgotten ; nor are God's great purposes of

---

tions, says : " The *doulos* was never a *hired* servant, the latter being
called by another name — *misthios*, or *misthotos.*" This testimony is
confirmed by every authority, ancient and modern, European and American, except a little clique of Abolitionists, who, to sustain their dogma,
would not only wrest the Scriptures, but overturn the very foundations
of the Greek language.

redemption capable of being defeated by an honest declaration of His truth everywhere and at all times. And yet this philosophy, so dishonoring to Christ and His Apostles, is moulding the character of our young men and women. It comes into our schools, and mingles with the very life-blood of future generations the sentiment that Christ and His Apostles held back the truth, and suffered sin to go unrebuked to avoid the wrath of man. And all this to maintain, at all hazards, and in the face of the Saviour's example to the contrary, the unscriptural dogma that slaveholding is sin.

But it must be observed, in this connection, that the Apostles went much further than to abstain from preaching against slaveholding. *They admitted slaveholders to the communion of the church.* In our text, masters are acknowledged as "brethren, faithful and beloved, partakers of the benefit." If the New Testament is to be received as a faithful history, no man was ever rejected by the Apostolic Church upon the ground that he owned slaves. If he abused his power as a master, if he availed himself of the authority conferred by the Roman law to commit adultery, or murder, or cruelty, he was rejected for these crimes, just as he would be rejected now for similar crimes from any Christian Church in our Southern States.*

---

* One of the grossest sins of Abolitionism, and one chief root of the bitterness that has sprung up between the North and the South, is its persistent slander on this subject. For example, some years ago it was asserted, and reiterated by Abolition journals and lecturers, that a minister at the South, without injury to his character, had tied up his slave on Sabbath morning, and, having inflicted a cruel punishment, left him

If parents abused or neglected their children, they were censured, not for having children, but for not treating them properly. And so with the slaveholder. It was not the owning of slaves, but the manner in which he fulfilled the duties of his station, that made him a subject for church discipline. The mere fact that he was a slaveholder no more subjected him to censure, than the mere fact that he was a father or a husband. It is, obviously, upon the recognized lawfulness of the relation, that all the precepts regulating the reciprocal duties of that relation are based.*

These precepts are scattered all through the inspired epistles. There is not one command or exhortation to emancipate the slave. The Apostle well knew that for the present emancipation would be no real blessing to

suspended, while he went to church to preach and administer the Lord's supper, and then returned to inflict additional stripes upon his lacerated victim. This is but a specimen. In regard to crimes against chastity, the Southern churches have been shamefully slandered. What wonder that Christian mothers, and even ministers of the gospel, are roused to a revolutionary indignation by such abuse?

* It is often said that this argument from the precepts of the apostles proves too much ; that it makes the Bible sanction despotism, even the despotism of Nero. In reply to this we quote a few sentences from Dr. Hodge's celebrated essay on slavery : "The argument for the lawfulness of slaveholding is not founded on the mere injunction, ' slaves obey your masters,' analogous to the command, ' let every soul be subject to the higher powers,' but on the fact that the apostles did not condemn slavery ; that they did not require emancipation; and that they *recognized slaveholders as Christian brethren.* To make the objection of any force, it must be shown that Paul not only enjoined obedience to a despotic monarch, but that he *recognized Nero as a Christian.* When this is done, then we shall admit that our argument is fairly met, and that it is just as true that he sanctioned the conduct of Nero as that he acknowledged the lawfulness of slavery."

him. But the master is exhorted to be kind and considerate, and the slave to be obedient, that so they might preserve the unity of that Church in which there is no distinction between Greek or Jew, male or female, bond or free.

It is often said that if the Bible does sanction slaveholding, it does not sanction *American Slavery ;* that it is not against slaveholding abstractly that the Abolitionist protests, but against the *system of American slavery taken as a whole.*

To this I answer, the Bible does not sanction *American marriage.* The system, taken as a whole, is full of evil and iniquity. The laws of the several States in regard to it, are, many of them, abominable ; and the fruits that grow out of it are heart-sickening and dreadful. Husbands beat and poison their wives. Multitudes of parents suffer their children to grow up in filth and ignorance ; and the details of the divorce cases with which our northern newspapers have been reeking for months past, are enough to poison the fountains of virtue in every family where they are read. But is any honest man and woman, who live together according to God's ordinance, to be charged with the iniquity of the statute-book of Indiana, or the misery and crime of the Five Points ? Neither is any honest slaveholder in Virginia to be charged with all the alleged or real evils connected with the system of slavery. And how will you correct the evils connected with marriage ? By railing at the whole system as an iniquity ? By joining the advocates of Woman's Rights, in their crusade against the divine law upon the subject ? By denouncing the relation itself as sinful ? No ! You acknowledge the relation as lawful, and seek to throw around it, and into the hearts of those who sustain it, the sanctifying influences of the blessed gospel. Just so, Christian men and ministers are striving to remove the evils connected with slavery in our Southern States. The gospel does not sanction either the *system* of American marriage or the *system* of American slavery, (if by system be meant everything connected with the practical workings of the two relations;) but then it *did* sanction both marriage and slaveholding under a system of laws, and in a condition of public morals, worse than now exist in either New York or Charleston. The Apostles did not endorse wicked laws in regard to slavery: they gave both master and slave the law of Christ. They did not sanction licentiousness or cruelty in any social relation; but sought to throw over all the sweet and sanctifying influences of the truth as it is in Jesus.

Oh, if ministers of the gospel in this land and age had but followed Paul as he followed Christ, and, instead of hurling anathemas and exciting wrath against slaveholders, had sought only to bring both master and slave to the fountain of Emmanuel's blood; if the agencies of the blessed gospel had only been suffered to work their way quietly, as the light and dew of the morning, into the structure of society, both North and South — how different would have been the position of our country this day before God! How different would have been the privileges enjoyed by the poor black man's soul, which, in this bitter contest, has been too much neglected and despised! Then there would have been no need to have converted our churches into military barracks for collecting fire-arms to carry on war

upon a distant frontier. No need for a sovereign State
to execute the fearful penalty of the law upon the invader, for doing no more than honestly to carry out the
teaching of Abolition preachers, who bind heavy burdens, and grievous to be borne, and lay them on men's
shoulders, while they touch them not with one of their
fingers. No need for the widow and the orphan to
weep in anguish of heart over those cold graves, for
whose dishonor and desolation God will hold the real
authors responsible. No occasion or pretext for slaveholding States to pass such stringent laws for the punishment of the secret incendiary and the prevention of
servile war.

I shall not attempt to show what will be the condition
of the African race in this country when the gospel shall
have brought all classes under its complete dominion.
What civil and social relations men will sustain in the
times of millennial glory, I do not know. I cordially
incline to the current opinion of our church, that
slavery is permitted and regulated by the Divine law,
under both the Jewish and Christian dispensations, not
as the final destiny of the enslaved, but as an important
and necessary process in their transition from heathenism to Christianity — a wheel in the great machinery of
Providence, by which the final redemption is to be accomplished. However this may be, one thing I know,
and every Abolitionist might know, if he would, that
there are Christian families at the South in which a patriarchal fidelity and affection subsist between the bond
and the free, and where slaves are better fed and
clothed and instructed, and have a better opportunity
for salvation, than the majority of laboring people in

the city of New York. If the tongue of Abolitionism
had only kept silence these twenty years past, the number of such families would be tenfold as great. Fanaticism at the North is one chief stumbling-block in the
way of the gospel at the South. This is one great
grievance that presses to-day upon the hearts of our
Christian brethren in the Southern States. This, in a
measure, explains why such men as Dr. Thornwell, of
South Carolina, and Dr. Palmer, of New Orleans —
men whose genius and learning and piety would adorn
any state or station — are willing to secede from the
Union. They feel that the influence of the Christian
ministry is hindered, and their power to do good to both
master and slave crippled, by the constant agitations of
Abolitionism in our national councils, and the incessant
turmoil excited by the unscriptural dogma that slaveholding is sin. They hope that under some other government they may have that peace for the prosecution
of their Master's work, which the Constitution of the
United States has hitherto failed to secure for them.
Whatever I may think of secession as a remedy for the
evils complained of, in my heart I do not blame them.
My soul is knit to such men with the sympathy of Jona-
than for David. Whatever be the result of this contest,
the union between their hearts and mine, cemented by
the word and Spirit of God, can never be dissolved.
Earth and hell cannot dissolve it. Though my lot is
cast in a colder clime, yet in the outgoings of that warm
affection to which space is nothing, I will ever say,
" Entreat me not to leave thee, for your people shall be
my people, and your God my God!" and though we
may be separated in body for awhile by the dark gulf

of political disunion, and by the absorbing strife for
which every sound man at the North will soon be
called upon to gird himself—the long, long rest of
eternity, will afford abundant opportunity for the inter-
change of our mutual charities.

II.—THE PRINCIPLES OF ABOLITION HAVE BEEN PROPA-GATED CHIEFLY BY MISREPRESENTATION AND ABUSE.

Having no foundation in Scripture, it does not carry
on its warfare by Scripture weapons. Its prevailing
spirit is fierce and proud, and its language is full of
wrath and bitterness. Let me prove this by testimony
from its own lips. I quote Dr. Channing, of Boston,
whose name is a tower of strength to the Abolition
cause, and whose memory is their continual boast. In
a work published in the year 1836, I find the following
words:—

"The Abolitionists have done wrong, I believe; nor is their
wrong to be winked at because done fanatically or with good
intentions; for how much mischief may be wrought with good
designs! They have fallen into the common error of enthusi-
asts, that of exaggerating their object, of feeling as if no evil
existed but that which they opposed, and as if no guilt could
be compared with that of countenancing and upholding it. The
tone of their newspapers, so far as I have seen them, has often
been fierce, bitter, and abusive. They have sent forth their
orators, some of them transported with fiery zeal, to sound the
alarm against slavery through the land, to gather together young
and old, pupils from school, females hardly arrived at years of
discretion, the ignorant, the excitable, the impetuous, and to organize these into associations for the battle against oppression.
Very unhappily, they preached their doctrine to the colored
people, and collected them into societies. To this mixed and

excitable multitude, minute, heart-rending descriptions of slavery were given in piercing tones of passion ; and slaveholders
were held up as monsters of cruelty and crime. The Abolitionist, indeed, proposed to convert slaveholders; and for this end
he approached them with vituperation, and exhausted on them
the vocabulary of abuse. And he has reaped as he has sowed."

Such is the testimony of Dr. Channing, given in the
year 1836. What would he have thought and said if
he had lived until the year 1860, and seen this little
stream, over whose infant violence he lamented, swelling into a torrent and flooding the land ?

Abolitionism is abusive in its persistent misrepresentation of the legal principles involved in the relation between master and slave. Its teachers reiterate, in a
thousand exciting forms, the assertion that the idea of
property in man blots out his manhood, and degrades
him to the level of a brute or a stone. " Domestic
slavery," says Dr. Wayland, in his work on Moral Science, " supposes, at best, that the relation between master and slave is not that which exists between man and
man, but is a modification, at least, of that which exists
between man and the brutes." Do not these Abolitionist philosophers know, that, according to the laws of
every civilized country on earth, a man has property in
his children, and a woman has property in her husband?
The statutes of the State of New York, and of every
other Northern State, recognize and protect this property, and our courts of justice have repeatedly assessed
its value. If a man is killed on a railroad, his wife
may bring suit, and recover damages for the pecuniary
loss she has suffered. If one man entice away the
daughter of another, and marry her, while she is still

under age, the father may bring a civil suit for damages for the loss of that child's services, and the pecuniary compensation is the only redress the law provides.* Thus the common law of Christendom, and the statutes of our own State, recognize property in man. In what does that property consist? Simply *in such services as a man or a child may properly be required to render.* This is all that the Levitical law, or any other law, means when it says, " Your bondmen shall be your possession, or property, and an inheritance for your children." The property consists, not in the right to treat the slave like a brute, but simply in a legal claim for such services as a man in that position may properly be required to render.† And yet Abolitionists, in the face of the Divine law, persist in denouncing the very relation between master and slave " as a modification, at least, of that which exists between man and the brutes."

This, however, is not the worst or most prevalent form which their abusive spirit assumes. Their mode of arguing the question of slaveholding, by a pretended appeal to facts, is a tissue of misrepresentation from beginning to end. Let me illustrate my meaning by a parallel case. Suppose I undertake to prove the wickedness of marriage, as it exists in the city of New

---

* If the law went further, as it ought to, and punished the minister who performs the marriage ceremony, the offence would not be so often repeated in this community.

† With a manifest design to prejudice the student against the idea of property in man, Dr. Wayland adopts a marvellous " Definition of the right of Property." Let Christian parents and teachers look at it. " The abstract right of property is the right to *use something in such manner as I choose.* But inasmuch as this right of use is common to all men, and as one may choose to use his property in such a way as to deprive his neighbor of this or of some other right, the right to use as I

York. In this discussion suppose the Bible is excluded, or, at least, that it is not recognized as having exclusive jurisdiction in the decision of the question. My
first appeal is to the statute law of the State.

I show there enactments which nullify the law of
God, and make divorce a marketable and cheap com-
modity. I collect the advertisements of your daily pa-
pers, in which lawyers offer to procure the legal separation of man and wife for a stipulated price, to say
nothing in this sacred place of other advertisements
which decency forbids me to quote. Then I turn to the
records of our criminal courts, and find that every day
some cruel husband beats his wife, or some unnatural parent murders his child, or some discontented wife or husband seeks the dissolution of the marriage bond. In the
next place I turn to the orphan asylums and hospitals,
and show there the miserable wrecks of domestic tyranny, in wives deserted and children maimed by drunk-
en parents.* In the last place, I go through our

choose is limited by the restriction that I do not interfere with the rights
of my neighbor. The right of property, therefore, when thus restricted, is the right to *use something as I choose, provided I do not use it so
as to interfere with the rights of my neighbor.*"— Page 229. Is that
so, Dr. Wayland? Has a man a right, if *he chooses*, to take his horse
into the woods, where his neighbors will not be disturbed by his cruelty,
and there torture or starve the poor beast? Does the master's claim to
property in his servant involve a claim to use that servant just as *he
chooses*, with no other restriction than the one you mention? No, sir,
the abstract right of property, is the right *to use some thing or person
according to the nature of that thing or person*, and under all the restrictions which the Divine law imposes, which restrictions go much further than my neighbor's rights. This is *Christian* philosophy. Your
definition would come with better grace from a heathen.

* There is in the Brooklyn Orphan Asylum, a little child who was
thrown into the fire, and almost roasted to death, by its father. If that

streets, and into our tenement houses, and count the
thousands of ragged children, who, amid ignorance and
filth, are training for the prison and gallows.

Summing all these facts together, I put them forth as
the fruits of marriage in the city of New York, and a
proof that the relation itself is sinful: If I were a nov-
elist, and had written a book to illustrate this same
doctrine, I would call this array of facts a " Key." In
this key I say nothing about the sweet charities and affections that flourish in ten thousand homes, not a word
about the multitude of loving-kindnesses that charac-
terize the daily life of honest people, about the instruction and discipline that are training children at ten
thousand firesides for usefulness here and glory hereafter ; — all this I ignore, and quote only the statute
book, the newspapers, the records of criminal courts,
and the miseries of the abodes of poverty. Now, what
have I done ? I have not misstated or exaggerated a
single fact. And yet am I not a falsifier and a slan-
derer of the deepest dye ? Is there a virtuous woman
or an honest man in this city, whose cheeks would not
burn with indignation at my one-sided and injurious
statements ? But this is just what Abolitionism has
done in regard to slaveholding. It has undertaken to
illustrate its cardinal doctrine in works of fiction ; and
then, to sustain the creation of its fancy, has attempted
to underpin it with an accumulation of facts. These
facts are collected in precisely the way that I have described. The statute books of slaveholding States are
searched, and every wrong enactment collated, newspa-

child had been a slave in Charleston, how the sad story would have rung
through the land !

per reports of cruelty and crime on the part of wicked masters are treasured up and classified, all the outrages that have been perpetrated "by lewd fellows of the baser sort,"— of whom there are plenty, both North and South — are eagerly seized and recorded ; and this mass of vileness and filth, collected chiefly from the kennels and sewers of society, is put forth as a faithful exhibition of slaveholding. Senators in the forum, and ministers in the pulpit, distill this raw material into the more refined slander " that Southern society is essentially barbarous, and that slaveholding had its origin in hell." Legislative bodies enact and re-enact statutes which declare that slaveholding is such an enormous crime, that if a southern man, under the broad shield of the constitution, and with the decisions of the Supreme Court of the country in his hand, shall come within their jurisdiction, and set up a claim to a fugitive slave, he shall be punished with a fine of $2,000 and fifteen years imprisonment. And this method of argument has continued until multitudes of honest Christian people in this and other lands, believe that slaveholding is the sin of sins, the sum of all villanies. Let me illustrate this by an incident in my own experience. A few years since I took from the centre-table of a Christian family in Scotland, by whom I had been most kindly entertained, a book entitled, " Life and Manners in America." On the blank leaf was an inscription, stating that the book had been bestowed upon one of the children of the family, as a reward of diligence in an institution of learning. The frontispiece was a picture of a man of fierce countenance beating a naked woman. The contents of the book were professedly compiled from the testimony of Americans upon the subject of slavery. I dare not quote in this place the extracts which I made in my memorandum. It will be sufficient for me to say that the book asserts as undoubted facts, that the banks of the Mississippi are studded with iron gallows for the punishment of slaves — that in the City of Charleston the bloody block on which masters cut off the hands of disobedient servants may be seen in the public squares, and that sins against chastity are common and unrebuked in professedly Christian families.

Now in my heart I did not feel angry at the author of that book, nor at the school-teacher who bestowed it upon his scholar ; for in Christian charity I gave them credit for honesty in the case. But standing there a stranger among the martyr memories of that glorious land, to which my heart had so often made its pilgrimage, I did feel that you and I, and every man in America, was wronged by the revilers of their native land, who teach foreigners that hanging, and cutting off hands, and beating women, are the characteristics of our life and manners.

But we need not go to foreign lands for proof that Abolitionism has carried on its warfare by the language of abuse. The annual meeting of the American Anti-Slavery Society brings the evidence to our doors. We have been accustomed to laugh at these vernal exhibitions of fanaticism, not thinking, perhaps, that what was fun for us, was working death to our brethren, whose property and reputation we are bound to protect. The fact is, we have suffered a fire to be built in our midst, whose sparks have been scattered far and wide ;

and now when the smoke of the conflagration comes back to blind our eyes, and the heat of it begins to scorch our industrial and commercial interests, it will not do for us to say that the utterances of that Society are the ravings of a fanatical and insignificant few ; for the men who compose it are honored in our midst with titles and with offices. The ministers who have thrown over its doings the sanction of our holy religion, are quoted and magnified over the land as the representative men of the age; and the man who stood up in its deliberations in the year 1852, and exhausted the vocabulary of abuse upon the compromise measures, and the great statesmen who framed them, is now a judge in our courts and the guardian of our lives and property.

It will, doubtless, be said that misrepresentation and abuse have not been confined, in the progress of this unhappy contest, to the Abolitionists of the North ; that demagogues and self-seeking men at the South have been violent and abusive, and that newspapers professedly in the interest of the South, with a spirit which can be characterized as little less than diabolical, have circulated every scandal in the most aggravated and irritating form. But suppose all this to be granted — what then ? Can Christian men justify or palliate the wrath and evil-speaking which are at their own doors, by pointing to the retaliation which it has provoked from their neighbors? If I were preaching to-day to a Southern audience, it would be my duty, and I trust God would give me grace to perform it, to tell them of their sins in this matter. And especially would it be

my privilege, as a minister of the gospel of peace — a
privilege from which no false views of manhood should
prevent me — to exhort and beseech them as brethren.
I would assure them, that there are multitudes here who
still cherish the memory of the battle-fields and coun-
cil-chambers where our fathers cemented this Union of
States, and who will stand by the compact of that constitution to the utmost extremity.   I would tell the
thousands of Christian ministers, among whom are some
of the brightest ornaments of the American pulpit, and
the tens of thousands of Christian men and women,
toward whom, while the love of Christ burns in me, my
heart never can grow cold, that if they will only be patient, and hope to the end, all wrongs may yet be right-
ed.   Therefore, I would beseech them not to put a great
gulf between us, and cut off the very opportunity for
reconciliation upon an honorable basis, by a revolution
whose end no human eye can see.   But, then, I am not
preaching at the South.   I stand here, at one of the
main fountain-heads of the abuse we have complained
of.

I stand here to rebuke this sin, and exhort the guilty
parties to repent and forsake it.   It is magnanimous
and Christ-like for those from whom the first provocation came, to make the first concessions.

The legislative enactments which are in open and acknowledged violation of the constitution, and whose
chief design is to put a stigma upon slaveholding, must
and will be repealed.   Truth and justice will ultimately
prevail ; and God's blessing, and the blessings of generations yet unborn, will rest upon that party, in this
unhappy contest, who first stand forth to utter the lan-

guage of conciliation, and proffer the olive-branch of peace. The great fear is, that the reaction will come too late; *but sooner or later it will come.* Abolitionism ought to, and one day will, change the mode of its warfare, and adopt a new vocabulary. I believe in the liberty of the press, and in freedom of speech; but I do not believe that any man has the right, before God, or in the eye of civilized law, to speak and publish what he pleases, without regard to the consequences. With the conscientious convictions of our fellow-citizens, neither we, nor the law, have any right to interfere; but the law ought to protect all men from the utterance of libellous words, whose only effect is to create division and strife.

I trust and pray, and call upon you to unite with me in the supplication, that God would give Abolitionists repentance and a better mind, so that in time to come they may, at least, propagate their principles in decent and respectful language.

III. — ABOLITIONISM LEADS, IN MULTITUDES OF CASES, AND BY A LOGICAL PROCESS, TO UTTER INFIDELITY.

On this point I would not, and will not, be misunderstood. I do no not say that Abolitionism is infidelity. I speak only of the tendencies of the system, as indicated in its avowed principles and demonstrated in its practical fruits.

One of its avowed principles is, that it does not try slavery by the Bible; but as one of its leading advocates has recently declared, it tries the Bible by the principles of freedom. It insists that the word of God must be made to support certain human opinions, or forfeit all claims upon our faith. That I may not be suspected of exaggeration on this point, let me quote, from the recent work of Mr. Barnes, a passage which may well arrest the attention of all thinking men : —

"There are the great principles in our nature, as God has made us, which can never be set aside by any authority of a professed revelation. If a book claiming to be a revelation from God, by any fair interpretation, defended slavery, or placed it on the same basis as the relation of husband and wife, parent and child, guardian and ward, such a book would not, and could not, be received by the mass of mankind as a Divine revelation." — *Barnes on Slavery and the Church*, p. 193.

This assumption, that men are capable of judging beforehand what is to be expected in a Divine revelation, is the cockatrice's egg, from which, in all ages, heresies have been hatched. This is the spider's web which men have spun out of their own brains, and clinging to which, they have attempted to swing over the yawning abyss of infidelity.* Alas, how many have fallen in, and been dashed to pieces! When a man sets up the

---

* It is not denied that man, as originally constituted by his Creator, was capable of discerning for himself between good and evil Even since the fall the law of God is still written in the heart, (Rom. ii. 8 , and would be a sufficient guide, if there were nothing to blot and pervert it. But what says the Apostle in regard to the whole world who have not the Scriptures? "They have become vain in their imaginations, and their foolish heart is darkened," &c., (Rom. i. 21—25) What are the *principles* by which, according to Mr. Barnes's theory, these men are to try " the authority of a supposed revelation?" Their principles teach them that human sacrifices, and all kinds of uncleanness, are right. Must a supposed revelation conform to these principles in order to secure their acceptance of it?

Mr. Barnes well knows, that in Christian lands the ablest and best men differ as to what are the principles of our nature. Who will as-great principles of our nature (by which he always means his own preconceived opinions) as the supreme tribunal before which even the law of God must be tried — when a man says " the Bible must teach Abolitionism, or I will not receive it," he has already cut loose from the sheet-anchor of faith. True belief says, " Speak, Lord, thy servant waits to hear." Abolitionism says, " Speak, Lord, but speak in accordance with the principles of human nature, or thy word cannot be received by the great mass of mankind as a Divine revelation." The fruit of such principles is just what we might expect. Wherever the seed of Abolitionism has been sown broadcast, a plentiful crop of infidelity has sprung up. In the communities where anti-slavery excitement has been most prevalent, the power of the gospel has invariably declined ; and when the tide of fanaticism begins to subside, the wrecks of church order and of Christian character have been scattered on the shore. I mean no disrespect to New England — to the good men who there stand by the ancient landmarks, and contend earnestly for the truth — nor to the illustrious dead whose praise is in all the churches ; but

sume to be the oracle on this subject ? The Abolitionist will declare that *hostility to slavery on moral grounds*, is one of these principles. But the great mass of mankind, including just as wise and good men as he is, do not admit any such principle, and are not willing that he should be dictator in morals. Besides, this whole appeal to natural principles presents a false and deceitful issue. The Bible is *admitted* to be a Divine revelation. The simple question is, what does the Bible teach ? Mr Barnes, while professedly expounding the Scriptures, finds certain texts, which, by every fair construction of words, seem to put God's sanction on slaveholding. From these texts he desires to extort a different meaning ; to justify which procedure, he appeals to the principles of our (i. e., *his*) nature.

who does not know that the States in which Abolitionism has achieved its most signal triumphs, are at the
same time the great strongholds of infidelity in the land?
I have often thought that if some of those old pilgrim
fathers could come back, in the spirit and power of
Elias, to attend a grand celebration at Plymouth Rock,
they might well preach on this text: — " If ye were
Abraham's children, ye would do the works of Abraham." The effect of Abolitionism upon individuals, is
no less striking and mournful than its influence upon
communities.

It is a remarkable and instructive fact, and one at
which Christian men would do well to pause and consider, that, in this country, all the prominent leaders of
Abolitionism, outside of the ministry, have become
avowed infidels; and that all our notorious Abolition
preachers have renounced the great doctrines of grace
as they are taught in the standards of the reformed
churches — have resorted to the most violent processes
of interpretation to avoid the obvious meaning of plain
Scriptural texts, and ascribed to the Apostles of Christ
principles from which piety and moral courage instinctively revolt. They make that to be sin which the
Bible does not declare to be sin. They denounce, in
language such as the sternest prophets of the Law never
employed, a relation which Jesus and his Apostles recognized and regulated. They seek to institute terms
and tests of Christian communion utterly at variance
with the organic law of the Church, as founded by its
Divine Head; and, attempting to justify this usurpation
of Divine prerogatives by an appeal from God's law to
the dictates of fallen human nature, they would set up

a spiritual tyranny more odious and insufferable, because more arbitrary and uncertain in its decisions, than Popery itself. And as the tree is, so have its fruits been. It is not a theory, but a demonstrated, fact, that Abolitionism leads to infidelity. Such men as Garrison, and Giddings, and Gerrit Smith, have yielded to the current of their own principles, and thrown the Bible overboard. Thousands of humbler men who listen to Abolition preachers, will go and do likewise. And whether it be the restraints of official position, or the preventing grace of God, that enables such preachers to row up the stream and regard the authority of Scripture in other matters, their influence upon this one subject is all the more pernicious, because they prophesy in the name of Christ. In this sincere and plain utterance of my deep convictions, I am only discharging my conscience toward the flock over which I am set. When the shepherd seeth the wolf coming, he is bound to give warning.

IV. — ABOLITIONISM IS THE CHIEF CAUSE OF THE STRIFE THAT AGITATES AND THE DANGER THAT THREATENS OUR COUNTRY.

Here, as upon the preceding point, I will not be misunderstood. I am not here as the advocate or opponent of any political party; and it is no more than simple justice for me to say plainly, that I do not consider Republican and Abolitionist as necessarily synonymous terms. There are tens of thousands of Christian men who voted with the successful party in the late election, who do not sympathize with the principles or aims of

Abolitionism. Among these are some beloved members of my own flock, who will not hesitate a moment to put the seal of their approbation upon the doctrine of this discourse. And what is still more to the point, there seems to be sufficient evidence that the man who has just been chosen to be the head of this nation, is among the more conservative and Bible-loving men of his party. We have no fears that if the new administration could be quietly inaugurated, it would or could Abolitionize the government. There are honest people enough in the Northern States to prevent such a result. But, then, while this is admitted, as a simple matter of truth and justice, it cannot be denied, on the other hand, that Abolitionism did enter with all its characteristic bitterness into the recent contest; that the result never could have been accomplished without its assistance, and that it now appropriates the victory in words of ridicule and scorn that sting like a serpent. Let me give you, as a single specimen of the spirit in which Abolitionism has carried on its political warfare, an extract from a journal which claims to have a larger circulation than any other religious paper in the land. I quote from the New York *Independent*, of September, 1856 : —

"The people will not levy war nor inaugurate a revolution, even to relieve Kansas, until they have first tried what they can do by voting. If this peaceful remedy should fail to be applied this year, then the people will count the cost wisely, and decide for themselves boldly and firmly, which is the better way, to rise in arms and throw off a government worse than that of old King George, or endure it another four years, and then vote again."

Such is the spirit — such the love to the constitution and Union of these States, with which this religious element has entered into and seeks to control our party politics.

This passage is not quoted as an extraordinary one for the columns of the Independent, for that paper is accustomed to breathe out threatenings and slaughter. It is but a fair illustration of the fierce spirit which this so-called *religious* journal infuses into the families where it is a weekly visitor, and of the opinions concerning the United States government it seeks to disseminate. The passage quoted has a special significance, however, in view of its date, *September*, 1856. The opinions of the Editors appear to have undergone a wonderful change in four years; and forgetting that they have been the violent advocates, not only of disunion but of civil war, they have become loud in rebuking secession at the South. The genius of the constitution might well say to such defenders, " What hast thou to do to declare my statutes, or that thou shouldst take my covenant in thy mouth?"

But we deceive ourselves, if we suppose that our present dangers are of a birth so recent as 1856. As the questions now before the country rise in their magnitude above all party interests, and ought at once to blot out all party lines, so their origin is found far back of all party organizations as they now exist.

An article published twenty years ago in the Princeton Review, contains this remarkable language : —

" The opinion that slaveholding is itself a crime must operate to produce the disunion of the States and the division of all ecclesiastical societies in this country. Just so far as this opinion operates, it will lead those who entertain it to submit to any sacrifices to carry it out and give it effect. We shall become two nations in feeling, which must soon render us two nations in fact."

These words are wonderfully prophetic, and they who read the signs of the times must see that the period of their fulfilment draws near. In regard to ecclesiastical societies, the division foretold is already in a great measure accomplished. Three of our great religious denominations have been rent in twain by the simple question, " Is slaveholding a sin ? "

It yet remains to be seen whether the American Tract Society, and the American Board of Foreign Missions, will be revolutionized and dismembered by a contest which, we are told, is to be annually renewed. In regard to the Union of these States, there is too much reason to fear that " we are already two nations in feeling," and to anticipate the near approach of the calamity which shall blot out some of the stars in our ensign, and make us two nations in fact.

And what has brought us to the verge of this precipice ? What evil spirit has put enmity between the seed of those whom God, by his blessing on the wisdom and sacrifices of our fathers, made one flesh ? What has created and fostered this alienation between the North and the South, until disunion — that used to be whispered in corners — stalks forth in open daylight, and is recognized as a necessity by multitudes of thinking men in all sections of the land ? I believe before God, that this division of feeling, of which actual disunion will be but the expression and embodiment, was begotten of Abolitionism, has been rocked in its cradle and fed with its poisoned milk, and instructed by its ministers, until, girded with a strength which comes not altogether of this upper world, it is taking hold upon the pillars of the constitution, and shattering the noble fabric to its base.

There was a time when the constitutional questions between the North and South — the conflict of material interests growing out of their differences in soil and production — were discussed in the spirit of statesmanship and Christian courtesy. Then such men as Daniel Webster on the one side, and Calhoun on the other, stood up face to face, and defended the rights of their respective constituency, in words which will be quoted as long as the English tongue shall endure, as a model of eloquence and a pattern of manly debate. But Abolitionism began to creep in. It came first as a purely *moral* question. But very soon its doctrines were embraced by a sufficient number to hold the balance of power between contending parties in many districts and States. Aspirants for the Presidency seized upon it as a weapon for gratifying their ambition or avenging their disappointments. Under the shadow of their patronage, sincere Abolitionists became more bold and abusive in advocating their principles. The unlawful and wicked business of enticing slaves from their masters was pushed forward with increasing zeal. Men who, in the better days of the republic, could not have obtained the smallest office, were elected to Congress upon this single issue ; and ministers of the gospel descended from the pulpit to mingle religious animosity with the boiling caldron of political strife. Nor was this process confined to one side in the contest. Abuse always provokes recrimination. So long as human nature is passionate, hard words will be responded to by harder blows. And now behold the result! In the halls where Webster and Calhoun, Adams and McDuffie, rendered the very name of American statesmanship illustrious, and revived the memory of classic eloquence, we have heard the outpouring of both Northern and Southern violence from men who must be nameless in this sacred place; and in the land where such slave-holders as Washington and Madison united with Hamilton and Hancock in cementing the Union, which they fondly hoped would be perpetual, commerce and manufactures, and all our great industrial and governmental interests, are trembling on the verge of dissolution. And as Abolitionism is the great mischief-maker between the North and South, so it is the great stumbling-block in the way of a peaceful settlement of our difficulties. Its voice is still for war. The spirit of conciliation and compromise it utterly abhors; and, mingling a horrid mirth with its madness, puts into the hands of the advocates of secession the very fans with which to blow the embers of strife into a flame. One man threw a torch into the great temple of the Ephesians, and kindled a conflagration which a hundred thousand brave men could not extinguish. One man fiddled and sang, and made his courtiers laugh amid the burning of Rome. And so, the Abolition preacher " feels good " and overflows with merriment, when he sees our merchants and laboring men running after their chests and the bread of their families, " as if all creation was after them," and snuffs on the Southern breeze

the scent of servile and civil war. Oh, shame — shame
that it should come to this, and the name of our holy
religion be so blasphemed! Let us hope, in Christian
charity, that such men do not comprehend the danger
that stares them in the face. Indeed, who of us does
fully comprehend it? In the eloquent words of Daniel
Webster, " While the Union lasts, we have high, exciting, gratifying prospects spread out before us — for us
and for our children. Beyond that I seek not to penetrate the veil. God grant that in my day, at least, that
curtain may not rise." I repeat the noble sentiment;
God grant that in my day the curtain may not rise! Let
the night of the grave envelop these eyes in its peaceful sleep, ere their balls are seared with the vision of
dissolution and civil war. He must be blind who does
not perceive that such a vision is just ready to burst
upon us.

A kind and wonderful Providence has so tempered
the body of these States together, so bound and inter-
laced them with commercial and social ties, to say nothing of legal obligations, that no member can be severed,
and especially no contest can be waged among the
members, without a quivering and anguish in every
nerve, and a stagnation in the vital currents of all.
Let one star be blotted out from our ensign, and the
moral gravitation which holds all in their orbits will be
paralyzed, if not utterly destroyed. The living example of successful secession for one cause, will suggest
the same course for another; and unless God gives our
public men a wisdom and forbearance of which the past
few years have afforded too little evidence, the dissolution of this Union will be the signal for the disintegra-

tion of its elements. In such a chaos, let us not flatter
ourselves that we shall be in entire peace and safety.
The contest, on whose perilous edge we stand, cannot
be merely sectional — all the North on the one side,
and all the South on the other. It is a conflict that
will run the ploughshare of division through every
State and neighborhood in the land. Abolition orators
may talk about what " we of the North " will do, and
will not do, as though all the people had bowed down
to worship the image they had set up; but other men
besides them will claim the right to speak — other interests will need to be conserved besides the cause upon
which they arrogantly assume that victory perches and
the smile of heaven rests. " Let not him who putteth
on his armor boast as he that putteth it off."

When the thousands of working-men whose subsis-
tence depends upon our trade with the South, many of
whom have been deluded by Abolition demagogues,
shall clamor in our streets for bread, free labor may present some problems which political economy has not
solved. And when the commerce of this cosmopolitan
city is paralyzed, and all her benevolent and industrial
institutions are withering in the heat of this unnatural
contest, it may become a question — nay, is it not already whispered in your counting-houses — whether this
great metropolis can be separated from the people with
whom her interests and her heart is bound up, and continue to be controlled by a legislative policy against
which she is continually protesting; or whether, following the great lights of history, she will, at all hazards,
set up for herself, and, unbolting the gateway of her
magnificent harbor, invite the free trade of the world

to pour its riches into her bosom. Such are a few of
the problems which bring the question of a dissolution
of the Union home to us. If we were sure of a peaceful solution, at whatever pecuniary or social sacrifice,
we would not feel so deeply nor speak so earnestly.
But who knows that it will be peaceful? Where is the
surgeon who can sever even one member from this body
politic without the shedding of blood? Where is the
statesman or political economist who will undertake to
control the parties, or direct the industrial interests of
any one State, amid the confusion and alarm of dissolution? Let us not deceive ourselves. The chasm before us is a yawning abyss, into whose depths no eye
but God's can penetrate. Other men may cry, "Who's
afraid?" and whistle to keep their courage up; but I
confess my fears. Through the curtain that is about to
rise, I see shadows at which the horror of a great darkness settles down upon my spirit, and the hair of my
flesh stands up. Oh, my country! I have loved thee
with an affection passing the love of woman! The glories of thy history, mingled with the life-blood of my
childhood; thy prosperity has been the pride and boast
of my riper years; and mingling in my heart the love
of country with the love of Christ, I have cherished the
hope that thy brightness would never be diminished until it blended with the glories of the millennial day;
that thy consummation would be like the setting of the
morning star,

> " Which goes not down
> Behind the darkened west, nor hides obscured
> Among the tempests of the sky, but melts away
> Into the light of heaven."

And must this precious hope be dispelled ? Must this light go out, and the brightest prospect the world ever beheld disappear amid confused noise, and garments rolled in blood ? Must the interest of thirty millions of white men be sacrificed, and the sun of civilization be turned back upon the dial of the world's history, by a fanaticism which all experience proves to be the black man's bitterest enemy ? Let us appeal to the God of peace, in whose hands are the hearts of all men, to dispel the fearful vision, to infuse His loving Spirit into our national councils, to give our public men the meekness of wisdom, and to bind the hearts of all the people once more in bonds of brotherly kindness.

But, if we would have these supplications answered, let us prove our faith by our works ; take the beam out of our own eye, and obey the two-fold precept of the text : " These things teach and exhort ; and if any man teach otherwise, from such withdraw thyself."

PATRIARCHAL AND JEWISH SERVITUDE NO ARGUMENT FOR AMERICAN SLAVERY.

PUBLISHED IN "THE WORLD" IN REPLY TO THE PRECEDING SERMON OF REV. HENRY J. VAN DYKE.

BY PROF. TAYLER LEWIS, D. D.,

To the Editor of *The World:*

MAY I ask for such space as may be conveniently given in your columns, to a reply to the late pro-slavery sermon of the Rev. Henry J. Van Dyke? The term pro-slavery is used, not by way of reproach, but as expressing, in the briefest terms, the true effect, as well as description, of the discourse. It is apparently aimed at the abolitionists, but, taken in connection with the times, it is a strong defence of slavery as it now exists in these United States; it is a defence of the men, who, for the sake of slavery, are breaking up the Union; it is a defence of slavery as it is now held by southern clergymen, as a normal, a perpetual, a divine institution; it would logically justify its unlimited extension; it is a giving ease to the consciences of its more ultra advocates; it is a virtual justification of their proceedings; it is condemnatory of that great vote in the North, which men as orthodox as Mr. Van Dyke, as sound on the Scriptures, as free from all fanaticism, cannot help regarding as a popular decision, as intelligent, as con-

8*

scientious, as sublime, as any that was ever before rendered by man upon this earth.

Not to waste time in preliminaries, I must notice a pervading fallacy which is to be found, not only in Mr. Van Dyke's sermon, but in most of similar productions in the Northern States. To take the extremest ground of the extremest South would be too odious. Hence, although the argument is almost wholly against the one side, and ever palliative of the other, there is still assumed something like the appearance of a *via media*. There is a charm in such a position for many readers. It seems an easy way of getting near the truth without the labor and difficulty of ascertaining its real place. *In medio est veritas.* We distrust the maxim. It is as likely to be false as true. It is not scriptural. Truth may not be in the middle. It seldom is precisely in the middle. It is more likely to be nearer to one side than it is to the other. It is sometimes, as history has well shown, far to the one side. But even admitting the maxim, still it may be said that, in the present argument, there is something utterly fallacious in the application of it. The gravitation to error, as Mr. Van Dyke would doubtless admit, being ever the strongest in this evil world, there is ever a demand for a new *via media*, running somewhere between the old one and the side to which the worldly current strongest tends, and then another, and still another, like that eternal subdivision of a mathematical space, which is ever approaching one extreme limit without ever exactly meeting it. It is so here. To make this easy middle path, we have placed before us, on one side, the abolitionists of the North ; on the other, the "fire eaters," as they are called, of the South. But there is forgotten, or wholly overlooked, what is very essential to a right understanding of the true bearing of this very plausible " middle way." The abolitionists proper, against whom Mr. Van Dyke's sermon would seem to be chiefly directed, are a mere handful of men ; they have been growing smaller ever since the formation of the republican party gave a constitutional and conservative vent to the anti-slavery feeling ; they are men without influence, without office, mostly without votes, without the shadow of political power. But what do we find in the other extreme, as it is so plausibly called ? We find men who rule their states ; men who are in Congress, in the Senate, on the bench, holding chief places in successive cabinets ; men who for long years have been the predominant power of the very government they are now seeking so unnaturally to destroy. Instead of running due east between two extremes, such a *via media* is, in fact, a line bearing E. 80° S., and nothing is more unfair than to represent such a course as justice to the North, or as giving a fair position for rebuking every rational and religious objection to slavery as the fruit of Northern fanaticism. Time has proved the truth of our statement. Every new move of the stronger extremist has drawn the mediist after him ; so that what was once thought a remote pro-slavery position is now claimed as a compromising middle way.

This is alluded to here because Mr. Van Dyke's sermon carries the form of an argument against the abolitionists. There can be no doubt that such men as are generally understood by this term have not treated slavery as the apostles treated it. It is true, as Mr.

Van Dyke says, that there is everywhere in this extreme class an anti-biblical and an infidel tendency.   It
is true that their mode of attacking slavery on the
ground of mere natural right, their view of man as confined chiefly to his secular destiny, and their consequent
attempt to secularize the philanthropy of the Gospel,
have produced this tendency — first to undervalue, and
finally to reject the authority of revelation.   There
may be other causes in the Christianity of the times
that might afford a palliation, if not a defence, of some
of these men.   But Mr. Van Dyke is right in the fact
stated, and if these were the enemies now chiefly de-
manding attention, it might be said that he has borne
himself right valiantly.   It is easy to answer the abolitionists ; they are poor interpreters of Scripture ; the
chief among them do not pretend to interpret Scripture
at all.   As against them, then, we should concur, at
least exegetically, in Mr. Van Dyke's view of 1 Tim.
vi., and other passages of the New Testament.   There
is, however, something in the more interior spirit of
those texts that he fails to see ; he does not take the
apostle's stand point ; he does not take into view the
vastly changed condition of the world ; he does not
seem to consider that whilst truth is fixed, eternal, immutable as God himself, its application to
distant ages, and differing circumstances, is so vary-
ing continually that a wrong direction given to the
more truthful exegesis may convert it into the more
malignant falsehood, making it, in fact, " the letter that
killeth instead of the spirit that giveth life."   It is vain
to say that this is a mere transcendental fancy, by
which the force of Scripture may be ever turned aside,

The danger we speak of is one against which inspiration itself expressly warns us.   The Bible is for all ages, but there is a "letter that killeth;" there is an "accommodation" that is true and holy.

I. — THE PATRIARCHAL SERVITUDE.

But, to take Mr. Van Dyke's interpretations in their Scriptural order: His argument from the Old Testament we are compelled to pronounce utterly worthless, even as against the abolitionist.   The change that has taken place — the difference, both in form and spirit, between what was called servitude in the days of the patriarchs and slavery *as it exists* in the modern states of Mississippi and Texas, is so immense that no fair comparison can be made between them.   The wholly domestic character of the former, the total absence of that feeling of caste, which is the curse of American slavery, the feudal or tribal form which gave it more the aspect of *government* than of *property*, the complete subordination of this latter idea rendering it, in this respect, the reverse of the modern servitude, the absence of the faintest Scriptural intimation that any patriarch (though he might buy) ever *sold*, or thought of selling, for money, the humblest of his dependent vassals — all these considerations make a difference so wide, so essential we may say, that the unselfish patriarchal and the mercenary American slavery should never be mentioned together.

Take the latter as defined so carefully by the South Carolina judge, Ruffin.   We would quote it in full were it not probably well known to most of our readers. Take that stern denial of all human rights, not merely social or political, but such as belong to the very essence

of humanity, and without which one ceases to be a man
in aught except his homo-animal life ; take that out-
casting from the State consummated in the late Dred
Scott decision, and which is so different from the close
ties that bound the ancient lord to his poorest follower
— that utter crushing out of humanity which the serious
Carolina judge is compelled to pronounce most cruel ;
while he sternly deduces it as the inevitable consequence of the peculiar form of property servitude ; take,
in short, that absolute reduction of a *person* to a *thing*,
a " chattel," an *organon empeuchon*, or " animated
tool," as Aristotle defines it, and compare it with the
relation existing between Abraham and Eliezer, or any
one, the poorest of that cherished clan which so promptly followed their aged leader to the rescue of Lot.
Four thousand years ! Have we, indeed, made progress
in this matter ? Have we steadily elevated the idea of
servitude, if we are not yet able to dispense with it
from the world ? Have we been constantly improving
it by giving it more of the social and less of the mercenary ; more of the humanizing and less of the dehumanizing character ; more of the fraternal and less of
the caste aspect ? Then may we quote the patriarchs
— if not to the honor, at least not the shame of our
Christianity.

Is the Texan slaveholder, or the Georgian cotton-
grower, more of the social *lord*, and less of the money
making *owner*, than in the days of Abraham ? It is a
vital question. Both ideas, *lordship* and *ownership*,
enter into slavery. Though actually mingled they are
logically distinct, and according as the one or the other
becomes predominant, so does the whole character of

the nation undergo an essential moral change. The claim of power, even where wrongful, is perfectly consistent with human dignity. There is no degradation in subjection to government of any form, even though it be of the most despotic kind. Frenchmen are still men — high spirited, intelligent men — though under the unlimited domination of Napoleon. Some of them, and not absurdly, do even find their glory in the very grandeur of its absoluteness. Power is not degrading. A man is still a man — he may be a man in his sublimest aspects, though the subject of an authority that places him at the cannon's mouth. The reason of this is found in the glory of the idea; in the essential assumption, although it may be false in practice, that government, as government, is ever unselfish — ever for the good of the governed.

But to be *owned* is degrading; to be *property*, and nothing more, is dehumanizing. The ideas are inseparable. It is degrading both ways. In the absence or subserviency of the other principle, a man cannot *own* his *fellow man*, a being like himself, without degrading himself. His own debasement is involved in the debasement of *his* race. Men *feel* this before they have objectively *thought* it, or reasoned about it. Hence it is, that in a Christianized slave holding community there is, there always must be, more or less of a hidden trouble of conscience. There is an obscure feeling, not allowed to come out in distinct thought, but which tells them there is, somewhere, something wrong about it. Hence, too, the never ceasing heave of unrest, that pervades such society. Hence the extravagant acts of their politicians, the extravagant doctrine of their clergymen, the continual overdoing of their social and political life. Perhaps, too, in this deeper ground, and not in the more superficial ones generally assigned, may we find the real cause of the turbulent madness that now characterizes certain portions of that unhappy region.

This smothered sense of the innate odiousness of the mere property slavery, seeks relief in two ways: The more honorable, although the more false, proceeding, is to find an assumed, if not a real shelter under the higher principle, or the unselfish government idea. When hard pushed with the moral argument, they forget the claim of carrying their property into Kansas, " just like any other property," and begin immediately to sermonize about the blessings of Christianity and good government they would confer upon Africa.

This, however, soon reveals its delusion. It is, moreover, only adapted to a special minority of minds. Relief failing here, it is more confidently sought by casting about, on the other tack, for arguments by which to throw the slave from the pale of humanity. It will not be so bad if we can, in some way, prove to ourselves that he is not a man. Any one may study this working of human nature as it has for some years been growing at the South, and penetrating the North. It is the most alarming feature in the whole business. Is the negro a *man* — a son of Adam? Then we are degraded ; we are all degraded by his being reduced to the rank of an animal, or a thing. It affects the dignity of us all, that any one believed to be of the same blood, to belong, in fact, to that same continuous stream of life which, at some historical point, was one with our own, should be

in so vile a state. We must either do something for
our " poor relation," or disown and cast him out. It
is this innate sense of what he would regard as due to
himself that has led the modern slaveholder, the politicians, if not *yet* the clergymen, to dehumanize the negro. We would solemnly warn our churches in this
respect. They are on the brink of an awful precipice.
The politicians are controlling our Christianity, instead
of being controlled by it. They are aided by certain
scientific tendencies, and such is the evident course of
things that but a short time will elapse before an orthodox clergyman at the South, who holds " the unity of
the race " as belonging truly to the very heart of our
theology, will be deemed as much a " fanatic " as any
of his anti-slavery brethren at the North. The moral
question, the theological question, the ethnological question, will stand no compromises. The course of things,
both North and South, shows that this new doctrine of
slavery as the " normal condition " of its subjects, as
something perpetual, never to be yielded, never relaxed,
except in some remote millenium, as Mr. Van Dyke
would savingly fancy in his sermon — that this new
doctrine of slavery, we say, which has sprung up within the last thirty years, is utterly at war with the proper
humanity of its victims. The negro must be dehuman-
ized ; and he is blind indeed who cannot see how rapidly, unless checked, everything is tending to that issue.

Now can we, as Christians, bear this thought ? Can
we think without pain of the brutalizing of our race, or
any portion of our race ? Every Christian man, as far
as he is a Christian man, must feel it. What thus degrades the negro, hurts *him* too, just as that which

touches the remotest member pains the whole body.   It
hurts him when the brutal politician at the South compares him with the horse or the " alligator ; " it hurts
him when the manufacturer of vile amusements at the
North makes a beastly caricature of the poor African in
his ribald minstrelsy.   It touches the heart, the *cor*, or
core, of our humanity ; it reaches that deep spot where
we are all one in Adam, and hope to be one in Christ.
May we not say with all reverence, He feels it, too, that
Ineffable One who took our sin-degraded nature and
now bears it in the highest heavens ?   In view of the
amazing thought that Christ should stoop so low to lift
us up ; how strange that we should be then thrusting
down a portion of our fallen brotherhood, that we
should be making castes, and hunting out arguments for
slavery, instead of feeling that it is each man's highest
interest, conservative of his own truest worth, as well
as his most solemn duty, to raise to the common level
of humanity, and if possible, above the common level
of humanity, the lowest of those degraded tribes that
still bear the form and the nature, though it be the
poorest nature of a man.

The sinking of a portion of the human race to this
low level of *property*, degrades us all.   The truth is so
important that we must be pardoned for dwelling upon
it.   It is an inevitable effect of the abominable doctrine
which would make some men semi-human, that it takes
away from the evidence of our highest human hopes.
It makes an inclined plane, or rather a gradation of
steps, between us and the brutes.   It thus links us on
with all the animality that is below us.   It destroys the
distinction on which we build our chief psychological

argument for immortality. It weakens in our minds
that other great argument from revelation, derived from
the incarnation, or Christ's taking our one common, universal humanity. What a coming down was there ! In
view of it, how unchristianlike when worldliness and
selfishness lead us to degrade ourselves by casting out
of the bound of human brotherhood any whose nature
Christ assumed, and for whose salvation He gave his
own human life. Yet all this is the inevitable tendency
of the property idea, when it becomes predominant.
Are our churches prepared for the issues it must in time
create ?

It is not the mere presence, but the predominance of
the one or the other of these ideas, the property or the
government idea, which gives its chief moral character
to servitude. In the patriarchal, we venture to affirm,
the former was altogether subordinate, or rather almost
wholly unknown, according to the modern mercantile
conception of it. There is mention of persons " bought
with money." It was, as we have said, an evidence of
the social change. With the heathen sellers it might
have had all the nature of mercenary traffic. That so
it was regarded by the patriarchs themselves, there is
not a particle of proof. There is the strongest inferen-
tial evidence to the contrary. We boldly challenge any
man to produce one line or word of Scripture to show,
directly or indirectly, that any patriarch ever sold a
slave to the heathen, or to any other patriarch ; that
ever a Jew, in later times, sold a bondman to a heathen
or to any other Jew. There may have been transfers
of neighborhood, or convenience, but nothing like *traffic*,
in our modern sense of the word. They were bought

with money, and, doubtless, in this way many a poor
stranger escaped death, or exchanged a hard vassalage
for a blessed patriarchal home; but there was no *domestic* slave trade.   Neither are slaves ever mentioned
as articles of " property."   They are never mentioned
in the Jewish statistics along with " the corn, the wine.
and the oil, the barley, the flocks, and the herds."
They are enumerated in the census of the household;
and in this way are named in connection sometimes with
lower things, but never as articles of traffic or merchandise.   They are mentioned, sometimes, as evidence
of their lord's power and greatness, but rather as followers and vassals than as slaves.   It is said " Thou
shalt not covet thy neighbor's man servant," and the
text is often quoted to prove the scriptural lawfulness
of the modern human bondage; but so is it also said,
" Thou shalt not covet thy neighbor's wife."   He who
would pervert the guileless scriptural language in the
one case, may do so with equal justice in the other.
Wives were sometimes bought with money; wives are
mentioned among the items of household prosperity; the
argument is as good in the one case as in the other.   In
neither does it present anything more than the painted
outside resemblance to our modern trafficking, whilst in
spirit it is as remote from it as the ages are from each
other.

   There was, doubtless, more of this property idea in
the ancient slavery as it existed in other nations — if
we may leave our Christianity, and go so far back for
conscience-silencing precedents — but this we may say,
that the oldest servitude, as it existed in the Homeric
age, and long after, was comparatively, if not wholly,

free from that peculiar species of degradation, that
odious caste feeling which is so prominent a feature of
our modern, and — shall we call it so ? — Christianized
bondage. In those early times it was a misfortune, a
loss, like the calamities of war ; it was a subjection, a
restraint, a toil ; there was much harshness in it, but
little or no degradation, such as we have been chiefly
regarding in these remarks in respect to its painful debasement of our common human nature. All were alike
in the risk. It might be the fate of any man to be
taken in war. It consequently retained a manliness
which is utterly wanting in our depredations upon the
miserable African. Every man can have his chance.
The master of to-day might be the *doulos*, the *demos*,
the subdued man, the *subject* of to-morrow. If the
chivalrous Carolinian would thus run the risk of becoming a slave himself, he might hold his captive as proudly
as any Ishmaelite of the desert, or any roving filibuster
of the Homeric age. Hence, the ancient servitude,
though severe, was not mean, as we think our modern
slavery is. It was consistent, too, with a social freedom neither awed by haughtiness nor insulted by a
humbling condescension. The old servant of Ulysses,
like the Eliezer of Abraham, was the trusted, confiden-
tial friend, at whose board his *lord* — the spirit of the
noble passage would rebuke us should we say *owner* —
sat and conversed without the least feeling of incon-
sistency or dishonor. It was like the feudal relation
of the middle ages ; harsh in some of its features, despotic, perhaps, to a degree beyond the condition of some
modern servants, but nothing degrading. It was power,
strong power, protection, mutual dependence, exacted

servitude, obedience, fealty — all dignified ideas, — and capable of growing, as they have grown in later times, into dignified social and political relations. But in the other, or caste aspect, all is base and debasing. The slaveholder, as the only way to get himself a quieting plea, must regard himself, not as the lord, or even the *despotes*, in its best sense, but as the owner of property that rises and falls with the times, and with the stocks. If he is a ruler, he is a ruler of chattels, of brutes, or of seeming men, who have only a half humanity. The whole scale sinks, the master as well as the slave. Beings that look like us, though brutalized in appearance, as we would be after generations of animalizing bondage ; beings that talk and think like us ; that are wonderfully like us in all our appetites and passions — such beings, treated as *things*, bought and sold continually, denied a political status, even the poor dignity of a local serfdom, claimed as property *everywhere*, property *in presenti*, property *in futuro*, bargained for before they are born, classed with the animals in the ignoble maxim *partus sequitur ventrem* — beyond all, doomed to this as their true and " normal " condition, from which they are never more to rise ! It degrades us all, we say. It is no mere transcendental conceit of human dignity that prompts the assertion, but a just appreciation of that ruined, yet costly nature, for which Christ died. There is no true parallel between the cases. Whoever reasons thus, whether in the pulpit, or elsewhere, from the patriarchal servitude, or even the most ancient heathen servitude, to the modern mercantile or mercenary slavery, is utterly deceiving both himself and his hearers.

We have given the more attention to this subject of the *patriarchal* slavery, because the argument is so often employed, and with such a conceit of its being unanswerable. There is another view of *Jewish* slavery, which we deem most important, and which may be presented in reply to Mr. Van Dyke's, and the common argument from the Old Testament! We make no other apology for the length or manner of this communication, than the great importance of the subject. If ever the moral aspects of the slavery question are to be discussed in its very roots, this would seem a proper time for such discussion. There is a right and a wrong, somewhere, in this matter; and we think they can be found. Too long has the appeal been made to everything else but truth. The writer may have overrated his own powers for the task, but it is certainly high time that from some quarter there should be addressed the intellect and the conscience as well as the passions and prejudices of the nation.

II. — THE JEWISH SERVITUDE.

Mr. Van Dyke next proceeds to what has been commonly regarded the scriptural Gibraltar of the slavery cause. It has been deemed so fundamental to the argument as to have a place in a late Carolina manifesto. We refer to the 25th chapter of Leviticus. What is there said of the servitude of Jew to Jew, Mr. Van Dyke sees at once cannot be employed in defence of southern slavery. "But not so," he says, "with those of foreign birth; there was no year of jubilee for them. For what says the law?" It is quoted as triumphantly as though he were citing a section of the Dred Scott

decision. "For what says the law ? "   Read the 44th
and 46th verses of the same chapter:

Both thy bondmen and bondmaids which thou shalt have shall
be of the heathen that are round about you. Of them may ye buy
bondmen and bondmaids. Moreover, of the children of strangers
that do sojourn among you — of them may ye buy, and of their
families that are with you, which they beget in your land, and
they shall be your possession. And ye shall take them as an
inheritance for your children after you, to inherit them as a possession ; they shall be your bondmen forever.

" There it is," he tells us like a triumphant advocate
who has made out his case from the statute and the reported decisions ; " there it is, plainly written in the
Divine law.   No legislative enactment, no statute
framed by legal skill was ever more explicit or incapable of perversion." We do not mean to pervert it,
and yet we would say to Mr. Van Dyke, very plainly,
though with all respect for his religious character as
well as his legal sharpness, that we do not think much
of his argument.   It has some force against those foolish people who contend that slavery, meaning thereby
the binding of one man to the authority of another, is
sin per se, but it is a very poor defence of those other
still more foolish people who maintain that slavery is
right per se, good per se, as well as *divine* by direct
statute enactment.   There are two answers to this argument.   There is one that greatly weakens any infer-
ences to be drawn from it to our present times ; there
is another that renders it utterly worthless.

As a preliminary to the first, we must express our
astonishment at the importance that some attach to

this passage of Scripture. Some of its phases sound like modern ones, and may, therefore, suggest modern ideas ; and yet, even in respect to them, the great remoteness of the times, and manners changing, more or less, the meaning of language, would lead a careful critic to suspect any such modern application as is sometimes given to them. But look again, and see how many things are lacking to complete the wanted parallel. How different the state of the Jews, lying in the midst of heathendom, and that of our slaveholding communities, lying in the midst of an all-surrounding Christendom ! How *far-fetched* any comparisons between that purely secluded nation, that agricultural, domestic, untrafficking theocracy, and our commercial, cotton-growing States ! How different the condition of the masters — how different must have been the condition of the servants, how remotely diverse the two relations — the simple, social status in the one case, and the growing property notion, with all its commercial adjuncts in the other.

But let us look at the passage closely, and even the seeming resemblances will begin to disappear. There is permission to *buy*. That looks mercantile. But does Mr. Van Dyke need to be told that in the old world, buying, in such cases, meant the payment of ransom — and the service to be returned was its equivalent recompense ; implying no idea of selling, unless with the consent of the *bought*. It was sometimes the ransom of the life, and then the service for such a costly favor might justly be for life — *in perpetuum*, indefinitely, or forever, as the guileless Hebrew word expresses it.

Again, they are permitted to *buy*, but not a word of *selling*, either to the heathen, or to any other Jew.

9

That is implied, it might be said. Not so certain, however. We must take care how we carry a familiar modern notion into ancient law and ancient language. If we *will* thus employ Scripture, we must take the *lex scripta* as we find it, just " that which is written, and nothing more." There is no such implication. Not only the whole style of the language, but also all we know of the ancient state, as well as the total absence of anything in subsequent Jewish history recognizing any such right to sell or trade, are all against it. Mr. Van Dyke quotes with an air of certainty. There can be no doubt about it. " There it is," says he, " plainly written in the divine law." " To the law and the testimony," he says, in another place, " if they speak not according to this word, it is because there is no light in them." To say nothing of his misunderstanding and misinterpretation of this latter passage, we will simply reply to him in his own style of challenge. The permission to sell is not *in the writing*, that is clear ; we mean, by way of traffic, as distinct from the original purchase from the heathen or the parent. Now, let him give us an adjudged case, an implication from any thing in the actual Jewish jurisprudence, a particle of inference from Jewish history, that there was a *traffic* in slaves, or anything like it, in Israel, even in its corruptest times. There is no evidence that any such traffic, any such selling, by a Jew to a heathen, or by Jew to Jew, was allowed, or would have been deemed reputable. There is no evidence as to the tenure or manner in which these bondmen were held, whether by individuals or by the nation, as was the case with the Gideonites and the public servants in Solomon's days.

Servants are reckoned among the elements of household state and grandeur, but they are not mentioned as property or income in the Jewish statistics. They are not reckoned thus, as has been already remarked, with " the corn, the wine, and the oil," the " flocks and the herds," the " wine presses and the barns." Servitude was, in short, a purely social status, that might have its inception in the payment of money. It was a protecting authority, reciprocally beneficial to both parties, but designed, benevolently, for the good of the servant. But all this falls short of the property idea in the modern sense. To make it perfect there must be sale, and not only that, but the unlimited power of sale. Property is not simply that which is bought, but that which is vendible, merchantable, marketable, and thus having a market value. Property rises and falls; is governed by current standards of exchange, with its laws of supply and demand. That such is the predominant idea in modern slavery (or the slavery of civilization, even so much more mercenary and degrading than that of barbarism or semi-barbarism) is evident from the fact that it is essential to its existence. Take away this predominant idea of marketable property, and no pleas for christianizing Africa would cause it to last a generation in our cotton growing states.

Such *has* become the character of slave property among us. Is there a syllable of evidence that there was anything like it in the secluded, domestic, untrading Israel? It is this distinction, too, that shows the absurdity of Mr. Van Dyke's argument, that " a man has property in his wife and in his child." Just so a wife has property in her husband, and a child in its father. Would he concede the same reciprocity between the slave and his master ? and would he give the slave, notwithstanding the Dred Scott decision, the right to sue in our courts for damages sustained in having a master killed upon a railroad ? If not, his parallel is good for nothing. It is only a deluding sophism, just adapted to the moral and intellectual state of any of his hearers, if he has any such, who might want to re-open the African slave trade for the benefit of Christianity. He might as well maintain that a man has property in every one of his neighbors. We are all bound together. There is something valuable to us in all our relations. They may have cost us money, too, or labor to obtain them. But here is the distinction between this kind of "property," if a man will allegorically call it so, and what the slaveholder means when he claims the right of carrying his slave to Nebraska, or insists upon the domestic slave trade between Virginia and Georgia ; it is the lack of vendibility. These relations are not vendible property, marketable property. They are not things that we buy to sell, even if we had power to sell, or it were reputable to sell them, or they had any market value as salable commodities. But the southern slave is thus regarded as property ; as their laws now stand, he is property in the most commercial sense, as much so as cotton or sugar.

This is getting, too, to be not merely an incidental but the predominant idea, and so, as we have shown before, completely changes the essential moral aspect of the whole matter. But Mr. Van Dyke's notion of property, absurd as it is, suggests the most unanswerable of fact-arguments against him. The Jewish servitude having little or nothing of the mercantile aspect, *could*, with some show of decency, be compared to the filial relation ; the cotton-growing slavery, if it ever had any, is fast losing every feature of resemblance. And this is the mighty difference between them.

The Jewish servitude may have tended in time to change its character, and to approach nearer the idea of traffic. If so, it was only in accordance with that strange yet most sure law, that slavery ever becomes worse — more degrading, at least, if not more cruel — with the advance of civilization. There are intimations in the Jewish history that it was at certain times more mercenary, and therefore more oppressive, than at others. But whenever it thus departed from the primitive mild idea, then we hear the thunderings of the prophets. No conservatism prevented their denouncing the vengeance of the Lord upon the whole thing. Read Isaiah lviii. 7 : "Is not this the fast day I have chosen, to loose your wicked bonds, to unbind the servile knots, to set free the oppressed, and to *break asunder every yoke*." We have no right to limit the language. The term "the yoke," is the same with the Hebraism by which the common servile condition is denoted in the New Testament.

But how is this, some may say, are you not making one part of Scripture contradict another ? Is it consistent that God should give a permission, and then rebuke men so sweepingly for taking the benefit of it ? He could not denounce it more sternly if it was a sin *per se*, which surely it cannot be, since it had his own divine sanction. Read Scripture more carefully, my orthodox friend. Read it not to get permits for this or

that, but to study humanity, to learn the dark mystery
of our fallen nature, to read ourselves, and the character and purposes of God as revealed in this human mir-
ror. "The letter killeth, but the spirit giveth life."
God does permit — we have like warrant for saying it
— God does permit what he rebukes men for doing.
He permitted Balaam to go to Balak, and then sharply
rebuked him for going. How much hair-splitting
verbal commentary has there been to reconcile the supposed discord in this passage? But take it aright, and
what a glorious truth comes out of the apparent contradiction! God gave him permission to go that he might
bless, but Balaam went to *curse;* and so "the anger of
the Lord was kindled against him *because he went,*"
the Scripture says, and the unreasoning beast was made
to rebuke the madness of the prophet in his unholy perversion of the divine word. The passage has been an
offendiculum, a stumbling block to the vulgar caviler
and to some of the vulgar learned, and this, both on
account of the miracle and the doctrine; to the spiritual discernment it is indeed a glorious passage, not only
in the light it sheds upon the divine ways, but in its
most fitting and rational mode of rebuking irrational
men. "God's ways are not as our ways, his thoughts
are not as our thoughts." "God is wiser than men,"
says Mr. Van Dyke, in one place where he would rebuke the abolitionists. We have no thought at all of
disputing the truth of that proposition, but might think
it capable of some application to others, who assume so
boldly to be the exclusive defenders of Deity.

Any one acquainted with the spirit of those times
must recognise, in this "permission," a merciful provis-

ion, intended, not for the selfish interest of the Jews
(they are too often reminded of the fact of their own
long bondage to allow that thought), but as a method
by which a person taken in war, liable to be put to
death, or to be sold into a far worse bondage might
find a refuge in Israel.   There is no permission to make
slave hunts in Moab and Idumea.   Solomon sent ships
to *Ophir* (the root, according to pretty good philology,
of our word Africa;) yet he never thought that the
divine grant allowed him to bring home a cargo of human chattels along with his "gold dust, asses and
ivory." If any one wishes to discover a more selfish,
or less merciful reason, let him hunt the letter until he
finds it. The one we have given, is in harmony with
the inward and outward life of ancient Israel; it is in
harmony with the declared destiny of the chosen people, as the light, the hope, the refuge, the ultimate blessing of a lost humanity.

The truth is, this permission was a branch of the
same humane law, Deut. xxiii., 15, 16, that forbids a
fugitive slave or servant to be delivered up to his master.   This is on the supposition that the injunction applies only to those that escaped from heathen masters,
and such is the view the writer was once inclined to
take of the text.   He must confess, however, that a
close examination has led him strongly to doubt its cor-
rectness.   Many commentators have adopted it, because they have thought that, otherwise, the lawgiver
would seem to nullify in one clause what had been permitted in another.   We must not however judge it by
modern ideas. If the above view be correct, the *permission* to hold bondmen was a permission " *to be con-*

strued strictly" as our lawyers would say, in favor of
the servant. If the master could not keep him, either
by force or kind treatment, he was to have no help from
his neighbor; he was not to put to trouble distant
tribes. The Hebrew word here rendered " escaped,"
is a strong one. It implies an escape made with difficulty — " *hath torn himself away.*" " Thou shalt not
shut him up; he shall dwell with thee where he chooses; thou shalt not be hard upon him," or " distress
him." There is no qualification. We might say to
Mr. Van Dyke — in his own chosen style — *ita scrip-
tum est; Thou shalt not surrender to his master the
servant that is escaped from his master unto thee; thou
shalt not trouble him.*

" There it is plainly *written* in the divine law; no
legislative enactment, no statute framed by legal skill
was ever more explicit." We might rest on this mere
absence of qualifying words, but the more the passage
is studied, the more it is seen that there is something
stronger. The expression, " from the nations that are
round thee," is expressly inserted in the other law,
which Mr. Van Dyke so exultingly quotes, and every
lawyer will tell him that, therefore, its absence in a perfectly similar enactment, where, if intended, it is equally
demanded, is equivalent to an express exclusion. " *Who
shall have escaped unto thee from his master.*" Had it
meant from the heathen, the language would not have
been personal and specific, as it is, but general and collective — " who shall have escaped from any of the nations that are round about thee." Besides, there
would have been no need of such a law. There is no
evidence of any national comity between the Jews and

the surrounding Moabites and Philistines, with whom
they were continually at war, which would have led
them to deliver up fugitive slaves without a divine law
forbidding it. We do not urge this at all as against
our duty to surrender fugitive slaves to the South ; for
we *have a lex scripta*, though a hard one ; we have a
constitution and a law, clear and explicit, and we are
bound, in truth and honesty, to execute it in spite of
feeling and in spite of provocation. But as against Mr.
Van Dyke, it is a perfect answer to the use he would
make of the old Jewish servitude.

God may grant a permission for many reasons, and
yet regard it as right and praiseworthy that men should
relax the extreme license that he himself may have giv-
en. The praise ever bestowed on liberation shows that
even the permitted bondage was regarded as an evil —
in one sense " a statute not good " (Ezek. xx. 25), such
as were made to " try Israel."   Hence, in the early
Christian church, it was esteemed a meritorious act to
" redeem the slave ; " it was thought a " good work,"
if we may use such a term without being suspected of
Pelagian heresy — a " good work " that Christ might
remember in the day of the world's last reckoning, to
" break the bars of the yoke and let the bound go free."
It is affecting, too, to find how often this is mentioned
in the Koran.   To redeem a slave might pay for the
neglect of fasting ; it would do much to atone for not
making a pilgrimage to Mecca.

It is in the light of this feeling, too, that we must
read the language of the Jewish prophets before referred to.   To this vehemence of style they are doubtless
excited by the most remarkable recollection in their

9*

own national history, as well as by that remarkable language frequently repeated in the law, and one instance of which lies overlooked so very near the text Mr. Van Dyke has so carefully quoted. — *Remember that ye were bondmen once yourselves.* To what purpose this admonition, coming so often and so close home ? Its nearest relation is, perhaps, to the milder servitude of a Jewish brother, but, *in spirit*, it applies to all ; for they are also told, with equal force and pathos, to " remember the stranger, for ye were strangers once " in a foreign land, as well as bondmen.

We have said that there are two views that may be taken of Mr. Van Dyke's and the common argument from Jewish servitude. One has already been given. It seems to us, to say the least, greatly to weaken the position. There is another that renders it utterly worthless. It is that derived from the relation of the Jewish to the Christian church, or rather the respective relation of each to the world.

III. — JEWISH SERVITUDE NO ARGUMENT FOR CHRISTIAN SLAVERY.

The view already presented is certainly sufficient to make one very cautious in applying to American slavery any argument drawn from what is called the Jewish servitude. But there is a second reply which, we are bold to say it, utterly sweeps away this stronghold of the pro-slavery cause. The Jew was secluded from the world. It was a nation kept apart, not for its own sake, but as the repository of special blessings for the race. It was a trustee for humanity. It was the first born, with the rights of primogeniture until the other

nations of the earth had closed their long minority. In
defence of this position they had many straitening pro-
hibitions. As a Divine signal, too, that they were the
princely, the conservative nation of the world, they had
some peculiar privileges, which may be considered as
types, or signs of fealty from other races to the chosen
people. It was in pursuance of the blessing of Jacob:
" Let people serve thee, and nations bow down unto
thee; be lord over thy brethren (the children of Esau,
Lot and Ishmael, Moab, Edom, the tribes of the desert),
and let thy kindred bow down to thee." — Gen. xxvii.
29. " It figured," says Mathew Henry, with his deep
spiritual discernment, " the bringing in of the Gentiles
to the service of Christ and His church." Thus Isaiah
says, lxi. 5: " Strangers shall stand and feed your
flocks, and the sons of the alien be your vine dressers."
" It was a people by itself." — Num. xxiii. 9. *Solus
habitabit, et inter gentes non reputabitur* — " it shall
dwell alone, it shall not be reckoned among the nations."

Israel, with all its imperfections, was the type of the
better humanity to come. It was the last refuge of the
world, and thus it was to be kept apart, in character
and in privilege, until the " desire of all nations "
should be born. Up to this period of time, Jew was to
Jew as he was not to the other peoples. The national
feeling, the sectional feeling, was to be preserved as
conservative of the great good it not only prefigured
but actually had in store for humanity. Hence Jew
was nearer to Jew than to any other race. Now, we
invite Dr. Van Dyke's attention to this point. As a
Christian, standing in a different position from his

Jewish co-laborer, Dr. Raphall; as a Christian man, valuing all that is most precious in Christianity, let him see if he can detect any fallacy in the use we are about to make of the great distinction. The Jew was allowed to hold bondmen from the heathen; whether as a merciful or a punitive provision; whether for his own mercenary profit, or for a higher reason, we will not, in this stage of our argument, inquire. But here is the vital question: who are heathen now? We once were such; our fathers once were such — " strangers to the covenant of promise, and aliens from the commonwealth of Israel." If, however, there is in Christianity one truth more prime than another, it is that " this wall of partition has been broken down," clean gone forever. There is no longer Jew nor Gentile, though Dr. Raphall may assert it on the one side and Dr. Van Dyke still plead for it in behalf of slavery, on the other. In Christ Jesus all are one — all are free — free spiritually, free socially, from all that degrades or casts out of the one common family of man; free from ownership, each one because he is a man and belongs to Christ, though subject to government, however imperial, as an institution truly ordained of God. We still speak of heathen, using the term geographically, and, to some extent, ethnologically; but theologically, ecclesiastically, Christianly, there are no heathen. The term was the antithesis of Jew, not of Christian; and it is only for the Jew, at the present day, to maintain it. As anciently, Israelite to Israelite, so in the " new covenant" with humanity, is every man to every man. All are brethren now. The language may sound radical, fanatical, some might say, but it is a precious truth — to us, practically, the

most precious of all Bible truths, inasmuch as it is the
most conservative of all real philanthropy. Reform,
progress, philanthropy, are all but empty words, mock-
ing delusions, without the doctrine of the incarnation
and its kindred dogma, the life or blood unity of the
race. Let us look again, then, to the old " statute,"
and see how it reads in the new version — " But of
your *brethren*, the sons of Israel, ye shall not make
bondmen; for ye are all my servants, whom I brought
from the land of Egypt." Translate it fairly into the
language of the more glorious dispensation, and it can
have but one meaning. To the Christian it says:
" Of your fellow men, your brethren, the sons of Adam,
your brethren redeemed by Christ, ye shall not make
slaves." Ye may *rule* them, sternly if necessary, but
ye may not *own* them. To treat them as chattels, to
hold slaves for gain (as a defending Presbyterian clergyman of late has boldly defined it), is a sin *per se;* a
sin in the thought, yes, in that which is deeper than the
thought, in the prime action, the mainspring, or *primum
mobile* of the soul. You may establish your political
and social relations with a wise or an unwise expediency, but you may not hold men, it seems to say to us,
you may not hold men as mercenary property, " for
they are my servants whom I have redeemed, saith the
Lord." The old seclusion has been broken up, " the
law has gone forth from Zion, the word of the Lord
from Jerusalem." It is long, long since the redemption
era was announced by the heavenly messenger.

> The year of jubilee has come,
> Return ye ransomed millions home.

The temple was for one people ; the Church is for all

nations, and it has no "inner or outer court." We
have all one mother now, one home, one brotherhood,
as well as one Saviour.

"And they shall be your *possession*," says the old
"statute," that "skillfully prepared enactment," which
Dr. Van Dyke and Dr. Raphall so proudly quote. But
that statute has been long since superseded by a new
grant. Ye cannot now plead it any more to make
bondmen of the nations that are round about you. God
has given them to Christ — "the heathen for an inheritance, the uttermost parts of the earth for a *possession*."
The modern rabbi may not hold to this, but the Christian doctor must certainly recognize the validity of the
grant. Well might the apostle say, in view of this
heavenly manumission, "Ye are bought with a price;
be ye not the servants of men." But of that pregnant
text in another place. There is light enough on this
subject, even in the Old Testament, if we were but to
look for it.

God has given to Christ "the heathen for a possession." It is our duty now to go in and occupy in His
name — in the old apostolical method, as bishops and
stewards, not as bailies or marshals. It is our high
privilege to bring to the Saviour his promised servants,
not by joining company with the King of Dahomey, or
forming a transportation partnership with the Sheik of
Borneo, but by going with the noble Livingstone into
the very center of that vast continent, carrying the Bible in the one hand and the instruments of civilization in
the other. It is ours to make them good servants of
Christ by christianizing them *where they are*, in that
home which was given to the African, and fitted for him

when "God made of one blood all nations of men to
dwell on all the face of the earth, having determined
the times appointed and the bounds of their habitation."
God meant there should be nationalities (see Deut.
xxxii. 8; Acts xvii. 26) as a better thing, and more
conservative of a hearty human brotherhood, than cosmopolitanism, whether it be that of an unscriptural radical philanthropy, or of a false conservatism, that would
break up this ancient "Divine constitution" by unnaturally bringing the labor of one part of the world to
raise cotton and sugar in another. Neither is this at
all opposed to what was said before about the common
life and brotherhood of the race. Cosmopolitanism will
not promote love. There is more unity in diversity
than in sameness; there is more true brotherhood in
separate nationalities than in a forced amalgamation,
whether it be that of radicalism or of commerce. God
hath not only "made of one blood all nations," but he
hath "made them to dwell on all the face of the
earth, having determined," by his own wisdom, "their
times and the bounds," that is the climatic tempera-
ments and local fitness "of their habitations." When
we shall have at length discovered the enormous evils
interfering with these divine arrangements, we may appreciate the wisdom of the saintly missionary who would
Christianize and civilize the African in his appointed
home, instructing him in the pure gospel without the
contamination of a degraded foreign life, and teaching
him to plant his own cotton fields on the banks of his
native Chadda and Zambesi.

Then let us go and tell him what we have so long
known, and so unfaithfully, but he has never heard, that

Christ has *bought him;* that there is a divine Goel, a
Redeemer, who claims him as his own " near kinsman,"
though dwelling far away, even in the " uttermost parts
of the earth." This is the scriptural mode of bringing
the world to Christ, and giving to him " the fruits of
his inheritance." How different from the proposed
method of Christianizing Africa by the slave trade.
Let us away with the impious cant, and all that is col-
lateral or consequential to it. The false, mercenary
spirit that prompts it is even more unchristian than the
cruelty. Every one knows that there would be neither
slavery nor the slave trade if the only reason for them
were the evangelizing of the negro, and every Christianized conscience must feel that the falsehood and
meanness of the assumed advocate of such a proceeding is really more odious to the Holy Saviour than the
undissembling barbarian ferocity which is stimulated by
it. How humiliating, as well as how sad, the thought
that, after the sun of Christianity has been shining on
us for nearly nineteen hundred years, there is still need
to contend against a plea so false, a doctrine so atro-
cious ! What a commentary, too, on the world's ethi-
cal progress, that the enslaving of those called heathen
should be justified by going back to this old Jewish
" statute," and perverting it to an end historically so
remote from anything intended by the ancient law-giver !
It might do for Dr. Raphall, for he is still a Jew — we
say it not offensively — he is still a Jew, with that " veil
upon the heart " in the reading of the Old Testament
which the recollection of Israel's ancient bondage and
long centuries of modern degradation has not been able
to take away. The Christian teacher has a higher law,

not an opposing revelation, but one that gives him the key to the right interpretation of the Old.

The trite argument from Ham, Dr. Van Dyke has wisely left out, though we see that his colleague in the slavery cause still employs it. Without a particle of authority from the text, he applies to the sons of Cush and Mitszalim, a prediction which the Scripture expressly pronounces against Canaan, and which was fulfilled when Dr. Raphall's ancestors reduced the Canaanites to subjection, or drove them from their land. But even as a prophecy against the Africans, would he as an interpreter of Scripture contend that it justified the acts and agents by which it had been fulfilled? We will cite him, then, another ancient prophecy, Deut. xxviii. 64, &c. — "And the Lord shall scatter thee among all people, and among these nations shalt thou find no ease, neither shall the sole of thy foot have rest, but the Lord shall give thee there a trembling heart, and failing of eyes, and sorrow of mind ; and thou shalt fear day and night and shalt have no assurance of thy life ; and thou shalt come down very low : And the Lord shall bring thee into Egypt again, and there shall ye be sold unto your enemies for bondmen and bondwomen and no man shall buy you." The same justification that this prophecy gives the Spaniard, the Saracen, the mad Egyptian Caliph Hakim, or to the cruel Plantagenet, in the oppression and bondage of the Jew, — just that same justification does the prediction in Genesis, even if it had any relation to Africa, afford to the slave transporter and slaveholder of modern times.

A few words more respecting this text, Lev. xxv. 44, 45. Carry out the common argument from it, and it lands us in utter absurdity. If the Christian church now stands to any, in any such relation as the Jew to the heathen, who shall dare to say that this divine right of enslavement now belongs to all the vile and ungodly men within its visible nominal pale? And how more revolting still the absurdity to claim it as a special privilege for the truly spiritual, the elect of God! Besides, when any one of those enslaved heathen becomes a baptized Christian — what then? Is he by fair implication of this " enactment," entitled to his freedom if he wishes for it? Will it be to him the year of his social as well as his spiritual jubilee? It may be said that that would be advancing Christianity by an appeal to mercenary motives. There would be some force in such an objection; but one should be careful in stating it, lest he affront the men who talk so plausibly of making the growing of cotton in America a means for Christianizing Africa. Still, it is a point we must meet in the fair interpretation of the text. Many of these poor enslaved beings do become Christians — all praise for it to the prayers and exertions of many faithful pious men and women in our southern states — and when any one is truly such, will he still be a heathen? Will he still be subject, himself and his unborn posterity, to the right of enslavement given by virtue of this " enactment " to his irreligious master? Or, instead of being entitled to his emancipation, as he would be by becoming a believer in some Mohammedan countries, would his value as a slave be increased by his Christianity, and the measure — we must present the query, though shrinking from it as impious and revolting — the measure of divine grace that is supposed to be in him?

These are home questions. We cannot perceive their impertinency, and we ask Mr. Van Dyke, or any of our religious advocates of modern slavery, to give them an attentive study and a serious answer.

IV. — SLAVERY AND THE NEW TESTAMENT.

As preparatory to the argument from the New Testament, we would call attention again to those two constituent ideas that enter into slavery. They may be variously named, as *power* and *property* — the *jus dominii* and *jus proprii* — the *governmental*, as distinguished from the *mercenary* idea. According to the predominance of the one or the other of these ideas, the relation changes. The parties change. The one becomes a *lord* or an *owner*, a *ruler* or a *trader*, the other a *subject* or a *slave*, a *doulos* or an *andra podon*, a *man* or a *chattel*, a *person* or a *thing*. The contract is fundamental to any right understanding of the morality of slavery, either in itself or as deduced from the silence of the Christian Scriptures.

But these are shadows, some might say, abstractions, ideas; give us something practical. And are we yet to learn that ideas have power? They will force us to recognize them, whether we would or not. Abstractions are, in the long run, the most practical of all things, the most officious, as well as the most efficient. They will not be put by. A southern abstraction is bringing this nation to the brink of ruin, whilst a northern abstraction is fiercely contending against it. It is a Titan war of ideas. We must make definitions as well as concessions, *distinctions* as well as *compromises*, if we would save the Constitution. What is property? What is local or territorial power? What is property natural and universal? The great reasoner, Time, has brought out these abstractions which are now agitating the very heart of the nation, and they must be settled.

The two constituent ideas of slavery may be practically confounded, but, they are legally distinct. We may not be able always to trace them in the individual action, but, in the long run, they manifest their power and predominance in the collective life. We take them, therefore, and reason from them in their essential assumptions. The first, or government idea, is *essentially* unselfish. It claims to be ever for the good of the governed. The *despotes*, whether of the empire, the clan, or the plantation, must make this assumption if he would justify himself to the world, or even to his own conscience. He claims to be " the father," the patron, the protector of his people. He rules for them, not for himself. The other idea is inseparable from selfishness, both logically and actually. The property holder can make no other or higher claim. He never does make any other claim, until the pressing odiousness of the naked idea drives him to seek shelter from it by some false hiding under the better principle.

In individual cases we cannot certainly know which of the two ideas, by its predominance, actually determines the moral character of the nation. We may form a safe judgment in regard to the slavery of an age, or of a nation, viewed in its general aspects, and in reference to its general results. But with the individual holder, the right or wrong is a matter which can only be judged *in foro conscientiæ*. The two elements are ever *ideally* distinct to our logic ; they are only actually distinct to the interior light. He who stands in the relation can alone certainly know, for himself, whether he regards himself as the *man-owner* or the *man*-ruler; as the true *despotes* — a stern one it may be, and rightly so ; or the capitalist, the trader, the trafficker, buying, holding, using, breeding, selling his *kind* — that is, his *kin* — for gain. His political duties as a citizen, if he has any such, in regard to the general known bearings of the system of which he forms a part, present a consideration by itself. But the law of the land having given to one man authority over other men (a proceeding which lies certainly within every form of state sovereignty, and whose wisdom is not for the individual conscience), then the man who has this authority is to determine for himself, *in foro conscientiæ*, and at his peril, whether he holds it unselfishly, Christianly, for the good of the governed, and, for this exacting service, or selfishly, unchristianly, solely or predominantly for his own gain. This he must decide for himself; and when he has thus decided, cautiously, self-denyingly, conscientiously, then he may be a ruler " ruling over men justly and in the fear of God." He may be an emperor, a king, a lord, a despotes, holding the reins of power that have been put into his hands with a clean conscience, and without regard to the fanaticism that may assail him on either side of the relation. As a *ruler*, to his own high Ruler he standeth or falleth. He is not bound to be as cruel as the law permits, nor as mercenary as the law would tempt. The statute may call him *owner*, but he determines his position, as well as his duties. by a higher law.

He may thus rule men, as doubtless the righteous

centurion in the Gospel ruled his soldiers — it being
very far from certain whether his " *boy* " (*ho pais au-
ton*), out of which Mr. Van Dyke has made such notable argument for slavery, was really an *andra podon*,
or even a *doulos*, in the servile sense of the word.   He
may rule men as Cornelius ruled them, or the Christian
despotai, whom Paul addressed as " believing and beloved." He may not shut his eyes to the manifest effects
of a similar power in others around him. He may not
ignore the facts which go to show that the relation, as
generally held, is predominantly mercenary. He may
not, as a citizen, ignore his own duties, growing out of
such knowledge, nor the vast difference, in this respect,
between himself and those old non-voting Christian
masters with whom the pro-slavery advocate compares
him.   Still, while a member of such government, con-
ferring upon him such responsible powers, his benevolent or mercenary, his Christian or unchristian exercise
of them is a question solely for his own private conscience, into which no other man has a right to intrude.

There is a path, then, which will guide us through
this vexed question. The moral character of slavery
may be theoretically determined. It depends on the
absence or presence, the predominance or subordinance,
of the one or the other of those two constituting ideas.
In regard to himself, each man judges from the intui-
tive glance which lights up the inner world of the true
conscience. For the study of the system at large he
employs an outward light. He must judge this predominant character from apparent motives and results,
as determined by a cautious, and yet, it may be, a very
safe and accurate induction. Under the one light he

acts as an individual *ruler*, clothed with a power for which he is morally responsible; by the other, he directs his political action as a member of a larger civil organism.

Guided by such a rule, we look at servitude in different ages of the world, and the broad inductions of history enable us to judge of its general character in an age or nation. We take four prominent divisions. There is, 1st, the patriarchal or most ancient; 2d, the Jewish; 3d, the Roman, and 4th, the modern form, with its *caste* and its *commerce* — that strange modern form which, in these latter days, has come up again, and grown exceedingly bold and strong, after Christianity had slain all the rest. Now in applying our test, it may be said, that in the patriarchal the mercenary idea existed as a *minimum*, the other, or ruling idea, was at a *maximum*. In the Jewish servitude, the property notion had assumed a larger proportion, but the *jus dominii* in distinction from mere *ownership* was still predominant. In the Roman, the mercenary idea had obtained the principal place, although in many, especially the eastern parts of the empire, the other still kept the preëminence. The modern slavery is the antipodes of the patriarchal. The property idea has become not only predominant, but a *maximum*; the other exists, not for its own sake, as the principal thing, but almost wholly as subordinate and subservient to the former, or the essentially selfish principle. Not but that the patriarchal relation may still be found in individual cases or localities — we hope there are many of them — but the predominant character of slavery, especially within the past thirty years, or since the full establishment of the Calhoun doctrine, is doubtless mercenary, mercantile, trafficking, used for gain, for producing gain, and for gain *per se*, to an extent which it never exhibited in the world before. We need bring no better proof of this than the fact that our present national troubles have come out of this change in slavery, this predominant property claim, and the difficulty of settling it, whilst the other idea, such as was more talked of and more truly existed thirty years ago, did not then produce, and would not now have produced, any such effect. A social status, a governmental relation, could have given no such trouble, because, every one sees at once, and without argument, that it must be the creation of local law. It has a home, and stays at home. Property is roving and trafficking; it seeks extension; it must have a supply and demand; it must have an outlet, and, of consequence, an inlet. Hence the confusion in which we are involved. This predominance of the purely mercenary principle has greatly complicated the political question; and hence, too, the difficulty which many minds encounter in determining the political as well as the moral boundaries of these two ideas.

We have placed the Roman above the modern slavery. Some may object to this. Mr. Van Dyke regards the former as much worse, and hence deduces an *à fortiori* argument from the silence of Christianity respecting it. If it were so, it would not affect our position that the enjoining of submission is not a justification of the wrong to be submitted to. But we would take issue with Mr. Van Dyke on this point. There are two things in which modern American slavery differs, to its discredit, from the Roman. It is more mercenary; it has more of caste. In this, we may say, it is almost exclusive, beyond any known slavery that ever existed upon earth. The Roman lawyers ever declared that slavery was against natural right, and it is the civil law, with that maxim, that has kept it out of Christian Europe. No Roman court ever made a decision so casting a man out of the state, and out of the pale of humanity, as the Dred Scott. Hence we are prepared to say that, though the Roman servitude gave a more despotic power to the master, it was not so debasing to the slave. It was more cruel, perhaps, but less dehumanizing. It did not leave such a long taint behind it after emancipation. The freed man was but little affected by the servile condition; his children rose up to the common level, and moved on, afterwards, without any degrading distinction in the common stream of social life. Horace's father was a freed man; Horace himself took rank with the noblest of his day. Teachers, artists, took their places in society, though coming from the servile ranks. From "being servants of man," others rose to be "freed men of Christ," and even Christian bishops.

Roman slavery may have been more cruel, we say, but it was less degrading. In other words, though it hurt the individual more, it hurt humanity less. This deep debasement has been reserved for the Christian slavery, and we have already given a reason for it in that trouble of conscience, or that troubled self-respect, which must either make a man let go the *ownership* of his *kind*, or get a plea for casting it down among the lower and animal races. We have divine authority for

10

saying, that what Christianity does not make better, it makes worse. If it is not a savor of life to an institution, it is a savor of death. So the actors in the old Roman drama were a higher class of men than our nominally Christian politicians. The reason is obvious enough. Where they are not true and hearty Christians, the hollowness of the common profession has taken away the native manhood which appears so grand in these old heathen, whilst the counterfeit Christianity has given no compensating grace. As with men, so it is with institutions. Christianity healed the old slavery ; the modern, which has come up in defiance of it, may be left to die of its own mercenary corruptions. This is doubly true of what may be called, not simply the modern, but the *most* modern slavery, with the new features it has assumed within the past thirty years. The Roman servitude was bitter enough ; it was Pandora's box of woes, but still with hope remaining at the bottom. Emancipation might speedily restore the *doulos*, or his children, to the level of society. It was, therefore, a better thing than this Calhoun, Hamitic bondage, " normal," endless, hopeless, to which no year of jubilee shall ever come.

We ask the reader's indulgence for dwelling on this distinction of property and power, of *ownership* and *rule*. Besides the other use we have made of it, it is vital to a true interpretation of those passages in the New Testament that, when taken without discrimination, have led some to such fearfully unchristian conclusions. To these passages, therefore, let us immediately proceed : Dr. Van Dyke gives us the leading one from 1 Timothy vi. 1–5. Servants, *douloi*, persons " under

the yoke," are enjoined to obey their masters, their believing masters, to count it as a gain to themselves that
they have such, that they are "sharers in such a benefit." Persons who teach otherwise (and there must
have been some such officious philanthropists) are condemned as conceited, ignorant, doting about *logoma-
chies* or word battles — "making godliness gain" — in
other words, secularizing Christianity, as many radicals,
and, we may also say, many conservatives, so called,
are now doing. It is, in short, a pretty fair picture of
some modern abolitionists, and Dr. Van Dyke's exegesis in these respects, or as against them, will pretty fairly stand the test of criticism. We do not think he
enters enough into the meaning of the expression,
"partakers of the benefit," or tells us what was that
peculiar change in the relation which necessarily arose
out of the master's conversion, and made so different
the relation of the *doulos*.

Right here, we think, is found the key that unlocks
the whole difficulty. A believing master never could
regard his believing *douloi* as *property* to be held for
his gain. And why do we say this? Simply because,
in the utter absence of anything affirming it, in view,
also, of our Saviour's golden rule, and the loving language of St. Paul throughout his epistles, the thing is
Christianly inconceivable. They were brethren under
his social rule. He remained *despotes*, though not in
the harsh sense we give the term, but *owner* no longer
— trader, buyer, above all, *seller* no longer. The
property idea had not only been reduced to a *minimum*,
but had vanished altogether. He could *rule* them, but
he could no longer *own* them, because they were his

kind, Adamically and Christianly, his *kin*, his " very dear brethren," yea, himself, even as they were all one in Christ Jesus. It is yet to be proved that, in teaching servants to be obedient, and masters to rule kindly, the mercenary idea, the idea of property, of one man's *owning* another, above all, of one Christian *owning* another Christian, ever came into the apostle's mind, ever could have had room among the unselfish, loving thoughts, that dwelt in that holy place. This is no mere sentimentality, but a direct application of the golden rule of Christ — that law of love which is perfectly consistent with the governmental relation, whether imperial or domestic, but ever presents the most distinct repulsion to the mercenary idea.

Masters and servants continued in their social relations. They were exhorted by the apostle to do so. The great *despotism* of the Roman empire overshadowed them all. Political changes, even if practicable, could have been of no avail. There were no duties of citizenship in the modern sense — no voting, no political rights — as there were no political duties but obedience and patience, until, in God's good time, this very obedience and patience would be found to be a power in the world vastly stronger than any seditious or revolutionary resistance. How utterly different the state of the world then ! How absurd to reason from it to the modern in regard to any of those social rights and social duties that are so boasted of in our proud democracy !

" Let every man continue in that condition wherein he is called." Masters and servants were to remain together. If both were converted, then there arose a new and holy brotherhood, having the outward semblance of the relation as it existed among the ungodly, but oh! how different in its spirit! Masters, it is often said, were not commanded to emancipate their slaves. So, neither, was Nero enjoined to abdicate the Roman empire. Even if the tyrant had become a Christian under Paul's preaching, we doubt very much whether he would have commanded him to turn democrat, and proclaim a popular election. Masters were not told to disperse their servants; but, can a case be found in which they were ever permitted to *sell* them, and put the money in their pockets? There is not a sentence, not a word or syllable, from which it can be inferred that evangelist or apostle ever conceived it possible that one Christian man could ever think of selling another, or that such a question of discipline or Christian morals could ever arise among them. It is astonishing, the one-sidedness in this matter, which has kept the clerical pro-slavery advocate from seeing that this is the real issue, and that here proof is utterly wanting. It is barely possible that there might have been, in certain cases, something with a resemblance of a sale, but which was merely a method taken by one brother for placing another brother in a better condition. There is not a particle of evidence, even, of this; but of *traffic*, that poisonous idea which underlies all American slavery — of traffic in men, of traffic in one another! — the thing is inconceivable; the very imagination of it is an insult to the blessed memory of our early Christianity. They had their imperfections; they were tempted by the old sensuality; they had a hankering, sometimes, for the showy scenes of the old idolatry; but this heavenly

law of love, this "new commandment" in the earth,
which had come as a new life into their souls — they
could not so soon have turned traitors to it.

There is not a word in the New Testament about buying and selling slaves, not a word that would justify a
Christian man in doing the one or the other, except in
some possible sense that would take the transaction out
of the mercantile idea. No such cases ever seem to
have arisen in the church's discipline, or to have been
regarded as conceivable. The thought is at war with
the precepts of Christ and the loving spirit that runs
through all Paul's epistles. Patience is enjoined upon
the poor, submission is taught to the enslaved, loving
kindness to the masters, *who still* remained in that social relation; contentment and quiet are preached to
all, on the ground of earth's small value as compared
with the spiritual glory. O, how far is this from making out a defense, much less a "*sanction*," for our
modern slavery — our *most* modern slavery — that
which Mr. Van Dyke means, or he means nothing.

We are astonished at this pretended argument from
the New Testament. It amounts to nothing, even in
the strongest light in which they can put it. "If a
man smite thee on the one cheek, turn to him the other." Does that justify the smiter and the smiting?
"Honor the King." Does that prove monarchy?
"Submit yourselves;" "resist not evil." It is sometimes the case in the Scriptures, that the severest rebuke to oppression is found in the very precept of patience and submission under it. "Let every soul be
subject to the higher powers." Why, in view of our

benign, genial government, is not that a good text
for the rebellious clergymen who have so long been
preaching "submission," "submission," to the slave?

Much learning has been exhibited in respect to the
word *douloi*. There is no doubt that it may denote the
servile condition. It is equally clear that it is a term
of government, and may signify a *subject* from the
highest to the lowest rank. It may imply both ideas.
But there *is* a word in the Greek language that has the
one, the lowest one, exclusively and forever. It is
always servile. It is ever used to denote slaves as
property, and in a property sense. As thus employed,
it is exceedingly common in the classical Greek —
always used, we may say, when the servile notion is to
be expressed simple and unmixed. It must have been
very familiar throughout Asia Minor, and wherever
Paul found the reality or the semblance to the relation.
It is the word *andra podon*. It is of the neuter form,
to express vileness, to denote that that to which it is
applied is regarded as a *thing* or chattel, without will,
or a true acknowledged personality. When slaves are
statistically enumerated as property, they are called
andra poda, just as cattle or flocks are called by similar
neuters, *ta kteno, ktenea, ktemata, probata*. It is an
interesting query: why is this servile word, so common
in Athenian Greek, never found in the New Testament?
It is because there is no idea acknowledged there which
it could properly express. The subject to which it had
been applied was there, but the servile thought was
gone. It could not live in the atmosphere of the
Christian life; and, therefore, the apostle, though so

often having the occasion, avoids it, we were going to
say; but no, that would be injustice to the holy Paul.
He does not avoid it. It never came into his mind,
though the word itself was as well known to him as
any term from the Grecian games. Property and a
brother Christian was an association of ideas that for
him had no existence.

There is once used in the New Testament a deriva-
tive of this word (1 Timothy, i. 10), but in such a way
that it will do the man who is hunting scriptural pleas
for slavery no good. It is *andra podistes*, rendered
man stealer, but clearly wrong. The form of the ending shows that it does not denote an occasional act, an
occasional theft, but a business, an occupation. *Andra
podistes* is not a *man-thief*, but a *man-trader*, a *slave-
trader*, or a slave-dealer; one whose business is to sell
an *andra podon*. Just as *kermatistes* (John ii. 14) does
not denote *money-stealer*, but *money-seller, broker*,
" *money-changer*." So in the Memorabilia, Socrates
metaphorically calls the Sophists who took pay for their
lectures *andra podistes*, men who sold themselves for
servile hire. Will Mr. Van Dyke look at the association, in which this term is found (1 Tim. i. 10), and
then judge for himself whether the idea of that thing
in which the *andra podistes* dealt, or the idea of human
property, could ever have been applied by the apostle
to a man, much less a Christian brother. What an ungodly crew!—" the unholy and profane murderers,
fornicators, *slave-traders*, liars, perjurers, and all else
that is opposed to pure doctrine."

These injunctions to patience and submission to

kindly treatment and gentle *ruling*, are frequent in the
New Testament.   Instead of shunning them as favoring
the pro-slavery cause, we should be glad, if space permitted, to set them forth in all that loving fullness of
style in which the apostle's noble heart indulged itself.
It is in such passages, in truth, we find the richest internal evidence of the super-human origin of the Scriptures.   When faith is failing at the thought of man's
unnumbered wrongs and truth's slow progress in the
earth, in some dark hour of unbelief, when shades of
skepticism are falling on the soul, it is here we may go
for relief and reassurance.   Open to these words of
love, see how the heavenly light is streaming from
them ; what an unearthly spirit is breathing from them !
" For perhaps he, therefore, departed for a season, that
thou should'st receive him back forever ; not now as a
slave," an andrapodon, or a doulos even — " not now as
a servant, but as *more than a servant*, as a brother, a
brother beloved, both in the flesh and in the Lord " —
both in thine old and in thy new humanity.   This is
not of the world ; it is " from above, where Christ
dwelleth " — our human, sympathizing Saviour.

   And now, to take these *holy things*, and make from
them an argument in favor of slavery as it exists in
these United States, of cotton-growing slavery, our
trafficking, mercenary, *property* claiming slavery, that
will sell a man, his children and his children's children
for its own worldly gain, and then content itself with
the poor, conscience soothing plea that, perhaps he may,
somehow, get Christianized in the process !   It is rank
sacrilege.   No other name can be given to it, unless we

suppose that they who thus abuse the Scripture are more the victims of an idea, a false idea, a foolish, false conservatism, more secular in its spirit than the unchristian radicalism with which it so vehemently contends.

BIBLE VIEW OF SLAVERY.

A DISCOURSE DELIVERED AT THE JEWISH SYNAGOGUE, NEW YORK, ON
THE DAY OF THE NATIONAL FAST, JAN. 4, 1861.

BY REV. M. J. RAPHALL, M. A. PH. DR.

"The people of Nineveh believed in God, proclaimed a fast, and put
on sackcloth from the greatest of them even to the least of them. For
the matter reached the King of Nineveh, and he arose from his throne,
laid aside his robe, covered himself with sackcloth, and seated himself
in ashes. And he caused it to be proclaimed and published through
Nineveh, by decree of the King and his magnates, saying: Let neither
man nor beast, herd nor flock, taste anything; let them not feed nor
drink any water. But let man and beast be covered with sackcloth, and
cry with all their strength unto God; and let them turn every individual from his evil way and from the violence that is in their hands. Who
knoweth but God may turn and relent; yea, turn away from his fierce
anger, that we perish not. And God saw their works, that they turned
from their evil way; and God relented of the evil which he had said that
he would inflict upon them; and he did it not."— *Jonah* iii. 5—10.

1. MY FRIENDS — We meet here this day under circumstances not unlike those described in my text. Not
many weeks ago, on the invitation of the Governor of
this State, we joined in thanksgiving for the manifold
mercies the Lord had vouchsafed to bestow upon us
during the past year. But "coming events cast their
shadows before," and our thanks were tinctured by the
foreboding of danger impending over our country.
The evil we then dreaded has now come home to us.
As the cry of the prophet, "Yet forty days and Nine-

veh shall be overthrown," alarmed that people, so the proclamation, " the Union is dissolved," has startled the inhabitants of the United States. The President — the chief officer placed at the helm to guide the vessel of the commonwealth on its course — stands aghast at the signs of the times. He sees the black clouds gathering overhead, he hears the fierce howl of the tornado, and the hoarse roar of the breakers all around him. An aged man, his great experience has taught him that " man's extremity is God's opportunity ; " and conscious of his own inability to weather the storm without help from on high, he calls upon every individual " to feel a personal responsibility towards God," even as the King of Nineveh desired all persons " to cry unto God with all their strength " — and it is in compliance with this call of the Chief Magistrate of these United States that we, like the many millions of our fellow-citizens, devote this day to public prayer and humiliation. The President, more polished, though less plain-spoken than the King of Nineveh, does not in direct terms require every one to turn from his " evil way, and from the violence that is in their hands." But to me these two expressions seem in a most signal manner to describe our difficulty, and to apply to the actual condition of things both North and South. The " violence in their hands " is the great reproach we must address to the sturdy fire-eater who in the hearing of an indignant world proclaims " Cotton is King." King indeed, and a most righteous and merciful one, no doubt, in his own conceit ; since he only tars and feathers the wretches who fall in his power, and whom he suspects of not being sufficiently loyal and obedient to his sovereignty. And the " evil of his ways " is the reproach we must address to the sleek rhetorician who in the hearing of a God-fearing world declares " Thought is King." King indeed, and a most mighty and magnanimous one — no doubt — in his own conceit ; all-powerful to foment and augment the strife, though powerless to allay it. Of all the fallacies coined in the north, the arrogant assertion that " Thought is King" is the very last with which, at this present crisis, the patience of a reflecting people should have been abused. For in fact, the material greatness of the United States seems to have completely outgrown the grasp of our most gifted minds ; so that urgent as is our need, pressing as is the occasion, no man or set of men have yet come forward capable of rising above the narrow horizon of sectional influences and prejudices, and with views enlightened, just, and beneficent, to embrace the entirety of the Union and to secure its prosperity and preservation. No, my friends, " Cotton " is not King, and " Human thought " is not King. *Adonai Meleck.* The Lord alone is King! *Umalkootho bakol mashala*, and His royalty reigneth over all. This very day of humiliation and of prayer — what is it but the recognition of His supremacy, the confession of His power and of our own weakness, the supplications which our distress addresses to His mercy? But in order that these supplications may be graciously received, that His supreme protection may be vouchsafed unto our Country, it is necessary that we should begin as the people of Nineveh did ; we must " believe in God." And when I say " WE," I do not mean merely us handful of peaceable Union-loving Hebrews, but I mean the

whole of the people throughout the United States : the
President and his Cabinet, the President elect and his
advisers, the leaders of public opinion, North and
South.   If they truly and honestly desire to save our
country, let them believe in God and in His Holy word ;
and then when the authority of the Constitution is to
be set aside for a higher Law, they will be able to appeal to the highest Law of all, the revealed Law and
Word of God, which affords its supreme sanction to the
Constitution.   There can be no doubt, my friends, that
however much of personal ambition, selfishness, pride,
and obstinacy, there may enter into the present unhappy quarrel between the two great sections of the Commonwealth — I say it is certain that the origin of the
quarrel itself is the difference of opinion respecting
slaveholding, which the one section denounces as sinful
— aye, as the most heinous of sins — while the other
section upholds it as perfectly lawful.   It is the province of statesmen to examine the circumstances under
which the Constitution of the United States recognizes
the legality of slaveholding ; and under what circumstances, if any, it becomes a crime against the law of
the land.   But the question whether slaveholding is a
sin before God, is one that belongs to the theologian.
I have been requested by prominent citizens of other
denominations, that I should on this day examine the
Bible view of slavery, as the religious mind of the
country requires to be enlightened on the subject.

    In compliance with that request, and after humbly
praying that the Father of Truth and of Mercy may
enlighten my mind, and direct my words for good, I am
about to solicit your earnest attention, my friends, to

this serious subject. My discourse will, I fear, take up more of your time than I am in the habit of exacting from you; but this is a day of penitence, and the having to listen to a long and sober discourse must be accounted as a penitential infliction.

The subject of my investigation falls into three parts: —

First, How far back can we trace the existence of slavery?

Secondly, Is slaveholding condemned as a sin in sacred Scripture?

Thirdly, What was the condition of the slave in Biblical times, and among the Hebrews; and saying with our Father Jacob, "for Thy help, I hope, O Lord!" I proceed to examine the question, how far back can we trace the existence of slavery?

I. It is generally admitted, that slavery had its origin in war, public or private. The victor having it in his power to take the life of his vanquished enemy, prefers to let him live, and reduces him to bondage. The life he has spared, the body he might have mutilated or destroyed, becomes his absolute property. He may dispose of it in any way he pleases. Such was, and through a great part of the world still is, the brutal law of force. When this state of things first began, it is next to impossible to decide. If we consult Sacred Scripture, the oldest and most truthful collection of records now or at any time in existence, we find the word *Ngebed* "slave," which the English version renders "servant," first used by Noah, who, in Genesis ix. 25, curses the descendants of his son Ham, by saying they should be *Ngebed Ngabadim*, the "meanest

of slaves," or as the English version has it, " servant
of servants." The question naturally arises how came
Noah to use the expression ? How came he to know
anything of slavery ? There existed not at that time
any human being on earth except Noah and his family
of three sons, apparently by one mother, born free and
equal, with their wives and children. Noah had no
slaves. From the time that he quitted the ark he could
have none. It therefore becomes evident that Noah's
acquaintance with the word slave and the nature of
slavery must date from before the Flood, and existed in
his memory only until the crime of Ham called it forth.
You and I may regret that in his anger Noah should
from beneath the waters of wrath again have fished up
the idea and practice of slavery ; but that he did so is
a fact which rests on the authority of Scripture.   I am
therefore justified when, tracing slavery as far back as
it can be traced, I arrive at the conclusion, that next to
the domestic relations of husband and wife, parents and
children, the oldest relation of society with which we
are acquainted is that of master and slave.

Let us for an instant stop at this curse by Noah with
which slavery after the Flood is recalled into existence.
Among the many prophecies contained in the Bible and
having reference to particular times, persons, and
events, there are three singular predictions referring to
three distinct races or peoples, which seem to be intended for all times, and accordingly remain in full force to
this day.   The first of these is the doom of Ham's descendants, the African race, pronounced upwards of
4000 years ago.   The second is the character of the
descendants of Ishmael, the Arabs, pronounced nearly

4,000 years ago; and the third and last is the promise of continued and indestructible nationality promised to us, Israelites, full 2,500 years ago. It has been said that the knowledge that a particular prophecy exists, helps to work out its fulfilment, and I am quite willing to allow that with us, Israelites, such is the fact. The knowledge we have of God's gracious promises renders us imperishable, even though the greatest and most powerful nations of the olden time have utterly perished. It may be doubted whether the fanatic Arab of the desert ever heard of the prophecy that he is to be a " wild man, his hand against every man, and every man's hand against him." (Gen. xvi. 12.) But you and I, and all men of ordinary education, know that this prediction at all times has been, and is now, literally fulfilled, and that it has never been interrupted. Not even when the followers of Mahomet rushed forth to spread his doctrines, the Koran in one hand and the sword in the other, and when Arab conquest rendered the fairest portion of the Old World subject to the empire of their Caliph, did the descendants of Ishmael renounce their characteristics. Even the boasted civilization of the present century, and frequent intercourse with Western travellers, still leave the Arab a wild man, " his hand against every man, and every man's hand against him," a most convincing and durable proof that the Word of God is true, and that the prophecies of the Bible were dictated by the Spirit of the Most High. But though, in the case of the Arab, it is barely possible that he may be acquainted with the prediction made to Hagar, yet we may be sure that the fetish-serving benighted African has no knowledge of Noah's prediction; which, however, is nowhere more fully or more atrociously carried out than in the native home of the African. Witness the horrid fact, that the king of Dahomy is, at this very time, filling a large and deep trench with human blood, sufficient to float a good-sized boat; that the victims are innocent men, murdered to satisfy some freak of what he calls his religion; and that this monstrous and most fiendish act has met with no opposition, either from the pious indignation of Great Britain, or from the zealous humanity of our country.

Now I am well aware that the Biblical critics called Rationalists, who deny the possibility of prophecy, have taken upon themselves to assert, that the prediction of which I have spoken was never uttered by Noah, but was made up many centuries after him by the Hebrew writers of the Bible, in order to smooth over the extermination of the Canaanites, whose land was conquered by the Israelites. With superhuman knowledge like that of the Rationalists, who claim to sit in judgment on the word of God, I do not think it worth while to argue. But I would ask you how is it that a prediction, manufactured for a purpose — a fraud in short, and that a most base and unholy one, should nevertheless continue in force, and be carried out during four, or three, or even two thousand years; for a thousand years more or less can here make no difference. Noah. on the occasion in question, bestows on his son Shem a spiritual blessing: "Blessed be the Lord, the God of Shem," and to this day it remains a fact which cannot be denied, that whatever knowledge of God and of religious truth is possessed by the human race, has been promulgated by the descendants of Shem. Noah bestows on his son Japheth a blessing, chiefly temporal, but partaking also of spiritual good. "May God enlarge Japheth, and may he dwell in the tents of Shem," and to this day it remains a fact which cannot be denied, that the descendants of Japheth (Europeans and their offspring) have been enlarged so that they possess dominion in every part of the earth; while, at the same time they share in that knowledge of religious truth which the descendants of Shem were the first to promulgate. Noah did not bestow any blessing on his son Ham, but uttered a bitter curse against his descendants, and to this day it remains a fact which cannot be gainsaid that in his own native home, and generally throughout the world, the unfortunate negro is indeed the meanest of slaves. Much has been said respecting the inferiority of his intellectual powers, and that no man of his race has ever inscribed his name on the Pantheon of human excellence, either mental or moral. But this is a subject I will not discuss. I do not attempt to build up a theory, nor yet to defend the moral government of Providence. I state facts; and having done so, I remind you that our own fathers were slaves in Egypt, and afflicted four hundred years; and then I bid you reflect on the words of inspired Isaiah (lv. 8.), "My thoughts are not your thoughts, neither are your ways my ways, saith the Lord."

II. Having thus, on the authority of the sacred Scripture, traced slavery back to the remotest period, I next request your attention to the question, " Is slaveholding condemned as a sin in sacred Scripture?" How this question can at all arise in the mind of any man that

has received a religious education, and is acquainted
with the history of the Bible, is a phenomenon I cannot
explain to myself, and which fifty years ago no man
dreamed of. But we live in times when we must not
be surprised at anything. Last Sunday an eminent
preacher is reported to have declared from the pulpit,
"That the Old Testament requirements served their
purpose during the physical and social development of
mankind, and were rendered no longer necessary now
when we were to be guided by the superior doctrines
of the New in the moral instruction of the race." I
had always thought that in the "moral instruction of
the race," the requirements of the Jewish Scriptures
and Christian Scriptures were identically the same;
that to abstain from murder, theft, adultery, that "to
do justice, to love mercy, and to walk humbly with
God," were "requirements" equally imperative in the
one course of instruction as in the other. But it appears I was mistaken. "We have altered all that
now," says this eminent divine, in happy imitation of
Molière's physician, whose new theory removed the
heart from the left side of the human body to the right.
But when I remember that the "now" refers to a period of which you all, though no very aged men, witnessed the rise; when, moreover, I remember that the
"WE" the reverend preacher speaks of, is limited to a
few impulsive declaimers, gifted with great zeal, but
little knowledge; more eloquent than learned; better
able to excite our passions than to satisfy our reason;
and when, lastly, I remember the scorn with which sacred Scripture (Deut. xxxii. 18) speaks of "new-
fangled notions, lately sprung up, which your fathers

esteemed not;" when I consider all this, I think you
and I had rather continue to take our " requirements
for moral instruction " from Moses and the Prophets
than from the eloquent preacher of Brooklyn. But as
that reverend gentleman takes a lead among those who
most loudly and most vehemently denounce slaveholding as a sin, I wished to convince myself whether he
had any Scripture warranty for so doing; and whether
such denunciation was one of those " requirements for
moral instruction " advanced by the New Testament.
I have accordingly examined the various books of
Christian Scripture, and find that they afford the reverend gentleman and his compeers no authority whatever for his and their declamations. The New Testament nowhere, directly or indirectly, condemns slaveholding, which, indeed, is proved by the universal practice of all Christian nations during many centuries.
Receiving slavery as one of the conditions of society,
the New Testament nowhere interferes with or contra-
dicts the slave code of Moses; it even preserves a letter written by one of the most eminent Christian teachers to a slaveowner on sending back to him his runaway
slave. And when we next refer to the history and
" requirements " of our own sacred Scriptures, we find
that on the most solemn occasion therein recorded,
when God gave the Ten Commandments on Mount
Sinai —

> There where His finger scorched, the tablet shone;
> There where His shadow on his people shone
> His glory, shrouded in its garb of fire,
> Himself no eye might see and not expire.

Even on that most solemn and most holy occasion,

slaveholding is not only recognised and sanctioned as
an integral part of the social structure, when it is commanded that the Sabbath of the Lord is to bring rest to
Ngabdecha re Amathecha, "Thy male slave and thy
female slave" (Exod. xx. 10; Deut. v. 14). But the
property in slaves is placed under the same protection
as any other species of lawful property, when it is said,
"Thou shalt not covet thy neighbor's house, or his
field, or his male slave, or his female slave, or his ox,
or his ass, or aught that belongeth to thy neighbor."
(Ibid. xx. 17; v. 21). That the male slave and female
slave here spoken of do not designate the Hebrew
bondman, but the heathen slave, I shall presently show
you. That the Ten Commandments are the word of
God, and as such, of the very highest authority, is acknowledged by Christians as well as by Jews. I would
therefore ask the reverend gentleman of Brooklyn and
his compeers — How dare you, in the face of the sanction and protection afforded to slave property in the
Ten Commandments — how dare you denounce slaveholding as a sin? When you remember that Abraham,
Isaac, Jacob, Job — the men with whom the Almighty
conversed, with whose names he emphatically connects
his own most holy name, and to whom He vouchsafed to
give the character of "perfect, upright, fearing God
and eschewing evil" (Job i. 8) — that all these men
were slaveholders, does it not strike you that you are
guilty of something very little short of blasphemy?
And if you answer me, "Oh, in their time slaveholding
was lawful, but now it has become a sin," I in my turn
ask you, "When and by what authority you draw the
line?" Tell us the precise time when slaveholding

ceased to be permitted, and became sinful?" When we remember the mischief which this inventing a new sin, not known to the Bible, is causing; how it has exasperated the feelings of the South, and alarmed the conscience of the North, to a degree that men who should be brothers are on the point of imbruing their hands in each other's blood, are we not entitled to ask the reverend preacher of Brooklyn, "What right have you to insult and exasperate thousands of God-fearing, law-abiding citizens, whose moral worth and patriotism, whose purity of conscience and of life, are fully equal to your own? What right have you to place yonder grey-headed philanthropist on a level with a murderer, or yonder virtuous mother of a family on a line with an adulteress, or yonder honorable and honest man in one rank with a thief, and all this solely because they exercise a right which your own fathers and progenitors, during many generations, held and exercised without reproach or compunction? You profess to frame your " moral instruction of the race " according to the " requirements " of the New Testament — but tell us where and by whom it was said, " Whosoever shall say to his neighbor, *Raca*, (worthless sinner), shall be in danger of the council; but whosoever shall say, thou fool, shall be in danger of the judgment." My friends, I find, and I am sorry to find, that I am delivering a pro-slavery discourse. I am no friend to slavery in the abstract, and still less friendly to the practical workings of slavery. But I stand here as a teacher in Israel; not to place before you my own feelings and opinions, but to propound to you the word of God, the Bible view of slavery. With a due sense of my responsibility, I must state to you the truth and nothing but the truth, however unpalatable or unpopular that truth may be.

III. It remains for me now to examine what was the condition of the slave in Biblical times and among the Hebrews. And here at once we must distinguish between the Hebrew bondman and the heathen slave. The former could only be reduced to bondage from two causes. If he had committed theft and had not wherewithal to make full restitution, he was "sold for his theft." (Exod. xxii. 3.) Or if he became so miserably poor that he could not sustain life except by begging, he had permission to "sell" or bind himself in servitude. (Levt. xxv. 39 *et seq.*) But in either case his servitude was limited in duration and character. "Six years shall he serve, and in the seventh he shall go out free for nothing." (Exod. xxi. 2). And if even the bondman preferred bondage to freedom, he could not, under any circumstances, be held to servitude longer than the jubilee then next coming. At that period the estate which had originally belonged to his father, or remoter ancestor, reverted to his possession, so that he went forth at once a freeman and a landed proprietor. As his privilege of Hebrew citizen was thus only suspended, and the law, in permitting him to be sold, contemplated his restoration to his full rights, it took care that during his servitude his mind should not be crushed to the abject and cringing condition of a slave. "Ye shall not rule over one another with rigor," is the provision of the law. (Lev. xxv. 46.) Thus he is fenced round with protection against any abuse of power on the part of his employer; and tradition so strictly interpreted the letter of the law in his favor, that it was a common saying of Biblical times and homes, which Maimonides has preserved to us, that " he who buys an Hebrew bondman gets himself a master." Though in servitude, this Hebrew was in nowise exempt from his religious duties. Therefore it is not for him or his that the Ten Commandments stipulated for rest on the Sabbath of the Lord ; for his employer could not compel him to work on that day ; and if he did work of his own accord, he became guilty of death, like any other Sabbath-breaker. Neither does the prohibition, " thou shalt not covet the property of thy neighbor," apply to him, for he was not the property of his employer. In fact, between the Hebrew bondman and the Southern slave there is no point of resemblance. There were, however, slaves among the Hebrews, whose general condition was analogous to that of their Southern fellow sufferers. That was the heathen slave, who was to be bought " from the heathens that were round about the land of Israel, or from the heathen strangers that sojourned in the land ; they should be a possession, to be bequeathed as an inheritance to the owner's children, after his death, for ever." (Levit. xxv. 44—46.) Over these heathen slaves the owner's property was absolute ; he could put them to hard labor, to the utmost extent of their physical strength ; he could inflict on them any degree of chastisement short of injury to life and limb. If his heathen slave ran away or strayed from home, every Israelite was bound to bring or send him back, as he would have to do with any other portion of his neighbor's property that had been lost or strayed. (Deut. xxii. 3.)

Now, you may, perhaps, ask me how I can reconcile

11

this statement with the text of Scripture so frequently quoted against the Fugitive Slave Law, " Thou shalt not surrender unto his master the slave who has escaped from his master unto thee" (Deut. xxiii. 16). I answer you that, according to all legists, this text applies to a heathen slave, who, from any foreign country escapes from his master, even though that master be an Hebrew, residing out of the land of Israel. Such a slave — but such a slave only — is to find a permanent asylum in any part of the country he may choose. This interpretation is fully borne out by the words of the precept. The pronoun " thou," is not here used in the same sense as in the Ten Commandments. There it designates every soul in Israel individually ; since every one has it in his power, and is in duty bound to obey the commandments. But as the security and protection to be bestowed on the runaway slaves are beyond the power of any individual, and require the consent and concurrence of the whole community, the pronoun " thou " here means the whole of the people, and not one portion in opposition to any other portion of the people. And as the expression remains the same throughout the precept, " With thee he shall dwell, even among ye, in the place he shall choose in one of thy gates where it liketh him best," it plainly shows that the whole of the land was open to him, and the whole of the people were to protect the fugitive, which could not have been carried out if it had applied to the slave who escaped from one tribe into the territory of another. Had the precept been expounded in any other than its strictly literal sense, it would have caused great confusion, since it would have nullified two other precepts of God's law ; that which directs that " slaves, like lands and houses, were to be inherited for ever," and that which commands " property, lost or strayed, to be restored to the owner." Any other interpetation would, moreover, have caused heartburning and strife between the tribes, for men were as tenacious of their rights and property in those days as they are now. But no second opinion was ever entertained ; the slave who ran away from Dan to Beersheba had to be given up, even as the runaway from South Carolina has to be given up by Massachusetts ; whilst the runaway from Edom, or from Syria, found an asylum in the land of Israel, as the runaway slave from Cuba or Brazil would find in New York. Accordingly Shimei reclaimed and recovered his runaway slaves from Achish, king of Gath, at that time a vassal of Israel (Kings ii. 39, 40). And Saul of Tarsus sent back the runaway slave Onesimus, unto his owner Philemon. But to surrender to a ruthless, lawless heathen, the wretched slave who had escaped from his cruelty, would have been to give up the fugitive to certain death, or at least to tortures repugnant to the spirit of God's law, the tender care of which protected the bird in its nest, the beast at the plough, and the slave in his degradation. Accordingly, the extradition was not permitted in Palestine any more than it is in Canada. While thus the owner possessed full right over and security for his property, the exercise of that power was confined within certain limits which he could not outstep. His female slave was not to be the tool or castaway toy of his sensuality, nor could he sell her, but was bound to " let her go free," " because he had humbled her " (Deut. xxi. 14).

His male slave was protected against excessive punishment; for if the master in any way mutilated his slave, even to knock a single tooth out of his head, the slave became free (Exod. xxi. 26, 27). And while thus two of the worst passions of human nature, lust and cruelty, were kept under due restraint, the third bad passion, cupidity, was not permitted free scope; for the law of God secured to the slave his Sabbaths and days of rest; while public opinion, which in a country so densely peopled as Palestine must have been all-powerful, would not allow any slave-owner to impose heavier tasks on his slaves, or to feed them worse than his neighbors did. This, indeed, is the great distinction which the Bible view of slavery derives from its divine source. The slave is a *person* in whom the dignity of human nature is to be respected; *he has rights.* Whereas, the heathen view of slavery which prevailed at Rome, and which, I am sorry to say, is adopted in the South, reduces the slave to a *thing*, and a thing can have no rights. The result to which the Bible view of slavery leads us, is — 1st. That slavery has existed since the earliest time; 2d. That slaveholding is no sin, and that slave property is expressly placed under the protection of the Ten Commandments; 3d. That the slave is a person, and has rights not conflicting with the lawful exercise of the rights of his owner. If our Northern fellow-citizens, content with following the word of God, would not insist on being " righteous overmuch," or denouncing " sin " which the Bible knows not, but which is plainly taught by the precepts of men they would entertain more equity and and less ill feeling towards their southern brethren. And if our

Southern fellow-citizens would adopt the Bible view of slavery, and discard that heathen slave code, which permits a few bad men to indulge in an abuse of power that throws a stigma and disgrace on the whole body of slaveholders — if both North and South would do what is right, then " God would see their works and that they turned from the evil of their ways ; " and in their case, as in that of the people of Nineveh, would mercifully avert the impending evil, for with Him alone is the power to do so. Therefore let us pray.

Almighty and merciful God, we approach Thee this day, our hearts heavy with the weight of our sins, our looks downcast under the sense of our ingratitude, national and individual. Thou, Father all bounteous, hast in Thine abundant goodness plentifully bestowed upon us every good and every blessing, spiritual, mental, temporal, that in the present state of the world men can desire. But we have perverted and abused Thy gifts ; in our arrogance and selfishness we have contrived to extract poison from Thy most precious boons ; the spiritual have degenerated into unloving self-righteousness ; the mental have rendered us vain-glorious and conceited, and the temporal have degraded us into Mammon-worshipping slaves of avarice. Intoxicated with our prosperity, we have forgotten Thee ; drunken with pride, we reel on towards the precipice of disunion and ruin. What hand can stay us if it be not Thine, O God ! Thou who art long-suffering as Thou art almighty, to Thee we turn in the hour of our utmost need. Hear us, Father, for on Thee our hopes are fixed. Help us, Father, for thou alone canst do it. Punish us not according to our arrogance ; afflict us not according to our deserts. Remove from our breasts the heart of stone, and from our minds the obstinacy of self-willed pride. Extend Thy grace unto us, that we may acknowledge our own transgressions. Open our eyes that we may behold and renounce the wrong we inflict on our neighbors. God of justice and of mercy, suffer not despots to rejoice at our dissensions, nor tyrants to triumph over our fall. Let them not point at us the finger of scorn, or say, " Look there at the fruits of freedom and self-government — of equal rights and popular sovereignty — strife without any real cause — destruction without any sufficient motive." Oh, let not them who trust in Thee be put to shame, or those who seek Thee be disgraced. Almighty God, extend Thy gracious protection to the United States! pour out over the citizens thereof, and those whom they have elected to be their rulers, the spirit of grace and of supplication, the spirit of wisdom and brotherly love, so that henceforth, even as hitherto, they may know that union is strength, and that it is good and pleasant for brethren to dwell together in unity. And above all this, Lord merciful and gracious, avert the calamity of civil war from our midst. If in Thy supreme wisdom Thou hast decreed that this vast commonwealth, which has risen under Thy protection, and prospered under Thy blessing, shall now be separated, then we beseech Thee let that separation be peaceable ; that no human blood may be shed, but that the canopy of Thy peace may still remain spread over all the land. May we address our prayers to Thee, O Lord, at an acceptable time ; mayest Thou, O God, in Thy abundant mercy, answer us with the truth of Thy salvation. Amen.

IRRELIGION, CORRUPTION AND FANATICISM REBUKED.

A SERMON PREACHED IN TRINITY CHURCH, NEW YORK, ON THE DAY OF THE NATIONAL FAST, JAN. 4, 1861.

BY REV. FRANCIS VINTON, D. D.

The people came to the house of God, and abode there till even before God ; and lifted up their voices and wept sore, and said, O Lord God of Israel, why is this come to pass in Israel, that there should be to-day one tribe lacking in Israel ? — *Judges* xxi. 2, 3.

THE text acquaints us with a time of great distress among the tribes of Israel. It was an era of lawlessness and confusion, when public sentiment was depraved ; when personal safety was endangered ; when law was dishonored and set at naught ; when piety was rare and worship of God neglected ; when good men retired into the sanctuary of their private and domestic firesides for the security and comforts of life which society denied them ; when the Commonwealth was abandoned to the control of " the sons of Belial," who, in the passionate rioting of pampered appetites and ravenous lusts, committed atrocities that appaled the community. (Judges xix. xx.) It was one of these horrible crimes that roused the tribes against the tribe of Benjamin, and gathered the congregation together as one man, from Dan to Beersheba. Ambassadors were sent to the offending tribe to demand the surrender of the children of Belial for punishment. But the tribe of Benjamin "would not hearken to the voice of their brethren," but made common cause with the offenders, and " gathered themselves together to go out to battle against the children of Israel." Civil war was the consequence, and the tribe of Benjamin was ruined nearly to extermination.

Those fearful times are described in the last verse of the Book of Judges, in these few emphatic words : — " In those days there was no king in Israel ; every man did that which was right in his own eyes." It was only when the fatal issue of that civil war was felt in the bereavements and desolation which ensued, that the pious sentiment was roused in the public heart and God was remembered. Under the pressure of the common woe, and in view of the impotency of mortal strife, " the people came to the house of God, and abode there till even before God, and lifted up their voices and wept sore ; and said, O Lord God of Israel, why is this come to pass in Israel, that there should be to-day one tribe lacking in Israel."

My brethren, your thoughts doubtless anticipate the suggestion of a likeness between the dark and revolting era of Israel's lawlessness and this present epoch in our country's history. We have not yet reached the extreme of wickedness, where law and government and public virtue and private security, wrecked and abandoned, were left a prey to the surging billows of a stormy sea of wild passions and slimy lusts; but we hear the storm howling around our ship of State, and behold confusion and dismay in those appointed to the command and pilotage of the Constitution, wherein we are all embarked with life's choice treasures. And while the staunch vessel is yet sound, we are summoned by the President, in one national voice of prayer to Him " who hath gathered the wind in His fists," (Prov. xxx. 4,) " who stilleth the voice of the seas, the noise of their waves, and the tumult of the people," (Ps. lxv. 7,) to implore His divine guidance and protection and deliverance, that, as in the ark, the world's hopes may be saved and we may come forth upon the mount, under the sunshine of His smile, united once more around the altar of thanksgiving.

The one bright spot that illumined Israel's night is reflected here to-day, and throughout the land, from ocean to ocean, where, with the single exception of one tribe — a loved one to whom our love would fain give Benjamin's fivefold portion — an united people acknowledge allegiance to the nation's law and render obedience to the nation's Chief Magistrate, in gathering ourselves together in the house of God, and lifting up our voices, saying — " O Lord God of our fathers, why is this come to pass in these United States, that there should be to-day one State lacking in our Union ? " Let us listen to the oracle of God's word. Let each consult the testimony of his conscience and observation, and trace the sure line of effect and cause in the law of Divine retribution. And let your preacher try to guide your meditations in humble dependence on the inspiration of the Holy Spirit, with all soberness and truth.

Why, then, is this come to pass, that there should be to-day one State lacking in our federal Union ? 1. My first answer to this inquiry is another question :

Why should we expect God's blessing on our Union
as one nation? There is one constitutional defect in
our organic law. It contains no acknowledgment of
God; no recognition of Jesus Christ. I am aware of
only one provision in our Constitution which distinguish-
es our civil polity from a heathen organization — that
provision is the oath of office. It has been noticed that
the normal principle of a nation's polity is stamped on
its coins. Look at the coins of Europe and you observe the legend, *Dei Gratia* — "by God's grace."
Look at our's and you read "Liberty" — man's independent free agency. In colonial times in this country,
the bills of lading were printed with a recognition of
dependence on God for the ship's favorable voyage;
but nowadays the bills of lading express trust in the
strong bolts and timbers of the craft and on the skill
of the shipmaster. But the scorner will ask: — What
profit is there in the acknowledgment of God in the fundamental Constitution of a nation and in the ordinary
ventures of commerce? Are the old nations any the
better for their pious formulas and pretended recognition of God? I answer, the profit is in telling the
truth and not hiding it. The profit is in keeping before
the eye of the nation the truth of God's presence and
power in the world, and thus educating the people so far
as a witness for God may. And if you ask if the old
nations are any better for it, I answer, how came they
to be old nations? With governments oppressive to
life and depressive of liberty and enterprise, they are
yet old nations whose cup of iniquity is not yet full,
while we are not yet out of the first century — the very
childhood of natural life — and are suddenly threaten-

ed with dissolution. But the best answer to the scoffing against the duty of a national acknowledgment of Almighty God may be witnessed in this national fast day, when trouble that no human wisdom has guarded against and no human foresight can foil, drives the nation to the mercy seat and compels the utterances of faith in God's presence and power and goodness. For if it be right and proper and conservative of our national being to confess God to-day, as a nation, it is right, proper and conservative to confess Him, not merely in a spasmodic way, but on principle, and in the solemnity of a constitutional act. But our fathers, in their opposition to a union of Church and State, with just apprehensions of the domineering exactions of bigotry and the predominance of sectarian intolerance, swung back on the extreme opposite of ignoring God as the Ruler of the nation.

It is a hopeful sign of the influence of Christianity that the laws and practices of most States and of the United States observe the Divine law of a Christian Sunday. And it is an omen of dark portent that the convention of the seceding State of South Carolina profaned the Lord's day in not observing it. For if there be any truth in physiology, it is that the seventh day's rest is wholesome and necessary to man. And when Robespierre and his godless and bloody band ventured to amend the Divine law, by appointing the tenth day as the decade of rest, the French army, both man and beast, fainted and succumbed under oppressive toil, compelling the First Consul to restore the seventh day Sabbath. And among the practical truths of Christianity is the fact that the people who, in the spirit of Jesus,

observe the Sunday for worship, for rest and for deeds
of necessity and charity, are blessed of God, both in
health of body and in cheerful piety of heart. Let it
be a lesson of this Fast day of the nation to train a public sentiment for the acknowledgment of God and Christ
in our civil constitutions and in the mandates of our
rulers and in the habits of the people.

Second. — A further cause of our national trouble
may be traced to our social and political corruption.
Pride and boasting, self-reliance and individual inde-
pendency; self-will and liberty, sprouting into licentiousness; violent competition in trade and in politics; covetousness for money and for place; reluctance to the
slow processes of labor in agriculture and in the me-
chanic arts; enterprise, pushed into impatience, through
haste to be rich. These are our national characteristics, in
some of which we observe virtues inordinately exercised
till they become perverted into vices.

But the crowning shame and the damning stigma on
the fore front of the Republic is Bribery. It is historical
that the decay of every republic has begun in the form
of a corruption most subtle, by influencing magistrates
and legislators and judges through some kind of purchase. It was the case, as every classical boy knows,
in the beginning of the downfall of the republics of
Greece and Rome. It was the premonitory symptom
of the end of the theocratic republic of Israel. When
good old Samuel resigned his vicegerency, he appealed
to the people to attest his personal fidelity : " Of whose
hand have I received a bribe to blind mine eyes there-
with ? " And they said, " Thou hast not taken aught
of any man's hand." And he said to them, " The Lord

is witness against you this day that ye have not found aught in my hand." And they answered, " He is witness." (1 Samuel, xii. 3—5.) So boldly and solemnly did that public officer purge himself from any suspicion of a crime which he considered the fatal blemish of character in a public man. But of the sons of Samuel it is written, that " his sons walked not in his ways, but turned aside after lucre, and took bribes and perverted judgment." (1 Sam. viii. 3.) And with this record, it follows, in the next verse, that the nation rejected God. " The Lord said to Samuel, they have not rejected thee, but they have rejected me, that I should not reign over them." In this short history is not the portrait of our country sketched ? Our fathers, like Samuel, could call God and the people to witness that no bribe had ever blinded their eyes to pervert judgment ; while their degenerate sons, in the high places of the nation, in the halls of the State and of the city — and, shall I say, in the tribunals of an elective and poorly paid judiciary — are, like the sons of Samuel, charged with turning aside after lucre, and taking bribes, and perverting judgment. The subtle temptation appears not at first in the glitter of gold, but in an agreement between parties to help one another in some favorite measure — the price is demanded and paid for a vote. This is bribery. Next, the promise or the hope of reward in some place of profit, is the motive to a vote. And by this selfish aim the heart is corrupted with bribery. At last the conscience gets hardened, and the people yield to the apparent necessity, and the public sentiment becomes defiled, and the itching palm of a covetous hand is overlaid with the bribe,

according to a tariff of each man's price. Alas! are
not these things notorious? Where is the pure man in
public life who exclaims, "Lord, I have loved the habitation of Thy house, and the place where Thine honor
dwelleth. Gather not my soul with sinners, nor my
life with bloody men, in whose hands is mischief, and
their right hand is full of bribes. But as for me, I will
walk in mine integrity. My foot standeth in an even
place; in the congregation will I bless the Lord." (Ps.
xxvi. 8—12.) Where is such a man? Here and
there he stands in his uprightness, "the observed of all
observers," "the cynosure of every eye," revered and
hated; a pattern of incorrupt virtue, sending forth the
beams of his light over the dark mass of people, like
the light-house on the headlands of the coast, to foil
the wreckers and to guide the voyagers in society. My
brethren, when an honest public agent becomes conspicuous and is praised for his fidelity, it is because of
a contrast with prevailing dishonesty. That he should
" be righteous in his generation," is to fix on him the
eulogium accorded to Noah in the Scriptures, because
of simple virtue in the midst of common wickedness.
And when such a state of society exists, God comes
with his deluge to destroy them all. God complains of
us in pathetic strains: — " How is the faithful city become an harlot! It was full of judgment; righteousness lodged in it; but now murderers. Thy silver is
become dross, thy wine mixed with water; thy princes
are rebellious and companions of thieves; every one
loveth gifts, and followeth after rewards; they judge
not the fatherless, neither does the cause of the widow
come unto them. Therefore, saith the Lord, the Lord

of hosts, the mighty One of Israel, ah ! I will ease me of mine adversaries, and I will avenge me of mine enemies." (Isaiah, i. 21—24.)

Such is the language of passing events, interpreted as Divine visitations. And when, as at this day, the public conscience becomes hardened, in tolerating bribery and in ministering to corruption, the nation is surprised only for a moment, at the discovery of fraud among the subordinates. And so we are startled at the tidings of a wholesale plunder of the national treasury, of nearly a million of securities, held in trust for the poor Indian tribes — a sacred fund, more sacred than any deposit in the nation's exchequer. Men are startled, I say, and then turn to their strong box to examine their securities ; and if there be no individual loss, we hear feeble reprobation of the public theft. These tokens are amongst us of a loss of virtue and integrity, which may well go to explain why God has permitted one star to be dimmed in the galaxy of our nation's flag.

3. But I now reach a third cause of the nation's woe. It is the question of slavery. I should be remiss if on such an occasion as to-day, I should avoid a question that so absorbs the public thought, and is freighted with such momentous issues. It is a problem which must be solved, for weal or for woe, and when the pulpit speaks according to the oracles of God, we may expect the Divine blessing, in the reconciling of opinions into a common faith.

In the extremes of abolitionism and propagandism, slavery is distorted. On the one side it is represented as the token of " the highest condition of Christian civilization ; " on the other, as " the sum of all iniquitics." These extremes are seemingly irreconcilable, and yet, like single truths, made errors by lack of union with other truths, wedded by Divine appointment, they may be seen to coalesce, when their affinities are developed and made manifest by the chemistry of God's word. It will be found, I think, that the Northern abolitionist reproaches the abuse of slavery, while the Southern propagandist confines his admiration to the spectacle of the benignant aspect of the institution. And if such be the case, then the remedy for the evil will be to correct the abuse ; and the point of coalescence will be the mutual effort, by moral and Christian persuasion, to redress the wrongs of the servant by the justice of the master, according to the golden rule of " doing to others what we would they should do to us," under like circumstances of relationship.

With this view, I proceed to the Divine law and to the testimony. Section 1. And noticing, first, God's constitution of society, we observe inequality. There are, everywhere, the relations of subordination and authority, whether in the family, or in the State, or in the church. But the characteristic of society, according to the Divine idea and Divine appointment, is mutual rights and correlative obligations. There is no such monstrous thing as an individual's prerogative that carries with it no corresponding duty ; but society is framed on the principle of mutual benefit, both to him who governs, and to him who is governed. So that, if it be the duty of the ruler to administer government as the Lord's vicegerent, it is the right of the subordinate to be ruled accordingly ; and if it be the right of the superior to receive the homage and obedience of the inferior, it becomes the duty of the inferior to render due homage and obedience to the superior, as to " God's minister to him for good." In these social relations we observe differences, both in degree and in the period of time, of the mutual service. In the relation of husband and wife, the bonds are for life, and dissoluble only for one cause. In the relation of parent and child, the rights and obligations are, in some respects, for life, and in others, for a term of years. In the relation of master and apprentice, the tenure of the relation is by agreement, for a specific time and purpose. In the relation of master and servant, the relation is for a specified time, or at will, or for life. When the term of service is for life, and with the condition of inheritance attached to property, the tenure is that of slavery. But in each of these relationships the principle of mutual benefit, to either party, is the ordained and unrevoked constitution of social life. In none is either party independent of the other ; in none is either party competent to take counsel only of his own self will. But each is servant to the other — bound by the sanctions of Divine authority to study each other's good, and to be governed by the principle of mutual benefit. All are, in some sense and degree, governors and masters ; all are, in some sense and degree, servants and subjects. Such is the Divine constitution of society. And if any man should rebel against it, through the arrogancy of self-will, he would be rushing on " the thick bosses of Jehovah's buckler," and would be crushed between the upper and nether mill-stones of the social rights and obligations of mankind.

If, then, slavery be subject to this law of God, where-

in the master must govern with an eye to the servant's
good as well as for his own interest, it will come to
pass that emancipation may be wrong, because unkind
and unjust to the slave. When not for the slave's
benefit, abolitionism would be a sin and a cruel thing.
And hence the question of emancipation can never be
determined justly as a *general* proposition, but must be
dealt with in each particular case. So neither does the
responsibility of determining this question of emancipation belong to any person but the master or some
superior authority that represents the master. Any foreign interference is, of necessity, obtrusive and tyrannical, and subversive of society, except such persuasions as
are derived from the Gospel of righteousness and peace,
which the master is willing to hear. For if the master's ear be heavy or his heart be hardened, it is no
apology for resorting to force to pierce the ear and
break the heart. We must trust in God to awaken and
convince him. John the Baptist might rebuke Herod
on his throne. But it was not every body's right and
duty in Judea to usurp the office of John the Baptist.
And so likewise, on the other hand, if the master hold
the slave for the master's exclusive interest; if he deny
him the privileges of mental, moral and religious culture; if he fail to recognise his manhood and withhold
the right of manhood to be trained for the service of
God and for the happiness of heaven; if he treat him
only as a brute or as a chattel inanimate; if he profane the relationship of marriage and violate the sanctity of the family, by violently sundering the ties that
God has instituted in Paradise, and which Jesus Christ
has restored to mankind in their sacredness and their

purity — if in any of these things, or others, the master deprives the bond servant of that which is " just and equal," governing, for his sole, exclusive benefit, then he abuses the power which God has given him, and the cry of the oppressed shall reach the ears of the Lord God of Sabaoth, appealing for deliverance and for justice. Such is a view of God's Providence.

2. Let us now resort to God's written words, and then regard the conduct of Jesus and his Apostles as the law and the testimony. The relation of apprenticeship was allowed among the Hebrews for a period of six years. "If thou buy a Hebrew servant, six years shall he serve, and in the seventh he shall go out free for nothing." (Exod. xxi., 2). But emancipation was *prohibited* if the servant chose to remain for life. " And if the servant shall plainly say, I love my master, my wife and my children; I will not go out free ; then his master shall bring him unto the judges ; he shall also bring him to the door, or unto the door post, and his master shall bore his ear through with an awl, and he shall serve him forever." (Exod. xxi., 5, 6 ; Deut. xv., 12 — 18.) Voluntary slavery was thus permitted out of regard to the slave's will and preference. In allusion to this fact and ceremony, the Spirit of prophecy, speaking in the name of Christ and foretelling His voluntary servitude for our salvation, describes Him as saying, " Sacrifice and offering thou didst not desire ; mine ears hast thou opened ; burnt offering and sin offering hast thou not required ; then said I, lo, I come to do thy will, O my God." (Psalms, xl., 6 — 8 ; compare Hebrews x., 5 — 9). The Apostle to the Hebrews employs this prophecy and its fami-

liar illustration to exemplify the voluntary mediatorial suffering of the Messiah. The slave, among God's ancient people, was as one of the family to whom privileges were allowed, not granted to the guest nor to the hired servant. As an example, the priest's portion of the sacrifices and the shew bread, " which it was not lawful for any to eat but the priest" and his family, was the meat of the bond slave. "There shall no stranger eat of the holy thing ; a sojourner of the priest, or an hired servant shall not eat of the holy thing. But if the priest buy any soul with his money he shall eat of it, and he that is born in his house, they shall eat of his meat." (Levit. xvii., 10, 11.) The special enactment which authorized bondage for life is in these words : — " Both thy bondmen and thy bondmaids which thou shalt have shall be of the heathen that are round about you ; of them shall ye buy bondmen and bondmaids ; moreover, of the children of the strangers that do sojourn among you, of them shall ye buy, and of their families that are with you, which they begat in your land, and they shall be your possession. And ye shall take them as an inheritance for your children after you, to inherit them for a possession : they shall be your bondmen forever." (Levit. xxv., 44 — 46).

Taking these permissive laws into one view, we see the institution of domestic slavery undoubtedly authorized ; but in every case the condition of the servant was improved by his servitude. It was an institution for the mutual benefit of the master and slave ; for, in the case of the voluntary slave, it was to gratify his affections, and in the case of the heathen slave it was to bring him into the midst of civilizing culture, both in mind and spirit. It was eminently a domestic institution. Yet, the Word of God does not fail to represent the condition of the slave as a hardship when the civilized man is reduced to bondage; for it is among the dreary punishments denounced against the apostate tribes, that they should be sold into bondage: — "Thou shalt be brought again into Egypt, and there ye shall be sold unto your enemies for bondmen and bondwomen. In the morning thou shalt say, would God it were even, and at even thou shalt say would God it were morning." (Deut. xxviii., 68, 69). In all this we recognise a certain authority for slavery which it would be uncandid to deny.

Yet it remains to examine the question by the light of the New Testament. And it is admitted on all sides that the institution of slavery was universal during the human life of Jesus and His Apostles. Yet we read of no instance where our Lord changed the ancient laws on the subject; but he taught those principles and precepts of equal love, which, if obeyed, would mitigate, if not bless, the relationship of master and servant. Idolatry was forbidden in the Old Testament, while slavery was permitted. And the Saviour and His Apostles denounced idolatry, but tolerated slavery. The Apostles, inspired on the day of Pentecost, taught bond slaves the Christian duty of obedience to their masters, and enjoined masters to "give unto their servants that which is just and equal." "Let as many servants as are under the yoke count their own masters worthy of all honor, that the name of God and His doctrine be not blasphemed. And they that have believing masters, let them not despise them, because they are

brethren, but rather do them service." (1 Tim. vi. 1,
2.) " Masters give unto your servants that which is
just and equal ; knowing that ye have also a Master in
heaven." " And there is no respect of persons with
Him." (Col. iii. 22 ; Eph. vi. 5, 9 ; Col. iv. 1.) Commentators of every complexion of religious persuasion
express no doubts that the " servants under the yoke "
were bondmen and bondwomen, the slaves of the Roman empire. And there is, moreover, a fugitive slave
law of the New Testament, in the Epistle of St. Paul to
Philemon. Onesimus, a fugitive slave[1] of Philemon,
flees to Rome, where he is converted by St. Paul.
(Verse 10.) The Apostle sends him back to his master (verse 12) ; for he would not keep him to serve
himself, out of regard to the master's right and the
slave's duty (verses 13, 14.) He enjoins Philemon to
treat him as a better servant than ever, even as a Christian brother (verses 15, 16) ; and he offers to pay Philemon all damage. (Verse 19.) If we believe this
Scripture and acknowledge the authority of this example, we must admit that it is a violation of the Christian law to retain fugitives from their masters, and for
the masters to treat them cruelly on their return. Such,
my brethren, is the statement of Holy Scripture as it
appears to your preacher, on this question of domestic
slavery.

Have the Southern States complied with the law of
God when they refuse to their servants manhood rights :
when they profane the sacred bonds of marriage ; when
they separate a family in the tenderness of their age ?
Have Northern fanatics fulfilled the Christian law when
they proclaim unqualified abolition, and lure servants

from their masters, or interpose hindrances to the fugitive's rendition ?

Public sentiment at the South is fast reaching the truth that separation of families is wrong, and some States have already forbidden the outrage by their statute law. Public sentiment at the North is sober and just and scriptural on the question of slavery, and profoundly respects the responsibilities, the rights, and the duties of master and servant. But passion has now usurped the throne of reason on both sides.

The Constitution of the United States still spreads its majestic folds around our country ; it regards slaves as persons having human rights of protection and of representation, yet as servants owing a life service to their masters. But the fury of political partisans has transferred a question purely spiritual from out of the moral code into the arena of a sordid calculation of selfish profit and sectional pre-eminence. And in that lustful controversy, the Battle of the Tribes is re-enacted in our country, and one fair State is lacking in our Union. Shall other States follow in the wake of that one ? I saw the meteor of last summer evening rise in light from the horizon to the zenith ; and at its highest ascension it exploded into two beauteous but divergent spheres ; and then they were both quenched in night. Was that the omen that presaged our country's doom ? Have we reached the height of our grandeur and prosperity to break and be extinguished ? No, no ; my brethren. The lacking tribe of Benjamin was not lost to Israel, but came back reformed and purified. And the eleven tribes, who, like us to-day, wept sore before God and asked of Him wisdom and forgiveness, learned to be considerate and kind to their seceding brethren. So, if it please God that we study the lesson of that record, shall our present disturbances promote our future welfare, as re-United States in the more perfect bonds of Christian brotherhood. I do not, I will not, despair of the Republic. Collisions of flint and steel produce sparks of light. The storm purifies the air. The very lightning whose voice is thunder, devours the vapors of miasma. This day's piety, at the behest of the Chief Magistrate of the nation, shall command God's blessing. And our children's children, in that better civilization which is in prospect, shall recur to these times as to a beacon which both warns and guides the pilgrim traveller to Eternity.

[1 He was a slave under the Phrygian code, which gave the master the power of life and death, without recurring to the magistrate.

PEACE, BE STILL.

A SERMON PREACHED AT PLYMOUTH CHURCH, BROOKLYN, ON THE DAY OF THE NATIONAL FAST, JAN. 4, 1861.

BY REV. HENRY WARD BEECHER.

———

" And there arose a great storm of wind, and the waves beat into the ship, so that it was now full. And he was in the hinder part of the ship, asleep on a pillow : and they awake him, and say unto him, Master, carest thou not that we perish ? And he arose and rebuked the wind, and said unto the sea, Peace, be still. And the wind ceased, and there was a great calm." — *Mark* iv. 37—39.

At the close of a laborious day, our Saviour entered a ship, upon the lake of Gennesaret, to cross to the other side. Wearied by his great tasks of mercy, which had filled the day, he fell asleep. Meantime, a sudden and violent wind, to which that lake is even yet subject, swept down from the hills, and well-nigh overwhelmed them. They were not ignorant of navigation, nor unacquainted with that squally sea. Like good men and true, doubtless, they laid about them. They took in sail, and put out oars, and, heading to the wind, valiantly bore up against the gale, and thought nothing of asking help till they had exerted every legitimate power of their own. But the waves overleaped their slender bulwarks, and filled the little vessel past all bailing.

Then, when they had done all that men could do, but not till then, they aroused the sleeping Christ and

12

implored his succor. Not for coming to him, did he
rebuke them; but for coming with such terror of despair, saying, Why are ye so fearful? How is it that
ye have no faith? He outbreathed upon the winds,
and their strength quite forsook them. He looked upon
the surly waves, and they hasted back to their caverns.
There is no tumult in the heavens, on the earth, nor upon the sea, that Christ's word cannot control. When
it pleases God to speak, tempestuous clouds are peaceful as flocks of doves, and angry seas change all their
roar to rippling music.

This nation is rolling helplessly in a great tempest.
The Chief Magistrate in despair calls us to go to the
sleeping Saviour, and to beseech his Divine interference.
It may be true that the crew have brought the ship into
danger by cowardice or treachery; it may be true that
a firm hand on the wheel would even yet hold her head
to the wind, and ride out the squall. But what of
that?

Humiliation and prayer are never out of order. This
nation has great sins unrepented of; and whatever may
be our own judgment of the wisdom of public men in
regard to secular affairs, we cannot deny that in this
respect they have hit rarely well. Instead of finding
fault with the almost only wise act of many days, let
us rather admire with gratitude this unexpected piety
of men in high places.

This government is in danger of subversion; and surely, while the venerable Chief Magistrate of this nation,
and all the members of his Cabinet, are doubtless this
day religiously abstaining from food, according to their
proclamation and recommendation to us, and humbly

confessing their manifold sins, it would ill become us to go unconcerned and negligent of such duties of piety and patriotism. Nor need we be inconveniently frank and critical. What if some shall say that fasting is a poor substitute for courage, and prayer a miserable equivalent for fidelity to duty? What if the national authorities had not only appointed the Fast, but afforded sufficient material in their own conduct for keeping it? It is all the more necessary on that account that we should pause, and humble ourselves before God, and implore his active interference.

But however monstrous the pretence of trouble may be, the danger is the same. Government is in danger of subversion. No greater disaster could befal this continent or the world; for such governments fall but once, and then there is no resurrection. Since there is no famine in the land, no pestilence, no invasion of foreign foe, no animosity of the industrial classes against each other, or against their employers, whence is our danger? from what quarter come these clouds, drifting with bolts of war and destruction? Over the Gulf the storm hangs lurid! From the treacherous Caribbean sea travel the darkness and swirling tornadoes!

What part of this complicated Government has at last broken down? Is it the legislative? the judicial? the executive? Has experience shown us that this costly machine, like many another, is more ingenious than practicable? Not another nation in the world, not a contemporaneous government, during the past seventy-five years, can compare, for regularity, simplicity of execution, and for a wise and facile accomplishment of the very ends of government, with ours. And yet, what is the errand of this day? Why are we observing a sad Sabbath? a day of humiliation? a day of supplication? It is for the strangest reason that the world ever heard. It is because the spirit of liberty has so increased and strengthened among us, that the Government is in danger of being overthrown! There never before was such an occasion for fasting, humiliation, and prayer! Other nations have gone through revolutions to find their liberties. We are on the eve of a revolution to put down liberty! Other people have thrown off their governments because too oppressive. Ours is to be destroyed, if at all, because it is too full of liberty, too full of freedom. There never was such an event before in history.

But however monstrous the pretence, the danger is here. In not a few states of this Union reason seems to have fled, and passion rules. To us who have been bred in cooler latitudes and under more cautious maxims, it seems incredible that men should abandon their callings, break up the industries of the community, and give themselves up to the wildest fanaticism, at the expense of every social and civil interest, and without the slightest reason or cause in their relations to society and to the country, past or future.

Communities, like individuals, are liable to aberrations of mind. Panics and general excitements seem to move by laws as definite as those which control epidemics or the pestilence. And such an insanity now rules in one portion of our land. Cities are turned into camps. All men are aping soldiers. For almost a thousand miles there is one wild riot of complaint and boasting. Acts of flagrant wrong are committed against the Federal Government. And these things are but the prelude. It is plainly declared that this Government shall be broken up, and many men mean it; and that the President-elect of this great nation shall never come to the place appointed by this people. Riot and civil war, with their hideous train of murders, revenges, and secret villanies, are gathering their elements, and hang in ominous terror over the capital of this nation.

Meanwhile, we have had no one to stand up for order. Those who should have spoken in decisive authority have been — *afraid!* Severer words have been used: it is enough for me to say only that in a time when God, and providence, and patriotism, and humanity demanded courage, they had nothing to respond but fear. The heart has almost ceased to beat, and this Government is like to die for want of pulsations at the centre. While the most humiliating fear paralyzes one part of the Government, the most wicked treachery is found in other parts of it. Men advanced to the highest places by the power of our Constitution, have employed their force to destroy that Constitution. They are using their oath as a soldier uses his shield — to cover and protect them while they are mining the foundations, and opening every door, and unfastening every protection by which colluding traitors may gain easy entrance and fatal success. Gigantic dishonesties, meanwhile, stalk abroad almost without shame. And this Puritan land, this free Government, these United States, like old Rome in her latest imperial days, helpless at the court, divided among her own citizens, overhung by hordes of Goths and Barbarians, seem about to be swept away with the fury of war and revolution.

If at such a solemn crisis as this, men refuse to look at things as they are ; to call their sins to remembrance ; to confess and forsake them ; if they shall cover over the great sins of this people, and confess only in a sentimental way, (as one would solace an evening sadness by playing some sweet and minor melody,) then we may fear that God has indeed forsaken his people. But if we shall honestly confess our real sins ; if we propose to cleanse ourselves from them ; if we do not make prayer a substitute for action, but an incitement to it ; if we rise from our knees this day more zealous for temperance, for honesty, for real brotherhood, for pure and undefiled religion, and for that which is the sum and child of them all, regulating liberty to all men, then will the clouds begin to break, and we shall see the blue shining through, and the sun, ere long, driving away the tumultuous clouds, shall come back in triumph, and like one for a moment cast down but now lifted up for victory.

1. It is well, then, that every one of us make this day the beginning of a solemn review of his own life, and the tendencies of his own conduct and character. A general repentance of national sins should follow, rather than precede, a personal and private conviction of our own individual transgressions. For it has been found not difficult for men to repent of other people's sins ; but it is found somewhat difficult and onerous to men to repent of their own sins. We are all of us guilty before God of pride, of selfishness, of vanity, of passions unsubdued, of worldliness in manifold forms, and of strife. We have been caught in the stream, and swept out into an ocean of thoughts and feelings

which cannot bear the inquest of God's judgment-day. And we have lived in them almost unrebuked. Each man will find his own life full of repentable sins unrepented of.

2. We should take solemn account of our guilt in the great growth of social laxity, and vice, and crime, in our great cities. We have loved ease rather than duty. Every American citizen is by birth a sworn officer of State. Every man is a policeman. If bad men have had impunity; if the vile have controlled our municipal affairs; if by our delinquencies and indolence justice has been perverted, and our cities are full of great public wickedness, then we cannot put the guilt away from our own consciences. We have a partnership in the conduct of wicked men, unless we have exhausted proper and permissible means of forestalling and preventing it. And I think every citizen of such a city as this, looking upon intemperance, upon vice, upon lewdness, upon gambling, upon the monstrous wickednesses that ferment at the bottom of society, should feel that he has some occasion to repent of his own delinquency and moral indifference.

3. We may not refuse to consider the growth of corrupt passions in connection with the increase of commercial prosperity. Luxury, extravagance, ostentation, and corruption of morals in social life, have given alarming evidence of a premature old age in a young country. The sins of a nation are always the sins of certain central passions. In one age they break out in one way, and in another age in another way; but they are the same central sins, after all. The corrupt passions which lead in the Southern States to all the gigan-

tic evils of slavery, in Northern cities break out in other forms, not less guilty before God, because of a less public nature. The same thing that leads to the oppression of the operative, leads to oppression on the plantation. The grinding of the poor, the advantages which capital takes of labor, the oppression of the farm, the oppression of the road, the oppression of the shop, the oppression of the ship, are all of the same central nature, and as guilty before God as the more systematic and overt oppressions of the plantation. It is the old human heart that sins, always, North or South; and the nature of pride and of dishonesty are universal. Therefore we have our own account to render.

4. There is occasion for alarm and for humiliation before God, in the spread of avarice among our people. The intense eagerness to amass wealth; the growing indifference of morals as to methods; the gradual corruption of moral sense, so that property and interest supersede moral sense, and legislate and judge what is right and wrong; the use of money for bribery, for bribing electors and elected; the terrible imputations which lie against many of our courts, that judges walk upon gold, and then sit upon gold in the judgment-seat; the use of money in legislation; and the growing rottenness of politics from the lowest village concern to matters of national dimension, from constables to the Chief Magistrate of these United States — is this all to be confessed only in a single smooth sentence?

Such is the wantonness and almost universality of avarice as a corrupting agent in public affairs, that it behooves every man to consider his responsibilities before

God in this matter. The very planks between us and
the ocean are worm-eaten and rotting, when avarice
takes hold of public integrity ; for avarice is that sea-
worm, ocean-bred, and swarming innumerable, that will
pierce the toughest planks, and bring the stoutest ships
to foundering. Our foundations are crumbling. The
sills on which we are building are ready to break. We
need reformation in the very beginnings and elements
of society. If in other parts of our land they are in
danger of going down by avarice in one form, we are
in danger of going down by avarice in another form.

Our people are vain, and much given to boasting ; and
because they love flatteries, those deriving from them
honor and trust, are too fond of feeding their appetite
for praise. Thus it comes to pass that we hear the favorable side of our doings and character, and become
used to a flattering portrait. Men grow popular who
have flowing phrases of eulogy. Men who speak unpalatable truths are disliked ; and if they have power
to make the public conscience uncomfortable, they are
said to abuse the liberty of free speech — for it is the
liberty of fanning men to sleep that is supposed to be
legitimate : the liberty of waking men out of sleep is
supposed to be license ! And yet we shall certainly die
by the sweetness of flattery ; and if we are healed, it
must be by the bitterness of faithful speech. There is
tonic in the things that men do not love to hear ; and
there is damnation in the things that wicked men love
to hear. Free speech is to a great people what winds
are to oceans and malarial regions, which waft away
the elements of disease, and bring new elements of

12*

health.   And where free speech is stopped miasma is
bred, and death comes fast.

5. But upon a day of national fasting and confession,
we are called to consider not alone our individual and
social evils, but also those which are national.   And
justice requires that we should make mention of the
sins of this nation on every side, past and present.   I
should violate my own convictions, if, in the presence
of more nearly present and more exciting influences, I
should neglect to mention the sins of this nation against
the Indian, who, as much as the slave, is dumb, but who,
unlike the slave, has almost none to think of him, and
to speak of his wrongs.   We must remember that we
are the only historians of the wrongs of the Indian —
we that commit them.   And our history of the Indian
nations of this country, is like the inquisitor's history
of his own trials of innocent victims.   He leaves out
the rack, and the groans, and the anguish, and the un-
utterable wrongs, and puts but his own glozing view in
his journal.   We have heaped up the account of treachery and cruelty on their part, but we have not narrated
the provocations, the grinding intrusions, and the misunderstood interpretations of their policy, on our part.
Every crime in the calendar of wrong which a strong
people can commit against a weak one, has been committed by us against them.   We have wasted their substance ; we have provoked their hostility, and then chas-
tised them for their wars ; we have compelled them to
peace ignominiously ; we have formed treaties with
them only to be broken ; we have filched their possessions.   In our presence they have wilted and wasted.

A heathen people have experienced at the side of a Christian nation, almost every evil which one people can commit against another.

Admit the laws of race; admit the laws of advancing civilization as fatal to all barbarism; admit the indocility of the savage; admit the rude edges of violent men who form the pioneer advance of a great people, and the intrinsic difficulties of managing a people whose notions and customs and laws are utterly different from our own, and then you have only explained how the evil has been done, but you have not changed its guilt, nor fact. The mischief has been done, and this is simply the excuse. It is a sorry commentary upon a Christian nation, and indeed, upon religion itself, that the freest and most boastfully religious people on the globe are absolutely fatal to any weaker people that they touch. What would be thought of a man who, when he became converted to Christianity, was dangerous to the next man's pocket? What would be thought of a man who, when he became perfect, was a swindler and a robber? And what must be the nature of that Christianization which makes this Republic a most dangerous neighbor to nations weaker than ourselves? We are respectful to strength, and thieves and robbers to weakness. It is not safe for any to trust our magnanimity and generosity. We have no chivalry. We have avarice; we have haughty arrogance; we have assumptive ways; and we have a desperate determination to live, to think only of our own living, and to sweep with the besom of destruction whatever happens to be where we would put our foot.

Nor is this confined to the Indian. The Mexicans

have felt the same rude foot.   This nation has employed its gigantic strength with almost no moral restriction.   Our civilization has not begotten humanity and
respect for others' rights, nor a spirit of protection to
the weak.

It is quite in vain to say that the land from which
we sprung did the same as we are doing.   A wicked
daughter is not excused because she had a wicked mother.   We boast of the Anglo-Saxon race ; and if bone
and muscle, an indomitable sense of personal liberty,
and a disposition to do what we please, are themes for
Christian rejoicing, then the Anglo-Saxon may well rejoice.   There are sins that belong to races ; there are
sins that belong to peoples ; there are sins that belong
to generations of the same people ; and the sins that I
have enumerated, are sins that belong to our stock, to
our kind.

But God never forgets what we most easily forget.
Either the moral government over nations is apocry-
phal, or judgments are yet to be visited upon us for the
wrongs done to the Indian.

6. But I am now come to the most alarming and
most fertile cause of national sin — slavery.   We are
called by our Chief Magistrate to humble ourselves before God for our sins.   This is not only a sin, but it is
a fountain from which have flown so many sins that we
cannot rightly improve this day without a consideration
of them.

In one and the same year, 1620, English ships landed
the Puritans in New England, and negro slaves in Virginia — two seeds of the two systems that were destined
to find here a growth and strength unparalleled in his-

tory. It would have seemed almost a theatric arrangement, had these oppugnant elements, Puritan liberty
and Roman servitude — (for, whatever men may say,
American slavery is not Hebrew slavery; it is Roman
slavery. We borrowed every single one of the elemen-
tal principles of our system of slavery from the Roman
law, and not from the old Hebrew. The fundamental
feature of the Hebrew system was that the slave was a
man, and not a chattel, while the fundamental feature
of the Roman system was that he was a chattel, and not
a man. The essential principle of the old Mosaic servitude made it the duty of the master to treat his servants as men, and to instruct them in his own religion,
and in the matters of his own household; while the
essential principle of Roman servitude allowed the master to treat his servants to all intents and purposes as
chattels, goods) — it would have seemed, I say, almost
a theatric arrangement had these oppugnant elements,
Puritan liberty and Roman servitude, divided the land
between them, and, inspiring different governments,
grown up different nations, in contrast, that the world
might see this experiment fairly compared and worked
out to the bitter end.

But it was not to be so. The same Government has
nourished both elements. Our Constitution nourished
twins. It carried Africa on its left bosom, and Anglo-
Saxony on its right bosom; and these two, drawing
milk from the same bosom, have waxed strong, and
stand to-day federated into the one republic. One side
of the body politic has grown fair, and healthy, and
strong: the other side has grown up as a wen grows,
and the wart, vast, the vaster the weaker. And this

nation is like a strong man with one side paralyzed, but nourished and carried along by the help of the other side.

We who dwell in the North are not without responsibility for this sin. Its wonderful growth, and the arrogance of its claims, have been in part through our delinquency. And our business to-day is not to find fault with the South, I am not discussing this matter with reference to them at all, but only with reference to our own individual profit. Because the South loved money, they augmented this evil; and because the North loved money, and that quiet which befits industry and commerce, she has refused to insist upon her moral convictions, in days past, and yielded to every demand, carrying slavery forward in this nation. You and I are guilty of the spread of slavery unless we have exerted, normally and legitimately, every influence in our power against it. If we have said, " To agitate the question imperils manufacturing, imperils shipping, imperils real estate, imperils quiet and peace," and then have sacrificed purity and honesty; if we have bought the right to make money here by letting slavery spread and grow there, we have been doing just the same thing that they have; for they have held slaves for the sake of money, and we have permitted them to hold them for just the same reason — money, *money*. It has been one gigantic bargain, only working out in different ways, North and South. It is for us just as much as for them that the slave works; and we acquiesce. We clothe ourselves with the cotton which the slave tills. Is he scorched? is he lashed? does he water the crop with his sweat and tears? It is you and I that wear the shirt and consume the luxury. Our looms and our factories are largely built on the slave's bones. We live on his labor. I confess I see no way to escape a part of the responsibility for slavery. I feel guilty in part for this system. If the relinquishment of the articles which come from slave labor would tend even remotely to abridge or end the evil, I would without hesitation forego every one; but I do not see that it would help the matter. I am an unwilling partner in the slave system. I take to myself a part of the sin; I confess it before God; and pray for some way to be opened by which I may be freed from that which I hate bitterly.

But this state of facts makes it to-day eminently proper for us to confess our wrong and sin done to the slave. All the wrongs, the crimes of some, the abuse of others, the neglect, the misuse, the ignorance, the separations, the scourgings — these cannot be rolled into a cloud to overhang the South alone. Every one of us has something to confess. Those who have been most scrupulous, if God should judge their life, their motives, and their conduct, would find that they, too, had some account in this great bill of slavery. The whole nation is guilty. There is not a lumberman on the verge of Maine, not a settler on the far distant northern prairies, not an emigrant on the Pacific, that is not politically and commercially in alliance with this great evil. If you put poison into your system in any way, there is not a nerve that is not touched by it; there is not a muscle that does not feel it; there is not a bone, nor a tissue, nor one single part nor parcel of your whole body, that can escape it. And our body politic is pervaded with this black injustice, and every one of us is more or less, directly or indirectly, willingly or unwillingly, implicated in it. And when it comes to the question of confession, we have a great deal to confess before we cast reproaches upon the South. And while I hold Southern citizens to the full and dreadful measure of their guilt before God, and would, if I were settled there, tell them their sin as plainly as I tell you your sin, it is for us to-day, and here, to consider our own part in this matter; and to that I shall speak during the residue of my remarks.

Originally, we were guilty of active participation in slavery. It seems very strange to take up the old Boston books, and read the history of slavery in Boston. Not that they have not slaves there now; but they are white! Once they were African and involuntary: now they are political and voluntary. We of the North early abandoned the practice of holding slaves. But it is said that ours is a cheap philanthropy; that having got quit of our slaves by selling them, we turn round and preach to the South about the sin of holding theirs. There is nothing more atrociously false than such a charge as that. There is nothing more illustrious in the history of the state of New York, and of the Northern states generally, than the method by which they freed themselves from slavery. This state decreed liberty at a certain period, and then passed a most stringent act making it an offence, the penalty attached to which no one would willingly inherit, for a man to convey away, or in any manner whatsoever to sell out of the State, a person held as a slave; and if a man, anticipating the day of emancipation, wished to make a

journey to the South with his slaves, he had to give
bonds for their return before he went away, and had to
give an account when he came back, if they did not
come with him. Nothing could have been more humane than the provision that the slave should not be
sold out of the state of New York, but should be emancipated in it. And what is true of New York in this
respect, is true of the States generally that emancipated
their slaves.

But we of the North participated in the beginnings,
and we are in part guilty of the subsequent' spread of
the system of slavery. When our Government came
into our hands, after the struggle of the Revolution, we
had gone through such a school in order to assert our
political independence, that the head, the conscience,
and the heart of this nation, in the main, were right on
the subject of human liberties. And at the adoption
of the Federal Constitution, nearly seventy-five years
ago, it might be said that, with local and insignificant
exceptions, there was but one judgment, one wish, and
one prophetic expectation — namely, that this whole territory should be dedicated to liberty, and that every
compliance or compromise was not to be made in the
interest of oppression, but was to be made only to give
oppression time to die decently ; and that was the spirit
and intent of every compliance or compromise that was
made.

The schools, the academies, the colleges, the intelligence, the *brain* of this nation, at that time, were in the
North — and in the North I include all the territory
this side of Mason's and Dixon's line. We were then
the thinking part of this country. The church, the

religious institutions, the moral elements that never
parted from the posterity of the Puritans, were then,
also, in the North.   When our Constitution was adopted ; when the wheels of our mighty confederacy were
adjusted, and the pendulum began to swing — at that
time the public sentiment was in favor of liberty.   All
the institutions were prepared for liberty, and all the
public men were on the side of liberty.   And to the
North, because she was the brain ; to the North, because she was the moral centre and heart of this confederacy, was given this estate — for in the first twenty-
five or thirty years the North predominated in the
counsels of the nation, and fixed the institutions, as the
South have fixed their policy since.   What, then, having this trust put into her hands, is the account of her
stewardship which the North has to render ?   If now,
after three-quarters of a century have passed away,
God should summon the North to his judgment-bar, and
say, "I gave you a continent in which, though there
was slavery, it was perishing; I gave you a nation in
which the sentiment was for liberty and against oppression ; I gave you a nation in which the tendencies were
all for freedom and against slavery ; I gave you the supreme intelligence ; I gave you the moral power in a
thousand pulpits, a thousand books, a thousand Bibles;
and I said, ' Take this nation, administer it, and render
up your trust ' " — if now, after three-quarters of a
century have passed away, God should summon the
North to his judgment-bar and say this, what would be
the account which she would have to render — the
North, that was strongest in the head and in the heart,
and that took as fair a heritage as men ever attempted

to administer? To-day, liberty is bankrupt, and slavery is rampant, in this nation. And do you creep out and say, "We are not to blame"? What have you been doing with your intelligence, your books, your schools, your Bibles, your missionaries, your ministers? Where, where is the artillery that God Almighty gave you, park upon park, and what has become of this nation under your care, that were provided and prepared for that special emergency? I take part of the blame to myself. Much as I love the North — (and I love every drop of Puritan blood that the world ever saw; because it seems to me that Puritan blood means blood touched with Christ's blood) — I take to myself part of the shame, and mourn over the delinquency of the North, that having committed to it the eminent task of preserving the liberties of this nation, they have sacrificed them. For to-day there are more slave states than there were states confederated when this nation came together. And instead of having three or four hundred thousand slaves, we have more than four millions; instead of a traffic suppressed, you and I are witnesses to-day of a traffic to be reopened — of rebellion, treasonable war, bloodshed, separate independence, for the sake of reopening the African slave-trade. So came this country into the hands of the North in the beginning, and so it is going out of her hands in the end. There never was such a stewardship: and if this confederacy shall be broken up; if the Gulf states shall demand a division of the country, and the intermediate states shall go off, and two empires shall be established, no steward that has lived since God's sun shone on the earth, will have such an account to render of an estate taken under such favorable auspices, as the North will have to render of this great national estate which was committed to her trust. It is an astounding sin! It is an unparalleled guilt! The vengeance and zeal of our hearts toward the South might be somewhat tempered by the reflection that we have been so faithless, so wicked, and that our account must stand before God in the end, as it does stand, for delinquency in our duty.

That is not the worst. That is the material side. The next step is this: that we have stood in the North with all the elements of power, boasting of our influence, and really swaying, in many respects, the affairs of this continent; and yet we have not only seen this tremendous increase of slavery, but we have permitted the doctrines of liberty themselves to take paralysis and leprosy. And to-day, *to-day*, TO-DAY, if you were to put it to the vote of this whole people, I do not know as you could get a majority for any doctrine of liberty but this: that each man has a right to be free himself. The great doctrine of liberty is concisely expressed by the Declaration of Independence; and it is this: that all men are free; born with equal political rights, of life, liberty, and the pursuit of happiness. And there is no true right that is not founded on this doctrine: "That liberty which is good for me, is indispensable for everybody." A right love of liberty inspires a man to say, "I will have it, and everybody shall have it." That is a poor love of liberty that makes a man a champion for the liberty of those that are capable of asserting their own liberty. But I doubt whether, so corrupt are the times, you could get a popular vote for the liber-

ty of all men. Why should you? I am ashamed of
what I must speak. The pulpit has been so prostituted,
and so utterly apostatized from the very root and substance of Christianity, that it teaches the most heathen
notions of liberty ; and why should you expect that the
great masses of men would be better informed on this
subject than they are? Do you believe that George
Washington, were he living, would now be able to live
one day in the city of Charleston, if he uttered the
sentiments that he used to hold? He would not. He
would be denounced as a traitor, and swung up on the
nearest lamp-post. Do you suppose that one single man
that signed the Declaration of Independence, if living,
could go through the South to-day, repeating the sentiments contained in that document? The lives of the
signers of the Declaration of Independence would not
be worth one day's lease in Alabama, Louisiana, Carolina, or Florida, if they were there to say the things
plainly which they said when they framed this government, so utterly have the South vomited up their political views; so radically have they changed their notions.
Was this country committed to our care? and is such
the lesson that we have taught our pupils? Shall the
schoolmaster render back the scholars that he undertook
to teach, with their minds debauched, and say that he
was not responsible for what they learned? And if
any part of the country was responsible for the education of the whole, it was the free-schooled, million-
churched North. And the result of our instruction is
this : slavery has spread gigantically, and the doctrine
of liberty is so corrupted, that to-day nothing is more
disreputable in the high places of this nation, than that

very doctrine. And at last, when the sleeper, long
snoring, having been awaked, raised himself up, and
like all new zealots, somewhat intemperately made crusade for liberty, the land was so agitated, and with
such surprise was this expression of the public sentiment of the North received, that the Chief Magistrate
of this nation declared that we were the cause of all
the trouble!

But this is not all. The most serious, the most
grievous charge, is yet to be made upon the North. So
far have we been delinquent in the trust that God committed to us, that the very centre of hope and expectation of success for humanity has been burned out; that
from the very fountain out of which flowed, as from the
heart of Christ, the first drops that were to cleanse men
from oppressions, has been extracted in our day, and in
our North very largely, the whole spirit of humanity
which breathes freedom.

It ill becomes, I think, one profession to rail against
another, or the members of the same profession to rail
against each other. I have no accusations to make
against any; but I will forsake my profession, for the
time being, and stand as a man among men, to lift up
my voice, with all my heart and soul, against any man
who, professing to be ordained to preach, preaches out
of Christ's Gospel the doctrines of human bondage.
When the Bible is opened that all the fiends of hell
may, as in a covered passage, walk through it to do
mischief on the earth, I say, blessed be infidels! Where
men take the Bible to teach me to disown childhood;
where men take the Bible to teach me that it is lawful
to buy and sell men, that marriage is an impossible

state, that laws cannot permit it, and that customs cannot permit it; where the Bible is held as the sacred document and constitutional guarantee of a system which makes it impossible that a man should go up on the path of development; where the Bible is made to stand and uphold one man in saying to another, "You are good for me in that proportion in which you are able to use the spade and the hoe, and I forbid you to read and expand your mind because knowledge will render you unmarketable;" where, according to the Bible, men, women, and children are legal tenders in the market, and anything that lessens their value there is an impediment, so that marriage and its sanctities are regarded as over-refinements; where a man takes the Bible and lays it in the path over which men are attempting to walk from Calvary up to the gate of heaven — I declare that I will do by the Bible what Christ did by the temple: I will take a whip of cords, and I will drive out of it every man that buys and sells men, women, and children; and if I cannot do that, I will let the Bible go, as God let the temple go, to the desolating armies of its adversaries. And I do not wonder that after so long an experience of the world, men who bombard universal humanity, men who plead for the outrage of slavery, men who grope to find under crowns and sceptres the infamous doctrines of servitude — I do not wonder that they are pestered with the idea of man's individuality. Why, that minister who preaches slavery out of the Bible is the father of every infidel in the community! I tell you that the most intelligent people in the world are infidels. In Germany I will pick out nineteen out of every twenty democrats who are infidels.

And why ? Not because they do not believe really in the Bible, but because the priests that the kings ordain in Germany have built up the whole kingly fabric and the archepiscopal throne on the Bible ; and when the democrat sees the oppression of the king, and feels the yoke of the priest, and protests against them, they stop his mouth by sticking the leaves of the Bible into it ! So he comes to hate the Bible, not for what it is in reality, but because it is made the bulwark of oppression ; and he spurns it that he may answer the call of God in his own nature — for to be free is a part of the sovereign call and election that God has given to every man who has a sense of his birthright and immortality. And in a community where the minister finds reason in the Bible for slavery, you may depend upon it that one of two things will take place : either there will be an inquisition to redeem the Bible from such abominable prostitution, or else the Bible will be spurned and kicked from under the feet of men, as it ought to be.

"I came to open the prison-doors," said Christ ; and that is the text on which men justify shutting them and locking them. "I came to loose those that are bound ;" and that is the text out of which men spin cords to bind men, women, and children. "I came to carry light to them that are in darkness, and deliverance to the oppressed ;" and that is the Book from out of which they argue, with amazing ingenuity, all the infernal meshes and snares by which to keep men in bondage. It is pitiful.

A hunter scorns a pigeon-roost ; because he would fain have some reward in skill and ingenuity ; and he feels that to fire into a pigeon-roost is shocking butchery.

But for that feeling I should like no better amusement than to answer the sermons of men who attempt to establish the right of slavery out of the Bible. It would be simple butchery! A man must be addicted to blood who would fire a twenty-four pounder into a flock of blackbirds or crows!

Now what has been the history of the Book but this: that wherever you have had an untrammeled Bible, you have had an untrammeled people; and that wherever you have had a trammeled Bible, you have had a trammeled people? Where you have had a Bible that the priests interpreted, you have had a king: where you have had a Bible that the common people interpreted; where the family has been the church; where father and mother have been God's ordained priests; where they have read its pages freely from beginning to end without gloss or commentary, without the church to tell them how, but with the illumination of God's Spirit in their hearts; where the Bible has been in the household, and read without hindrance by parents and children together — there you have had an indomitable yeomanry, a state that would not have a tyrant on the throne, a government that would not have a slave or a serf in the field. Wherever the Bible has been allowed to be free; wherever it has been knocked out of the king's hand, and out of the priest's hand, it has carried light like the morning sun, rising over hill and vale, round and round the world; and it will do it again! And yet there come up in our midst men that say to us that the Bible is in favor of slavery. And as men that make a desperate jump go back and run before they jump, so these men have to go back to the twilight of

13

creation and take a long run ; and when they come to
their jump, their strength is spent and they but stum-
ble !

It is in consideration of this wanton change which
has taken place (and which ought never to have been
permitted to take place, in view of the instruments that
God put into our hands, and in view of the solemn responsibility that he has put upon us) — it is in consideration of this change which has taken place in the material condition of the country, and in the opinions of
this people respecting the great doctrine of liberty, and
the worse change which has corrupted in part the
church at its very core, that I argue to-day the necessity of humiliation and repentance before God.

I shall first confess my own sin. Sometimes men
think I have been unduly active. I think I have been
indolent. In regard to my duty in my personal and
professional life, I chide myself for nothing more than
because I have not been more alert, more instant in season and out of season. If sometimes in intemperate
earnestness I have wounded the feelings of any ; if I
have seemed to judge men harshly, for that I am sorry.
But for holding the slave as my brother ; for feeling
that the Spirit of God is the spirit of liberty ; for loving my country so well that I cannot bear to see a stain
or a blot upon her ; for endeavoring to take the raiment
of heaven wherewith to scour white as snow the morals
of my times, and to cleanse them to the uttermost of
all spot and aspersion — for that I have no tears to
shed. I only mourn that I have not been more active
and zealous, and I do not wish to separate myself from
my share of the responsibility. I am willing to take

my part of the yoke and burden. I will weep my tears before God, and pray my prayers of sincere contrition and penitence, that I have not been more faithful to liberty and religion in the North and the whole land. And you must make this a day of penitence. You must do your part.

But be sure of one thing: He that would not come when the sisters sent, but tarried, has come, and the stone is rolled away, and he stands by the side of the sepulchre. He has called, " Liberty, come forth!" and, bound yet hand and foot, it has come forth; and that same sovereign voice is saying, " Loose him, and let him go!" and from out of the tomb, the dust, the night, and the degradation, the better spirit of this people is now emerging at the voice of God. We have heard his call, we know the bidding, and Death itself cannot hold us any longer; and there is before us, we may fain believe, a new lease of life, a more blessed national existence. That there will not be concussions, and perhaps some garments rolled in blood, I will not undertake to say : there may be some such things as these ; but, brethren, this nation is not going to perish. This confederacy is not going to be broken and shivered like a crystal vase that can never be put together again. We are to be tested and tried; but if we are in earnest, and if we stand as martyrs and confessors before us have stood, bearing witness in this thing for Christ, know ye that ere long God will appear, and be the leader and captain of our salvation, and we shall have given back to us this whole land, healed, restored to its right mind, and sitting at the feet of Jesus.

Love God, love men, love your dear fatherland; to-

day confess your sins toward God, toward men, toward
your own fatherland ; and may that God that loves to
forgive and forget, hear our cries and our petitions
which we make, pardon the past, inspire the future, and
bring the latter-day glory through a regenerated zeal
and truth, inspired by his Spirit, in this nation.   Amen,
and amen.

THE CRISIS OF OUR NATIONAL DISEASE.

A SERMON PREACHED AT ALL SOULS CHURCH, NEW YORK, ON THE
DAY OF THE NATIONAL FAST, JAN. 4, 1861.

BY REV. HENRY W. BELLOWS, D. D.

"These shall make war with the Lamb, and the Lamb shall overcome
them : for he is Lord of lords, and King of kings ; and they that are
with him are called and chosen and faithful." — Rev. xvii. 14.

———

THESE words fitly describe the eternal conflict going
on in the world between the false principles, the organized sins, the political errors and mistakes of our common humanity, and the eternal laws of God and his
Christ. The truth is always charged with creating the
violence that opposes its progress, while really it is
always the Lamb on whom the Wolf is making war, but
who is destined by God to overcome and convert him.
At this moment our institutions, in their legitimate operation, are the Lamb, on whom Error and Wrong and
Ignorance are making war, and it remains to be seen
whether now, as always before, the Lamb shall overcome
them. If our country be Christ's true heritage, in as-
sailing it, he is assailed, and in that case we have
nothing to fear ; for he is Lord of lords, and King of
kings, and they that are with him are called and chosen
and faithful.

We have come together, Christian brethren, in obedience to the proclamation of the President of these United States, backed by the proclamation of the Governor of New York, to fulfil the duties of a day of Special Humiliation, Fasting, and Prayer, in view of the distracted and perilous condition of our country. A proper respect for the recommendations of our rulers obliges us to join our fellow-citizens in the religious observance of this day. Humiliation before God, and prayer to the Divine Majesty and Fatherhood, are always in season ; fasting, as a religious service, never, and particularly not when all our bodily vigor and endurance may so shortly be required to meet the enemies of our national existence. But it would be gross hypocrisy in me to leave it to be inferred that I share any of the feelings or opinions, political or religious, which are avowed in the call for this special fast.

The proclamation of the President assumes that our present difficulties and perils are the result of some special wickedness on the part of the people at large — of some recent guilt in our conduct as citizens, that we have suddenly fallen under the high displeasure of the Almighty, and that nothing but confession of guilt and implorations for mercy can produce that interposition from his holy hand, without which we are inevitably ruined. I believe, on the contrary, that our present difficulties and perils grow out of the awakening virtue and increasing humanity of the people at large; that a stronger and more efficient desire to keep the Divine commandments — to fulfil the precepts, and realize the spirit of the Gospel — is the moving cause of the agitation and conflict which threatens the stability of our Union. I see no evidence of any Divine displeasure in the commotion which rocks our Government; nor do I believe that vague confessions of a guilt we do not feel, and formal prayers for an interposition we do not expect, are likely to produce anything but the ordinary fruits of hypocrisy.

The cause of our present agitation and insecurity, as it has been the cause of all the political trials and griefs of our whole history as a nation, is the anomalous existence in a republican and democratic Government, based on respect for human rights, political equality, universal representation, free speech, public discussion, general enlightenment, and progressive reform, of an institution for maintaining and perpetuating the bondage of one vast portion of the human family — an institution upholding and strengthening, in the freest country in the world, the most abject and mercenary system of domestic slavery — exactly contradicting every principle and sentiment in our Declaration of Independence, and reversing, in its spirit, operation, and tendencies, the theory, objects, and working of our Constitution and our National inspiration.

Whatever necessities, accidents, or antecedents planted slavery in the nation, however innocent and pardonable its heirs and present representatives may be, its own essential character is not changed, nor its anomalous position and influence altered. It remains what it always was and always must be — an abuse of the natural rights of man, a denial of real and proper humanity to beings in the human form, a state of war upon its subjects which brute force and nearly absolute power can alone render successful, and of irresponsible, corrupting, and debilitating influence on the dominant race who uphold it. Slavery is not a new thing in the world; its nature and effects are not open questions. It has proved the ruin of all the ancient and modern states that have yielded to its seducing temptations, until its quality and consequences are stamped by the historic, the political, the social, the religious experience and wisdom of the wide world, with fixed, decisive, and unalterable abhorrence.

And here is this instituted outrage upon God and man — upon the spirit of Christianity and the ethics and political instincts of the nineteenth century — planted in the capital of American liberty, become the foundation of fifteen sovereign States of this Union, wielding the authority of our Senate, the chief solicitude of the head of the Government, and menacing the downfall of our Nationality, if the majority of the American people do not disown their disgust, retract their reprobation, and pronounce property in man not a local and legal fiction, but a national fact, and the fundamental and permanent article of our political creed.

In a nation founded on the supposed intelligence of the people, the diffusion of intelligence has become, under this condition of things, the worst injury one part of the country can commit against the other; in a nation where labor was to be honored as nowhere else in the world, as the necessary corollary of universal equality, it has been degraded into a menial and servile necessity; in a land of free speech and free discussion, the safety of our institutions is endangered by the utterance of the veriest common-places of political thought, and the first principles of Christianity, and no crime is so great as humanity and justice! The noble system of government which invites into the free States of this Union almost the whole emigration of Europe, is a high offence against this anomalous system of slavery in the South ! Our growth in numbers, intelligence, equality ; our progress in morals, civilization, and religion — all, in short, that wins to us the respect and admiration of the rest of the world, increases the fear, the antipathy. and the jealousy of the slave power. Our purest morals are pronounced fanaticism ; our most efficacious piety, infidelity ; our most civilized and enlightened communities, hot-beds of treason and error. We cannot exercise, develop, and enjoy the very principles, ideas, rights, and feelings, which this free government was established to embody and protect, without imperilling the lives and fortunes of our fellow-citizens in that portion of our country whose domestic institutions are based on negro slavery. Our press, if it meets and represents the honest feelings of the civilized world, becomes a fire-brand at the South, and cannot be permitted to circulate there. Our most acceptable and advanced literature is dangerous to the peace of that community. The most legitimate exercise of our political rights is, as we are now seeing, the highest injury and most intolerable insult we can offer to our Southern countrymen !

How idle it is, in this state of things, to look for any other cause of disaffection, agitation, and conflict than the simple fact that the natural and inevitable progress of civilization on this continent is essentially threatening to the barbarous institution of slavery, and that the only real issue before the country and the world is this : Shall modern civilization and free institutions deny

themselves and lose their nature? or shall slavery accept its doom as a temporary and decaying institution,
under the rightful censure of Christendom, and beneath
the crushing feet of human progress? In pronouncing
this the real moral issue now open, I am far from saying or allowing that this is the political issue. There
is not a handful of Northern citizens who would consent, under any temptations or circumstances, to interfere with the existence of slavery in the States. It is
not party power, or direct action of any sort, now or
at any future time, which threatens slavery. It is simply civilization in its necessary progress which is doom-
ing it to ruin, as the steady rising of the sun drives
night away.

You will observe that I am bringing no charges
against slaveholders—pronouncing no sentence on them.
They are, for the most part, the innocent and helpless
victims of an hereditary system, and their existing
opinions the inevitable opinions of men in their circumstances. It is against slavery itself, considered as
a terrible social wrong, and a frightful political error,
and an essential immorality, that I bring the accusation
of being the cause of all our national troubles. So far
from blaming the slaveholder as such, I hold him to be
the most unfortunate and pitiable of men — the imper-
illed victim of a system which wrongs equally the bonds-
men and their masters. It is the greatest of mistakes
to confound hatred of slavery with hatred for slaveholders. It is the love of the slaveholder which inspires our hatred for what is ruining him, as it is God's
love for sinners which animates his wrath against sin.
There is no proper conflict between the Northern free-

man and the slaveholder. They have identical interests, if they did but know it. It is only between Civilization and the barbarous institution of Slavery that
an irrepressible enmity exists, and this enmity is impersonal, compatible with the most fraternal and the most
Christian feelings toward our Southern brethren.   I
know the incredulousness with which such professions
are received, and I do not forget that Jerusalem crucified Him who wept over it, while he condemned its
blindness.   But I believe that it will one day be known
to the South, as it is now known to God and the world,
that it is love for man, white and black — love for man,
slaveholding or otherwise — love for man, South or
North of the Potomac — that creates the ever-growing
and ever-blessed hatred of slavery, which is the necessary accompaniment, in those not blinded by immediate
interest, of the love of liberty, of Christ, and of God.

The real issue, then, is an issue between the Christian
civilization recognized by all the rest of the civilized
world, and a false, pernicious, and wicked institution
called domestic slavery, upheld by a minority of our
countrymen, in the face of the moral sentiments and
political convictions and Christian scruples of all men
besides.   As to the final result of such an unequal controversy — a controversy of opinion and sentiment
merely — not admitting of direct or political interference, nor aiming at any result which is not accomplished
by moral suasion and public opinion — but, nevertheless, armed with tremendous powers of reason, justice,
Christian truth, and Divine will — there can be no difference of opinion, outside of the immediate domain of
slavery — and there was, till very lately, little differ-

ence of opinion even there. Of the final result — the destruction of slaveholding with the glad consent of the slaveholder himself — no student of history, no philosopher, no wise observer of the providence of God, can doubt. The immediate and practical question for us is, How is this to be permitted to bring itself about (for I propose and desire no action to precipitate, or even interfere with its self-destroying energies) with the least injury to all concerned — the country, the North, the South, the slaveholder, the slave — in the present providential circumstances and dispositions to which the nation is brought?

There are many of our best and wisest men who have come to the conclusion that the only possible course open to us now is absolute and final separation between those States of the Union who choose slavery for their first and highest good, and the rest of the Confederacy. They think that the public sentiment of the political majority will inevitably become more and more impatient of the complicity of the Federal Government with slavery, and that the Southern States are justified in their fears that their position will thus become more and more uncomfortable. What the slave power, as represented by its most intelligent leaders, apprehends, is not the seizure of any unconstitutional power, or the enactment of any illegal measures by the Free States, but the dangers to them proceeding from the growth of their legal power, and the exercise of their Constitutional rights, and the embodiment in thoroughly orderly ways of their honest and conscientious conviction. They fear the effects of the Constitution and the Union in their most legitimate operations. And there cannot be the small-

est question, that without the least wish to interfere
with slavery in the States where it is established by law,
and without the smallest infringement of the Constitution, and after the most complete and persistent fulfilment of the Fugitive Slave Law, and every other constitutional obligation, slavery is in the greatest peril
from the public opinion, from the example, from the
contagious sympathy, from the actual and irrepressible
moral reprobation of the free States, and most of all
from their prosperity and their glorious destiny. The
steps made necessary at the South to defend slavery
from these influences — namely, the exclusion of our
newspapers, the greater stringency of police regula-
tions, a more active jealousy of all private opinions at
home, and a tyrannical espionage over all travellers —
will only increase this danger, by making the contrast
between the slave and the free States more offensive
and intolerable.

Sagacious and candid men at the South say what they
feel, that the necessary and inevitable progress of civilization in the free States is the real peril of slavery,
as it is the inexpiable offence of the North. They say,
and say sagaciously, therefore, No more mock compromises! no more impracticable engagements! Slavery
cannot live safely, comfortably, permanently, with free
discussion, free thought, free institutions — cannot live
under the same government, in short, as that which the
North glories in and can alone endure. " Let us peacefully separate. We will form a great Gulf Republic —
where your political power and influences cannot touch
us further. We will trade with you, but we cannot any
longer live under the same flag and the same Constitu-

tion." If I were a Southern man, a slaveholder, and entertained the opinions which seem inevitable in that state of society, I do not doubt that would be the ground I should take. The frightful unanimity of the population of the extreme Southern States — of all the States permanently committed by circumstances to slavery — on the doctrine of secession, shows how clearly they agree with us in perceiving that this Government cannot go on treating slavery and liberty as twin children of the Constitution; that either slavery or liberty must be nationalized — either slaves must be universally recognized as property in the ordinary sense of that word, with all the rights of property, or an entire check must be put to the extension of slavery, and its ultimate extinction recognized as the policy and hope of the future. That they do not expect the first to be granted, and that they are not disposed to submit to the second, is sufficiently proved by the fact that they demand the right of peaceable secession. Their leaders have been plotting it these twenty years, as the only refuge from the intolerable pressure of the preponderant national sentiment.

Why not, then, consent to what they so necessarily demand? We know in our hearts that they are justified in their fears of Northern sentiment — and that if they stay in the Union, they are in a Union whose legitimate and constitutional action henceforth will be and must be damaging to slave property, and perpetually favorable to emancipation! Why not consent, then, to pacific and amicable and just terms of separation? Are we prepared to hold them to the Union by the exercise of perpetual force? are we prepared to

enter into a state of civil war in defence of a Constitution which is hateful to fifteen States of the Confederacy?

I say, No! When it is proved that fifteen States of
this Confederacy prefer slavery to the Constitution and
Union as it is; when it is proved that they agree in
thinking that they need new securities for their domestic institution, and are not willing that the political
majority, necessarily opposed to the least extension of
slavery, should govern and shape the public policy of
the nation; when it is proved that new compromises
are required by them to stay in the Union, they ought
to be permitted to go out of it in peace. They should
not be bribed to stay by concessions on paper which
cannot be carried out. They should not be seduced by
political trickery into new complications, destined to
increase these difficulties. Anything more than the
Constitution as it is cannot honestly be granted or supported. It could not be re-created, were it to be done
over, in a shape even as favorable as it now is to the
Slave power. But the people, in their reverence for
its framers and their respect for its age, can be made,
and will be found faithful to its letter and its spirit.
Anything beyond it granted to the slave power, I fear,
would be a fraud on Southern credulity, because a political misrepresentation of the actual and growing sentiment of the North and North-west.

Standing on the Constitution, unchanged, and, I believe, unchangeable; ready to fulfil all its obligations,
painful as they are, for the sake of union and peace;
unwilling to yield, however, an inch of constitutional
right in favor of a local institution which we hold to be

a curse to its own people, a scandal to civilization, and
an eye-sore to Christendom; determined to concede
nothing to the threats or the delusions of slaveholders—
I declare unhesitatingly in favor of allowing the Slave
States to secede, if they deliberately, formally, and unitedly prefer and desire to do so. I admit no right of secession. I acknowledge no theory of State sovereignties as coëqual with or superior to the national sovereignty of the people. It is merely a question of expediency, of the least of two evils — separation, or a
long and bloody civil war! It is the numbers, the extent, the power, of the fifteen slave States, if united
among themselves, which makes it so frightful an alternative to enter upon a civil war, of indefinite extent
and inevitable and unspeakable horrors, in vindication
of the Federal Union, or to allow them peaceably to retire. I consider separation the least of the three evils
before us: 1. War with the united slave power — involving, as I believe it would, ruin to the South —
frightful insurrections, terrible slaughter of the people
and desolation of their property — with universal emancipation as its only blessing. 2. Further concessions
to the principle of slavery — which I hold to be immoral, fatal to our national honor and character, ruinous to our prospects as a Government, and to our duties as custodians of modern and Christian civilization
on this continent. 3. Peaceable separation, a serious
blow to our national pride and prosperity, but which
might end, after a shorter or longer experiment, in re-
union on a basis more favorable to Liberty and Right.

But now returns the question of fact. Are the fifteen
Slave States unitedly and deliberately in favor of seces-

sion? If Slavery cannot receive new guarantees, are
they — the obligations of the Constitution being punc-
tiliously fulfilled — desirous of going out of the Union?
I have very serious doubts of this. From the best of
the information I can obtain, most diligently sought, the
present monstrous unanimity, even in the Gulf States,
is artificial and temporary, the result of misrepresentation, ignorance, and conspiracy among a few interested
and ambitious political leaders, who, for party purposes,
have, in the recent campaign, disseminated falsehoods
which have produced a conflagration of popular feeling
utterly uncontrollable by those who kindled it — such
as that the President elect would, on the 4th of March,
proclaim universal emancipation; that the Vice-Presi-
dent elect was a mulatto; and that the victorious party
in the election intended to violate the constitutional
rights of the Slave States! A reign of terror evidently
prevails in South Carolina, where the earlier scenes of
the French Revolution are already repeated in forced
loans, in the proscription of suspected citizens, and in
the threatened confiscation of property, to say nothing
of treasonable seizure of the Federal structures and
functions. If, as is surmised, a few *doctrinaires* of the
Calhoun school are seizing the occasion of a sectional
defeat in a political canvass to further certain long-
cherished schemes of local independence — if, playing
upon the ignorance and passions of the populace (the
so-called mean whites, who, having nothing to lose, are
the most intemperate and reckless material in the
South), they are really nullifying the actual wishes and
opinions of the larger slaveholders, thought to be conservative of necessity, as property always is, whether in

slaves or money, then this alleged and seeming unanimity, even in the Gulf States, is an appearance and a
spectre that will shortly be laid.

I suppose it to be a great mistake to imagine the
present conflict one between slaveholders considered as
representatives of property, and Northern sentiment. I
doubt not the four hundred thousand slaveholders of the
South are really the sincerest lovers of the Union in
that whole country, and that it is the ambition and
jealousy of those who for fifty years have been using
the peculiar institution as an engine of their political
schemes, gradually making of the non-slaveholding millions of the South ignorant, inflamed, and misguided
constituency, who are represented in Congress by new
men like Hammond and Keitt, who are at the bottom
of this dreadful conspiracy. If, moreover, as is thought
by the wise, the border Slaves States are favoring the
Gulf States only for the purpose of working sufficiently
on the fears and patriotism of the North to secure new
and more favorable terms for Slavery, then unflinching
firmness in the North will soon develop their ultima-
tum and we shall know whether we have to deal with
politicians, factions, schemers, and conspirators, or with
a great and united people, convinced of the inexpe-
diency of union with us. To this great and united
people, when their wishes for separation are in proper
and unmistakable form made known, I see nothing to
be said but, Be it so! and be the consequences on your
mistaken and deluded heads! But to the politicians,
factions, schemers, conspirators, or to individual States
attempting secession, or little coteries of States proposing or enacting it, I see no dignified, safe, constitutional,

and Christian method of dealing with them, but with all the authority and force of the Federal Government. Great revolutions must, in modern times, be made peaceful revolutions; little revolutions must be instantly quenched. If this Union is to be — I will not say dissolved — but divided, it must be done by mutual consent, after comparison of views, and a formal expression of the will of the people on both sides, made known in legal ways. To break up in caprice, wilfulness, and passion, without form of law, and in unconstitutional ways, can never, ought never to be submitted to; for there is something more than union and nationality involved in such proceedings, viz.: the very existence of civil society — the sanctity of government itself.

Those who do not much value the Union at the North, value law and order; and they are determined to maintain it. It must not be supposed that it is the enemies of Slavery-extension alone who have the custody of order, and the maintenance of Federal authority on their consciences. Many who are perfectly ready to let the South go where she pleases when she makes her wishes known in a proper and orderly manner, will not consent, cost what it will, that the Federal authority of the nation shall be trampled upon by any or all the Slave States while the compact is in force. It will not be a war for or against slavery — a war between one party and another party, or one section and another section, which will be precipitated, if the Federal and Constitutional authorities of the United States are gravely insulted and despised; but a war in defence of civilization against anarchy — a war of law and order upon piratical and barbarous assailants of the public peace and security, which could not fail to be short, bloody, and decisive! Already the indecision of the National Executive has obliterated party lines, and united in a new party of order and civilization the complete North. How vast must be the sympathy secretly felt by all property-holders and patriots in the South, with such conservators of all the precious interests of civilization! This party must grow. Its issue must, for the time, supersede every other. Are we a nation? Have we a Government? Is the Constitution to be respected by its own subjects? These are questions, in my judgment, which will be positively and finally settled, if necessary, with any cost of blood and treasure — settled affirmatively, before the secondary questions of the union or separation of the States will admit of debate and adjustment.

Let us not make a false issue with our exasperated and unhappy fellow-citizens of the Slave States about the Union. We are not going to war, I trust, to force fifteen States to live under a Government they hate. But we will go to war to save order and civilization, with any faction, conspiracy, rabble, or political party that strives, in illegal and treasonable ways, to break up the Government. We owe it to the intelligence and worth of the South, to believe that they are silenced and tyrannized over by a mob that does not understand nor value their interests and wishes. The sobriety and sense of that region has a right to be heard. They are entitled to the protection of the General Government, and to the evidence that they live under a Constitution and an Executive capable of enforcing the laws of the land. We are not to believe, until we have made the experiment, that Federal authority would not be obeyed, and that a dignified demonstration of national force would not restore order and peace. Who knows how the hearts of the real patriots and real men, even in South Carolina, may be even now anxiously expecting efficient interference from the General Government? To assume the weakness, the inadequacy, the unpopularity of the Federal power, is to invite contempt, rebellion and secession. I would not harshly judge the Executive of the Union. The vast responsibilities of his position, the varied means of his information, the contrariant influences brought to bear upon him, entitle him to our utmost charity. We may possibly see, in due time, that his policy has been wiser and more patriotic than it appears. But there can be no difference of opinion on one point. The National Government must be not merely submitted to, but obeyed, or we are in a state of revolution and anarchy, and in a little while shall be cutting each other's throats, beginning in South Carolina, where anarchy commenced, and ending at Washington, where liberty will be buried in the bloody waters of the Potomac, and lapse away to stain the sods of WASHINGTON'S grave.

In the providence of God, and in the natural course of affairs, we have been brought to this crisis. It could not have been avoided. With such an anomalous element as Slavery in the Constitution, a tremendous trial of its strength, and of the strength of the Union and the Government, was inevitable, sooner or later. It has not come an hour too soon. If we are not strong enough in our centripetal principles to hold together upon the original compact, if the Federal power is inherently too weak for the State powers, it is better to know it now — better abandon a Union which will presently, with increased weight, fall upon our children's heads, and destroy our successors. But I will believe in no such weakness until it is proved. The Government is strong in the hearts and in the interests of the vast majority of the people. The Constitution is strong enough to outlive its one congenital disease. The Union is strong enough to bear even the tremendous strain now trying its hoops. We want only faith in the Constitution as it is; faith in the right of political majorities to exercise their legitimate power; faith in the original wisdom of our fathers; faith in humanity; faith in Christ and in God, to carry us triumphantly through this glorious but awful hour, when the grandest political structure the providence of God ever allowed to be erected is to be finally tested by earthquake, and to prove, I doubt not, that it rests on the rock of ages, and will endure while time shall last.

PRAYER FOR RULERS, OR, DUTY OF CHRIS-TIAN PATRIOTS.

A SERMON PREACHED IN THE MADISON SQUARE PRESBYTERIAN CHURCH, NEW YORK, ON THE DAY OF THE NATIONAL FAST, JAN. 4, 1861.

BY REV. WILLIAM ADAMS, D. D.

" I exhort, therefore, that first of all supplications, prayers, interces-sions, and giving of thanks, be made for all men ; for Kings, and for all that are in authority, that we may lead a quiet and peaceable life in all godliness and honesty." — 1 *Timothy* ii. 1, 2.

APPROPRIATENESS is the first law of discourse. My theme, on this occasion, has been chosen for me by the circumstances which have called us together. The Pres-ident of the United States, and the Chief Magistrate of this Commonwealth, have recommended that this day be observed as one of humiliation, fasting, and prayer, in view of the present distracted and perilous condition of the country. Such a recommendation from such a source cannot be disregarded by the Christian ministry.

For one, I confess to a feeling of humiliation already. Less than two months ago I returned from a visit to foreign countries on the other side of the sea. Travel-ling under despotic governments, where the Press is stifled, and speech is guarded, and your personal move-ments subject to espionage, I had prided myself much

on the privileges of an American citizen ; and as our
noble ship entered the bay of New York, on one of the
brightest days of our golden Autumn, it was with a
swelling heart and a suffused eye that I exclaimed,
" How goodly are thy tents, O Jacob, and thy tabernacles, O Israel " — believing that the sun that day did
not shine upon a people having more of real prosperity
and happiness and peace than our own. Less than forty days ago we had our annual festival of Thanksgiving, to consider the bounties of Providence towards us
as a nation, when I endeavored to guide your thoughts
into the channels of gratitude. To-day we are summoned
to the altars of religion to humble ourselves, to fast and
pray, in view of public calamities. A reversal so sudden,
so entire, so unnecessary, so gratuitous, so unreasonable,
as we should say, brought upon us by no descent of fire
or pestilence from heaven — by no invasion of a foreign
foe — but altogether engendered within our own borders — is itself enough to afflict and mortify us. Hu-
miliated we are before the world, by anything which
touches the honor or integrity of our nationality, or implies the weakness of our much-boasted form of government.

We are assembled also to pray in behalf of our country. But to pray intelligently we should comprehend
the import of our prayers. There is need, therefore,
of instruction concerning the proper objects of prayer.
To give that instruction in the spirit of Christian patriotism is the duty we have undertaken, in coincidence
with the appointment of this day. On the Christian
Sabbath we occupy ourselves chiefly and directly with
those topics which concern man in his higher and spi-

ritual relations. Not that these are without their influence upon man as a citizen of this present world, for
our belief is that the indirect effect of Christianity on
human society has more potency than all the direct efforts of mere human politics; that liberty and law, and
restraint, and Governments, and civilization — all these
and more are included in and spring from the central
doctrines of the Gospel. For this very reason, and for
others which are infinitely higher and greater, the pertinency of our Sabbath instructions is directly with the
spiritual and eternal relations of man, from that point
of perspective which constitutes the peculiar characteristic of the Christian ministry. There are other topics
concerning which every minister of religion, in common
with his fellow-citizens, has his personal opinions. His
own self-respect would be wounded if he were not able,
in the proper place and in the proper manner, to hold
his own independent judgment on all these subordinate
subjects. It does not follow from this that he should
make use of his official position on the day which Christ
has hallowed for a specific purpose, to enforce his private interpretations of irrelevant matters. I hold to
the right and duty of preaching politics — as that expression is properly defined — meaning not the squab-
bles of party, but the application of Christian truth to
every relation and duty of life, just as the duty and the
relation are presented in the New Testament. But this
should be done with appropriateness, with sound judgment, and with proper regard to relevancy and edification, and the due proportion of faith. I have never
felt, for example, that it was wisdom or duty for me to
discourse, directly and frequently, on the subject of

14

American Slavery — not that I ever so much as imagin-
ed there was any disposition on the part of the pews to
restrict the liberty of the pulpit — not that I have not
my own opinions on the subject, as a citizen — nay more,
my own opinions as a student of Providence and the
Bible — but because I have never judged that it was for
edification to insist upon this subject before those who
constitute this pastoral charge. Had it been my lot in
life, as a Christian minister, to preach to those who
were personally related to Slavery, I should have endeavored, to the best of my ability, to instruct them on
the subject, as every other, with pertinence and direct-
ness. There is no preaching which is so easy, measured by the time and intellectual effort of preparation,
as controversial preaching in regard to matters on which
the public mind is already inflamed ; and one's manliness and Christian wisdom are often more demonstrated
by holding himself in restraint concerning many political topics, rather than falling in with prevalent opinion,
and riding along on the wave of popular excitement.
While, therefore, pertinency and appropriateness require us, on the Sabbath day, to hold our minds in
contact with our own bosom sins, and our personal relations to Christ and eternity, the same law of appropriateness makes it necessary for me, on this occasion,
to speak with direct reference to the circumstances
which have led to our convocation.

We are invited by magistrates to pray for our country ; to pray for our rulers ; and the text before us
enjoins it upon us, for a reason annexed, to do the same
thing. Perhaps some may think that it would be wiser
to do nothing but pray. I am myself reminded of what

was once said by the pious and discreet FENELON, in a time of great trouble and turbulence: " *Parlez à Dieu pour la paix de l'Eglise et ne parlez point aux hommes*" — " Speak to God for the peace of the Church, and speak not to men." But we are safe always when we speak in accordance with the letter and spirit of the Scriptures. Our text is, "*Pray* for Kings and for all those in authority, that we may lead a quiet and peaceable life." The emphasis given to this matter shows that there were special reasons which led the Apostle to give it the prominent place which it holds in this epistle. Any one informed as to the state of the Christian mind at the time this epistle was written, in regard to the heathen magistracy, under which Christianity was born and developed, and especially the deluded expectations of the Judaist mind in reference to what was about to ensue, can understand how pertinent this counsel was. Then there is a design in the accumulation of expressions — supplications, prayers, intercessions, and giving of thanks. All the synonyms of the language in reference to the subject are employed, inculcating prayer in all its forms, looking to the supply of what is needed, the averting of what is evil, and the obtaining of what is good. Not only have we this emphatic form of expression in reference to prayer for the civil magistracy, but the reason is appended why we should thus pray. Not for what will inure to the benefit of the magistrates themselves — not merely for the conversion of the men thus described ; but this is the end, the object of our prayer in behalf of the civil power : That we may lead a quiet, peaceable life, in all godliness and honesty. This latter expression, " in *all godliness and propriety of conduct*," denoting the ultimate end, of which a quiet, peaceable life is the condition. We have outlived the old error which was installed in ancient treatises on government, that, because the Holy Scripture refers to *Kings*, requiring men to pray for Kings, and to honor the King, therefore monarchy was the only form of magistracy which had the Divine sanction, for the scriptural injunction making reference to the form of government which then and there existed is not even thus restricted, but includes all forms of authority and magistracy. Such a form of government as our own was not in existence when Holy Scripture was written, but never was there one under which prayer had such scope and pertinency, for the very reason that those who pray are the source of all power and sovereignty.

To give some order to our thoughts, let me say, in the first place, as explanatory of all the emphasis given to this subject, that the reason here assigned why we should pray for such as are in authority lays bare at once the whole design and office of civil government: "*That we may lead a quiet and peaceable life.*" We present this as the very best definition that can be given of the province and end of the civil power. Writers on political economy have fallen upon manifold mistakes by assigning to the ruling authority prerogatives which do not belong to it at all. A most notable instance of the kind comes to mind in the very clever book written by Mr. GLADSTONE, then a member of the British Parliament, some twenty years ago, entitled, *The State in its Relations with the Church.* The object at which he aims is, to prove that one of the prin-

cipal ends of civil government, as such, is to propagate
religious truth; and that, as a means to this, it is obligatory on every Government to profess and support a
religion. Once allow the premises from which he
starts, in his logic, and you cannot escape his conclusion. The error lies in the very foundation of his argument. He assumes a major premise which is too
large, and includes too much. He begins with affirming that it is the province of government to attend to
all which is vital to human interests. This would seem
to be very plausible and very good. But it contains
the mischief of a tremendous sophistry. We join issue
at the very beginning, and deny that such is the province of civil government. Ten thousand things vital to
the happiness of individuals and families there are
which do not pertain to the civil magistracy at all.
The province of government is not universal, but limited and restricted. We should say that this was the design of government, that we may lead a quiet and
peaceable life, or, to expand the definition somewhat —
government is to protect our lives, our persons and property, as inhabitants of this present world. It is to
help men to settle their difficulties, not by individual
force, but by processes of law and justice; to protect
from violence and invasion — in short, to furnish a sub-
stratum on which the social system may stand and develop itself. This is not to affirm, as some good people
have feared, that the temporal interests of man are of
greater consequence than his spiritual. Far from this.
But it is the province of government to care for one,
but not for the other. Men of all religions and of no
religion have an equal interest in this, that life, and

person, and rights be protected by the civil powers.
Men holding opinions the most antagonistic that can be
conceived on many subjects — Gentile and Jew, Papist
and Protestant — all agree in this, that they need the
protection of a good government. Whether they have
any faith in a future world or not — whether they can
harmonize on this or that theory of morals or not —
here is something which is admitted by all, there must
be a ruling power in this world, or we could not live at
all. The right conception of the province of government is very important, since it has always been true
that men are in danger of extending the civil power
over and beyond its just limits. We are jealous of
such encroachments. We are unwilling that affairs
should be thrust into the province of government which
do not belong to it. This definition of government, its
use and object, has another advantage. It meets the
scruples of such as have conscientious objections to being associated in the same government with those whose
opinions and practices, on many subjects, they disap-
prove and detest. The Apostle instructs us on this
very point: "I wrote unto you," says he, "in an epistle, not to company with fornicators; yet not altogether with the fornicators *of this world,* for then
must ye needs go out of the world. But if any man
that is called a *brother* be a fornicator or an idol-
ater," then withdraw from him. Within your own
communion of the church you may have laws of fellowship which you cannot apply to the social organization
at large. Idolaters and Christians, pure and impure,
sober and drunken, whatever are men's notions or habits in reference to other matters, in this they have all a

common interest and necessity, that they should be protected by the ruling power from rapine, and violence,
and carnage. Starting, then, with this object and end
of government full in our eye, *that we may lead a quiet
and peaceable life*, as the result for which we are to
pray, let me remind you that this is an object of vast
importance, of indispensable necessity. We have fallen
upon the evil habit of speaking slightingly of government. In the too common custom of abusing the men
who administer government, many have come to think
and speak disparagingly of government itself, as though
we could do as well or better without it. Without it,
not to speak of living quietly and peaceably, we could
not live at all. Government is God's ordinance for human protection. The word does not define the form,
the mode, in which the governing power shall be administered ; but there is, in the very nature of things a
necessity for some government — the worst is better
than none — and in this sense the powers that be are
ordained of God. And by government we do not mean
a fortuitous assemblage of forces, but an organized form,
adequate for the purpose ; not an accidental convenience, but a stable power on which society may repose
and develop itself safely and happily, and the Church
of God may build her nest and lay her young. Government, as an ordinance of God, is a *power*. Designed for this very end to keep impulses and passions
under restraint, within legal processes, it must have the
means of protecting itself, and enforcing its own enactments. Without this it is a nullity — it is nothing.
Therefore says the Scripture, the magistrate beareth the
sword, and not in vain, a sword not made of a shingle,

but the veritable symbol of a veritable power, able to accomplish the legitimate object for which government was instituted.

Surely here is something worth praying for. That government is the best in kind which, like the great forces of nature, works so smoothly and quietly that we take but little notice of its working. If ours has been, and is a government, which is adapted to secure for us a quiet, peaceable life, then it is a government which ought to be preserved ; and for this end prayer should invoke Divine aid, and the hearts and hands of all patriots should be combined in one. Greatly mistaken shall I be, if the result of events now in progress in our country is not to diffuse wider than ever the conviction that government, organized government, is with us a most benignant thing, to be valued for time to come as it has never been valued before. Men have been trifling, in both extremes, with most sacred interests, till we are in danger, at last, of being consumed. Without a government, a power worthy of the name, able to protect us, where are we ? What becomes of us and our children ; if society is to become disintegrated, if theories are to be allowed which, carried out to their legitimate consequences in States, and counties, and cities, and families, would destroy the very idea of government, and leave us altogether at the mercy of passion, the power of mobs, and the turbulence of physical strength ? The right of *revolution* — that word of hope and of terror — remains with every people, as the last resort of necessity ; otherwise we should be forced to blush at the bend of illegitimacy and shame in our own coat armorial ; but that right can be justified only after all legal methods of redress have been exhausted, and the power which resorts to it must first plead before the bar of reason and the judgment of the civilized world, that it has been compelled to this final and dread necessity in view of a greater good, which thereby, and thereby only, it is sure to accomplish. It is time for this subject to be taken out from the sway of passion into the domain of Christian reason. The time has come for all party and sectional lines to be effaced in the broad claims of patriotism. All subordinate matters, prejudices and antipathies, must give way before this simple question, Whether we have, and are to have, a Government beneath which, as the ordained protection of God, we can lead honest, and quiet, and peaceful lives? When all irrelevant matters are brushed away, and that simple question is presented naked and alone in its own merits, the heart of this whole American people will be found to be true, and sound, and loyal. God grant that this question may be settled in his own wise and blessed way — by inclining the hearts of a praying people to consider candidly, seasonably, and wisely what is meant by his ordination of civil government as the means of securing for all quiet and honest lives.

With this reason which inspiration has assigned as the result and object of prayer, we come next, by a natural order, to consider why we should pray, in a special manner, in behalf of our rulers. Such an act of prayer, let me say, promises two results, and is to be justified by two reasons: 1st, The persuasive power of prayer in the way of securing for those in authority, as a gift from God, what is needful to the discharge of their duty ; 2d, The reactive influence of prayer on the minds of those who offer it, as the best mode of adjusting all perilous and difficult questions of polity. Let us consider these in their order.

All but Atheists believe that God presides over nations and individuals, and that by means and influences beyond our sight he can turn the hearts of men as rivers of water are turned. Now by fears and terrors as he did the heart of PHARAOH, and now by gentler processes as he did the hearts of DARIUS and CYRUS. Who that has read history aright can doubt the power of the Almighty higher, stronger, and mightier than that of kings and cabinets ? It was God who bestowed wisdom on Solomon — a wisdom so singularly displayed in his first judicial act, before he had reached his majority — with no intention of cruelty to a living child, yet proposing its dismemberment, that he might test the instinct of maternity, discovering which of the two claimants would first cry out against the violent division ; and God it was who turned the counsel of AHITHOPHEL into foolishness. He it is who still instructs us to pray for our rulers as dependent for success in their office upon Him. Let us pray that our " officers may be peace, and our exactors righteousness." That those who are invested with authority may be firm and faithful to their trusts : administering government without fear or favor. That they may be inspired with that wisdom which is profitable to direct, that they may fear God and do justly, and hate bribes, and remember their obligations to Him who has said : " Counsel is mine and sound wisdom. I am understanding, I have strength. By me kings reign, and princes decree justice. By me princes rule, and nobles, even all the judges of the earth." And prayer of this description should go up from unfeigned lips. Never should devotion be subsidized to prejudice, nor partisanship make use of prayer for expressing its own pique. These are the prayers which have been prepared for us by the Divine Spirit, and such we should unceasingly offer in public worship, in true loyalty, and Christian patriotism.

Times like these lay bare to our eye the weaknesses and perils of our Government, as storms expose the leaks of a ship. We are wise if we come to see that our rulers are subject to manifold dangers, from which nothing but Divine wisdom can shield them. We boast much before the world of the freedom of our institutions, of the perfect equality of our citizenship, so that no man is debarred from office by the accident of birth and condition. But we must remember that there is another side and aspect to this subject. If there is an advantage of this kind, there are many disadvantages and dangers connected with it. If all offices of trust and power are open to all, then all may seek them, and there will be scrambling and corruption, and most unworthy rivalries. The frequency of our popular elections multiplies the mischief from this source, and society is upturned from its discolored depths. It is not strange in such a state of things, that we are shocked by revelations of fraud, and dishonesty, and corruption. Men will intrigue for office for selfish ends, who are not fitted for it by education or character. They will employ methods which ought never to be used. It has come at last — it humbles us before God and man to admit it — to be understood that all is fair in politics.

Nothing can be more unscrupulous than the strictly party Press of this country. So strong have become the chains of party, that the last thing to be expected of a political opponent is chivalric fairness and candor and courtesy and truth. An irreparable mischief has been done to the morals of the country by this shameless perversion and falsehood, which waxes worse and worse. The public conscience is debauched. Nor can I see relief from all this mischief in any quarter but this one : — a deeper sense of religion, such as is implied in the act of prayer to Almighty God. Some put their trust in universal education ; but intelligence is not the thing which is wanting in such a crisis ; for who is so shrewd as your thorough-bred politician ? The more you educate the faculties in the wisdom of this world, without the virtuous restraints of religion, the more you sharpen the edge which will wound and kill us.

> " Yon Cassius *thinks* too much ;
> Such men are dangerous."

Our safety lies in that acknowledgment of Divine control, of obligation and modest trust which finds expression for itself in holy prayer, without " wrath and doubting."

Beyond all this power of prayer, considered as a means of helping our rulers to act wisely and faithfully, working their deliverance from all selfishness and partisanship and venality, there remains a most important and blessed effect of prayer, as it is reflected upon the hearts of those who offer it. If prayer had no power nor promise of securing a gift of light from the Throne, its influence would be immeasurably good and great upon those who offer it. It calms the passions, clarifies the judgment, enlightens the intellect, composes the spirit, and pervades the conduct with serenity, and charity, and patience, and meekness, and hope.

Does any one doubt that the causes which more than any endanger our institutions proceed from excited passion rather than sober reason? That at this very moment our peril is from exasperated feeling, from threats, and wrath, and bitterness, and menaces, and taunts, and objurgations, and not from the spirit which would refer all matters of difference to legal adjudication, and to the wisdom and guidance which are never withheld from filial prayer?

Not for the purpose of recrimination, of which we have had so much, but for the very opposite — of suppressing it, and fostering a better temper — let me come at once to the very subject, which, more than any other, has occasioned the present embarrassment. I shall trust to your candor to say, when I have finished, whether the statement of the case has been made in truth and fairness.

Anterior to our own time and generation, without personal complicity of our own, by the persistent agency of the mother country, African Slavery was introduced and entailed upon this country. In the original draft of the Declaration of American Independence, by the hand of Mr. JEFFERSON, himself a slaveholder, one of the reasons alleged for the act was that Great Britain, notwithstanding the remonstrances and expostulations of the Colonies, had persisted in forcing upon them this very system. The time was, and not so long ago, when, throughout the whole of this country, and

especially in the Southern States, which, in the origin and prosecution of measures at emancipation, anticipated others, and outstripped others in the amount
of costs and sacrifices looking to that end — the time
was, I say, when throughout the whole country there
was a remarkable unanimity in reference to Slavery, as
a political, social, and moral evil.   Legislatures of
States where it existed, and ecclesiastical bodies more
immediately connected with it, scarcely without an exception, took action, looking to its gradual and ultimate
removal.   I shall not undertake to describe the manner
in which a change in regard to the treatment of the
subject was effected ; enough to know, what cannot be
denied, that a change has taken place, and that this has
led to extreme views, acrimony, and active antagonism.
Men have driven each other wide apart by contrary
opinions, as ivory balls are separated by concussion.
On the one hand are those who regard the act of slaveholding as necessarily and unexceptionably sinful.
They pronounce those who are involved in this relation
as the greatest of criminals.   Churches in the Northern
interior, who never saw either a slaveholder or a slave,
and were never in the way of such a probability, took
action, denouncing this relation as one of the most atro-
cious of all crimes, forbidding any one connected with
it to approach their communion.   Epithets could not
be found too strong by way of expressing detestation
of this particular act, and those there are who have
publicly avowed their purpose to put the Constitution
and the Bible under their feet for a supposed complicity with this one unpardonable sin.   In the opposite extreme are those who now assert that this relation is of

Divine origin and sanction, and that to " conserve, extend, and perpetuate it," after the same manner as the relation between parent and child, to the end of time, is a Christian duty. Moreover, the proposal has been made and publicly advocated, in consistency with this sentiment, to reopen and legalize the African Slave-trade, which the whole civilized world, and none more emphatically than our own country, has stigmatized as piracy.

But these, you say, are extreme views. Certainly they are. I describe them as such. I refer to them as such. But do you not know that these are the very agencies which work mischief; for that which is ultra — beyond fairness and truth — is the parent of fanaticism ; and fanaticism is a fire which, once kindled, burns you know not where or what. I use that word with philosophical accuracy. Enthusiasm is a noble quality. We all admire earnestness and zeal ; the expression of one's own sentiments with an honest heartiness. But fanaticism has this peculiarity, that always it has in it an element of malignity ; a spirit that would do harm to its object after some form or method ; a spirit which would lift its hands and sharpen its tongue in wrath ; which would strike, and bite, and retaliate, and devour. Extremes to be sure. But does any one question that it is these extreme notions which are now flying through the troubled air ; which are repeated backwards and forwards, exasperating a bad temper ? Is not this spirit, wherever it has existed, the parent of misapprehension, and prejudice and hate ? If Sir Walter Raleigh found it so difficult to arrive at the exact truth of facts, occurring almost under his own eye, in his own castle-

yard, what may truth expect when the very air is full
of a malign spirit, excited to a most inflammable and
explosive pitch ? The consequence has been, that while
the extremists on either wing have understood each other well, and hated each other heartily, the great body
lying between, on both sides, have not known and understood each other at all. When, at length, the
subject became involved with political legislation,
then a thousand other forces came in to intensify the
feeling. Now it was that legislative acts themselves
partook of the prevalent sentiment on either side, increasing the exasperation. The real cause which made
the Fugitive Slave Law so obnoxious to many in the
North was, that they interpreted it as containing a
crack and a jeer which was intended to humiliate them ;
while the people of the South, in their turn, put the
same interpretation upon every Northern Liberty Bill,
its animus, whatever ingenuity may have been in the
letter, being understood as one of defiance and insult.
And so it is that the great mass of the nation, innocent
of all evil designs, intending no wrong, and doing no
wrong, are yet, by the great law of social liabilities, involved in perils engendered by others, which threaten
now the whole domain. The question now before us,
is whether it is possible for this matter to be lifted up
and lifted out from this region of distemper into the
court of reason, and before the supremacy of providential facts ? The stars in their courses fought against
Sisera — and there is no place for passion, or impatience, or fretfulness, when we put ourselves in contact
with the great calm facts of Nature, and Providence,
and Revelation. Our hope is not so much in legislation

and discussion, for it has long been our national vice to legislate and talk too much, for mere effect, on abstract questions, instead of meeting each and every case upon its own merits. In cases of disputed rights, let supreme law be arbiter, — and I believe there are many questions of law in connexion with this subject which should employ the highest legal talent of the country — and every citizen be prompt to recognize its solemn authority. Though it is the most difficult of all conditions in which to act wisely and freely when put under threats, yet it is a token for good, that, already in our own Northern community, there is a disposition to repeal whatever may have been judged in its spirit and intention to be contrary to faith, and honesty, and law. I speak of the spirit and the temper, for this is the whole matter. If by any process, if, by a special answer to special prayer, there could be such a return to a reasonable and charitable temper, in which all shall be convinced that nothing is intended, and nothing will be tolerated which is not right, then, indeed, fear would give place to hope, and apprehension to peace.

How is this subject presented to us in the New Testament? Perhaps we shall see the better if we look first at the Christian method of treating another subject which is free from all doubt in our minds. I refer to despotic Government, the object of our implacable abhorrence. When Christ and his Apostles were upon the earth, they lived under Roman despotism; and what that was, a superficial acquaintance with history will suffice to show. Did they ever make a *direct assault* upon this tremendous power? Did they excite to insurrection? Did they draw the sword against it? Did

they arm the tongue against it? Never. The very opposite. "Render unto Cæsar the things that are
Cæsar's" was the rule of Christ. It was in regard to
this old Heathen despotism that Paul counselled his
contemporaries to be obedient and loyal, recognizing
its authority himself, and appealing to its jurisdiction.
Are we, then, to infer that Christianity sanctions irresponsible and cruel tyranny, aiming to extend and perpetuate it? Never, never! For its own spirit fosters
justice. It looks at the universal diffusion of what is
right. Tell us, then, why the New Testament does not
contain one direct assault upon those ancient and stub-
born-tyrannies. Some reason there must have been,
and that reason the very best. Do you say that it
would have done no good; that it would have reacted
upon the heads of those who took part in it, and, therefore, it was deferred till a more auspicious opportunity?
Then you admit that there is such a thing as wise expediency, and that this is a Christian virtue, employing
the best means and occasions for its own good ends.
So we believe. Like the sun in the heaven, Christianity lifts itself up to its central position, and its warmth
melts the ice, and its attractions gradually, but certainly, draw all lesser orbs around itself obediently.
Would you know what Slavery was in the days of the
Cæsars? Read Tacitus, the contemporary of Paul.
Yet you do not find in the New Testament one *direct
assault* upon it, as a thing to be overthrown by instan-
taneous violence. The relation is recognized as an existing fact. Masters and slaves — there is no mistak-
ing the word — those that were under the yoke, are instructed in their relative duties; while the hand is not

once lifted to sever at a blow the relation itself. What, then? Must we infer that this is a relation which Christianity ordains, and conserves, and perpetuates, as one of her own institutions? By no means. Read the epistle of Paul to Philemon; a most extraordinary thing it is that such an epistle, from such a man, to such a man, on such a subject, should have been handed down to us — and I confess to you that I find it always hard to read that epistle, so full of the very spirit of Christian gentleness and courtesy, without a moistened eye — and you need not wonder long or be in doubt as to the process by which the religion of Christ reforms abuses and removes evils. Men may be impatient, fret and goad themselves and others into madness, but God has his own time and method, and we do well sometimes to think of the slow yet certain processes of his Spirit and Providence.

On the one hand, we of the North — I say *we*, since I speak of a prevalent habit — must cease from all vituperation and angry reproaches. We must not speak of our southern brethren as oppressors and barbarians, nor vilify them, nor taunt them, nor goad them, as if they were sinners above all others. We must bear in mind that had we been born in the same circumstances with themselves, in connexion with a system which sends its roots through the whole social structure, there is no reason to suppose that we should have been more humane, more kind, more wise than they. We must acknowledge that among them, familiar with this relation, are some of the best specimens of philanthropy and religion the world can furnish, men and women worthy to stand by the side of the man in the New Testament, who held the same relation to a *doulos*, whom Christ healed, of whom Christ said, " I have not seen so great faith, no, not in Israel."

On the other hand, we say to our brethren of the South, while we acknowledge and defend every right guaranteed to you by the Constitution, you must not take new ground which is untenable ; you must not force us to join a new issue ; nor give resurrection to questions which have long ago been considered as settled by the civilized world ; you must not resort to violence ; if the solemn tramp of the census instructs you as to the certainty of prospective changes, you must meet the fact as an appointment not of man, by which to be irritated, but of God, with acquiescence, with equanimity ; you must not forswear reason, nor put the torch to that edifice which we occupy in common, and in which we and our children, and children's children, have such incomparable and ineffable advantages.

Surely, then, we find abundant occasion for prayer, full of faith in God, and charity for our fellow men, in the presence of this great embarrassment. If any man pretends to know by what method this great problem of our history is to be solved without detriment to either race, our own or the African, for as Christians our regard is for all, in Christ all are our brethren ; if any one, I say, pretends to know the future of this history, without aid from divine wisdom, I pity his self-sufficiency and arrogance. No man can look with indifference upon that which in any way affects the prosperity of the country or any part of it. We may have no direct personal relation to this or that system. But here comes in the great law of organic life and social liabili-

ties. We may be innocent, and yet suffer the conse-
sequences of others' actions. Children may be harm-
less as doves, but they are involved in the results of
their parents' conduct. Our fathers were immediately
related to the introduction and extension of slavery.
If wrath, and bitterness, and objurgations could produce
any good, they would be most inappropriate and unbe-
coming in us. Then we have a real interest in everything which concerns the welfare of every part of our
Confederacy. The whole is our country. There is not
a right which belongs to any State which we would not
defend. Not a wrong can be inflicted upon one which
all the rest do not suffer. Whatever infidels may say
on the subject, objecting to the ethics of the New Testament, that it omits from its injunctions this virtue of
patriotism, we know that there is such a thing as patriotism, a true love for country, a sentiment which may
run to excess and folly in the absence of Christianity,
but which Christianity cherishes, and fosters, and mod-
erates, infusing into it her own celestial temper.

It is time for us to make some peculiar expression of
our loyalty. Partizanship must be merged in patriotism. Sectionalism must give place to an intense love
for the whole nationality. If revolution is actually to
occur, let it not be till men have opened to each other
their honest hearts of patriotic love, and the conviction
is justified to the waiting world that there is some imperative necessity which makes that ultimate resort inevitable. Does that exist? How would you define it?
What is the question which forces any to such a necessity? Differences of opinion? But men may live under
constitutional law with conscientious sentiments of ut-

most diversity. Differences of opinion leading to antagonism of claims? Let them be referred to the tribunal which law describes, and a loyal people must ever acknowledge. Revolution! — for what? Disappointment, temper, impulse, passion — none of these are to supersede law, and to displace that constitutional Government which is our protection. Revolution! What memories are associated in our minds by the word? It was only last week that the last survivor of the Battle of Bunker Hill died in the State of Maine. Surely it cannot be possible that within so short a time from the beginning of the Revolution which resulted in our independence, there should, in any quarter, even be thought of another revolution, for what good end we cannot imagine, against the very Constitution which our fathers framed. As the later Athenian orators, when their country was in danger of distraction and dismemberment, were wont to shout "Marathon! Marathon!" recalling the field where patriotism and valor prevailed against desperate odds, so will we repeat the names of the men and the fields whose renown has come down to us as a common heritage, associated with our common ancestry and our earlier strugglos. More than all, will we call aloud on the name of our God, beseeching him by the very arguments which he has put upon our lips, not to give us up to reproach. Political zealots may scoff at the inutility of prayer. But I speak to-day to men and women who have faith in its efficiency. Before the spirit of prayer, the false guides of passion and an evil temper disappear, and the great lights of charity, and meekness, and hope, come forth to point us in the way. What will the nations say if our experiment of self-government should thus early prove a failure? How should we be ashamed to confess before the world our weakness and imbecility, if the bond of our Confederated States should prove a rope of sand, instead of a chain of gold. We cannot pretend to dictate or mark the way for Divine Providence — but with all the heart we have, we will pray for the peace and prosperity of our country. Let us confess our sins most heartily before God. "Think you," said Christ, "that they on whom the tower of Siloam fell were sinners above all others? I tell ye nay. But except *ye* repent, *ye* shall all likewise perish." Sin of every name and form is a leak in the ship, and humbling ourselves before God is our strength and security. For the sake of all the hopes and prospects of mankind — for the sake of rational liberty — for the sake of the Christian Church, with its new domains and auspices — for our brethren and companions' sakes — we will pray for our rulers, and pray to Almighty God for ourselves — that here, beneath the vines and trees which our fathers planted, we may lead a quiet and peaceful life. Should reason be borne down by passion; should it prove that a fire has already been kindled which may not by any human power be quenched, still will we not let go our hold on faith and the guardianship of God. Still we cling to the altars of religion, and invoke the grace of the Almighty. Still will we pray that we may keep a conscience void of offence before God and man, so that in any extremity we may have the security which springs from confidence in Supreme direction, believing that He, in the day of evil, will say to his own wherever they are, "Come, my people, enter thou into thy chambers, and shut thy doors about thee, hide thyself, as it were, for a little moment, until this indignation be over-past." But prayer and faith will win a blessing. After the storm behold the bow in the clouds, and bright-ness covering the whole heavens.

THE END.